'Se van, se van, y nunca volverán'

'They're going, they're going, and never shall come back'

— Popular slogan in Argentina as the military withdrew to
barracks in 1983

Latin America

The Transition
to Democracy

Ronaldo Munck

Zed Books Ltd
London and New Jersey

Latin America: The Transition to Democracy was first published
by Zed Books Ltd, 57 Caledonian Road, London N1 9BU, UK, and
171 First Avenue, Atlantic Highlands, New Jersey 07716, USA,
in 1989.

Cover designed by Andrew Corbett.
Typeset by EMS Photosetters, Rochford, Essex.
Printed and bound in the United Kingdom
at Bookcraft (Bath) Ltd, Midsomer Norton.

British Library Cataloguing in Publication Data

Munck, Ronaldo *1951–*
    Latin America: the transition to democracy
    1. Latin America. Democracy
    I. Title.
    321.8'098

    ISBN 0-86232-818-7
    ISBN 0-86232-819-5 Pbk

Library of Congress Cataloging-in-Publication Data

Munck, Ronaldo
    Latin America: the transition to democracy/
        Ronaldo Munck.
        p.   cm.
    Includes bibliographical references.
    ISBN 0-86232-818-7.–ISBN 0-86232-819-5 (pbk.)
        1. Representative government and representation
    – South America – Case studies.   2. Socialism –
    South America – Case studies.   3. Argentina –
    Politics and government – 1983-.   4. Brazil –
    Politics and government – 1985-.   5. Uruguay –
    Politics and government – 1973-.   6. Chile –
    Politics and government – 1973-.   I. Title.
    JL1866.M86   1989   CIP
    320.98–dc20   89-36323

Contents

Tables

Acknowledgements

There are many people and organizations who have made possible the writing of this book. A field trip to Latin America in 1986 was generously financed by The British Academy and the McCrea Research Award at the University of Ulster. While in Latin America I visited several social research centres in the various southern cone countries where I was kindly assisted by the following. In Argentina, CEDES (Marcelo Cavarozzi, Andrés Thompson and Leonor Platte), CLADE (José Nun), CLACSO (Fernando Calderón) and IIPAS (Anna Proietti-Bocco). In Chile, CES (Manuel Barrera), ILET (Guillermo Campero), CIEPLAN (Patricio Meller) and FLACSO (Manuel Antonio Garretón). In Uruguay, CIESU (Carlos Filgueira and Danilo Veiga), CLAEH (Martin Gargiulo and Romeo Perez), CIEDUR (José Perez, Geronimo da Sierra and Guillermo Martorelli). In Brazil, CEBRAP (Jose Arthur Gianotti, Francisco de Oliveira and Ruth Cardoso), CEDEC (Roque Aparecido de Silva) and IDESP (Marcus Figueiredo). At CEBRAP I also met fellow Argentinian Guillermo O'Donnell who generously discussed his own project on democratization and encouraged my own, more modest, endeavours. My heartfelt thanks go to all the above.

This book is dedicated to my parents, whose hospitality in Argentina turned a research project into a memorable holiday.

Introduction

By the mid-1980s the countries of the southern cone of Latin America had returned to democratic rule, with the exceptions of General Pinochet's Chile and the long-standing rule of General Stroessner in Paraguay. Does this mean we can now say 'farewell to the dictators' and look forward to an uninterrupted period of democratic renewal? Or was this, rather, simply a change of masks by capitalism and imperialism from their 'military face' to their 'civilian face'? These were questions of more than academic interest to the social scientists and political theorists of Latin America when I began to think about this book in 1985. When my earlier book, *Politics and Dependency in the Third World: The case of Latin America* (Zed Books), appeared in 1984 these issues were already being posed, but the book had been written in 1982, when the dictatorships seemed firmly established. In *Politics and Dependency* I surveyed the populist–nationalist regimes of the 1950s and 1960s and the military regimes of the 1970s, but only touched on the possible transitions to democracy which, we now see in retrospect, were then commencing. The present study is thus, in many ways, a necessary sequel to *Politics and Dependency*, building on its analysis of social forces and political regimes in Latin America. It is also, however, an implicit critique of the earlier book in terms of its theoretical underpinnings and, to some extent, of its political orientation.

Without wishing to engage in the once fashionable self-indulgent art of 'auto-critique' I would like to make explicit some of the shifts from *Politics and Dependency* so as not to clutter up the main text. It goes without saying that these changes are due to changes in the objective situation and advances in critical thought rather than personal revelations. In its title and substantive concerns, *Politics and Dependency* reflected the impact of the dependency paradigm across the social and political sciences in Latin America since the late 1960s. My own position was by no means uncritical of the so-called dependency theory — 'so-called' because its original proponents saw it simply as a framework for concrete analysis and not a full-blown theory on a par with that of capitalism, for example. I argued that the dependency perspective often placed undue emphasis on external factors, to the detriment of internal social and political processes, in determining the development of each country. Furthermore, my own emphasis was much more historical than structural, and gave a primary role to the interaction between social classes. Nevertheless,

Politics and Dependency still sought an all-embracing or totalizing theory to account for the underdevelopment of Latin America. I was driven towards the concept of 'dependent reproduction' which had the merit of being dynamic rather than static, and of being able, at least potentially, to integrate the economic, political and social aspects of development. Today, I feel this line of enquiry has definite limitations.

For twenty years or so now we have had grand theoretical debates on the ultimate cause of underdevelopment, in which various theories of imperialism, dependency, modes of production, unequal exchange or world systems are juggled about without much engagement with the complex historical and social process of development. To be honest, this unease springs from a broader dissatisfaction with the more orthodox or 'literal' readings of Marx. To seek justification in the sacred texts for this or that theory of imperialism is now worse than a curious anachronism. Dogmatisms of various sorts were, as we shall argue, contributing factors to the long night of the dictatorships in the southern cone. It is now necessary to move (back) to a 'concrete analysis of a concrete situation' which in the Latin America of the late 1980s means the incipient process of democratization, its causes, limits and prospects. It is not a crass empiricism which leads to a distrust of endless theorizing, but a healthy dose of practical political engagement which teaches better than any text what is important to any process of social and political transformation. Struggles are engaged in not to prove or disprove Marxist classics but because of a deep human will to surmount oppression. It is in this spirit that I began a study of the democratization process in the southern cone of Latin America.

As to its political orientation, *Politics and Dependency* paid lip-service, albeit critical, to the then orthodox leftist position that the ultimate choice in Latin America was between socialism and fascism. I was prone to detect a 'general crisis of the state' and was not immune to the apocalyptic political vision of leftist circles of post-1968 vintage. Although it is no longer fashionable, I would still argue that socialism is part of the solution to the deep-seated social and economic problems of Latin America. The question of democracy, however, has to be far more central to our analysis than it ever was in the 1970s. The late unlamented military dictatorships were not the *only* possible solutions for capitalism in the 1970s, and the democratic regimes of the 1980s may well prove more viable for the long-term prospects of capitalism in the region. As to socialism, it can hardly be discussed in isolation from the issue of democracy because only a democratic socialism which springs from the mobilization of the people can meet the liberatory aspirations of the great socialist thinkers. Nor, of course, is a socialist regime a magic answer to all the problems of underdevelopment; that is another question (and the subject of my next book). In a more general sense, Marxism still provides many tools for critical social analysis in its method and insights into particular issues, but it cannot be the exclusive and totalizing theory we deploy in every concrete analysis.

In *Politics and Dependency* there was some attempt to distance the text from the crass reductionism of 'orthodox' Marxism but I now feel that the break was incomplete. We must feel free to ask new questions and develop novel interpretations unconstrained by any theoretical or political straitjacket. It is now widely accepted that Marxism is ill equipped to deal with issues such as gender, race, nation and culture. Democracy is, of course, another area where the classics tend to provide us with pat formulas and facile interpretations. We need to consider the symbolic dimension of politics as much as the classic concerns of party and class. For example, the process whereby Alfonsín's democratic discourse was constructed in Argentina is far more relevant and interesting than the comings and goings at the US Embassy and how many CIA agents were in Argentina at the time. If these concerns could be accommodated by the theoretical framework within which *Politics and Dependency* operated, there were others which were simply outside its terms of reference. These other concerns are difficult to categorize but I can give one example.

While walking and driving around the cities of Buenos Aires and São Paulo recently I was struck (again) by the ferocious, bordering on criminal, behaviour of many car drivers. I could remember this endearing characteristic from when I lived there but it seemed to have got worse. Having experienced more civilized driving habits in other countries, I knew this was not an innate human condition. Yet this was not something I thought of in theoretical, let alone political, terms, it was merely something I experienced 'personally' while I went about my real business of collecting statistics and interviewing political actors. Then I read an article by Guillermo O'Donnell on macro- and micro-authoritarianism which recounted (in gory detail) his own driving experiences. This alerted me to the social, political, even theoretical significance of apparently trivial matters such as driving practices. Marxism, bar one or two moralistic texts, had never paid much attention to the problems of everyday life. Yet could an aggressive, sexist, possible sadistic driver get out of a car and be transformed miraculously into a responsible citizen when arriving at a polling station? An even bigger question was whether the savagery of torture and forced disappearances was entirely unrelated to the daily aggression and butchery in the streets of the city. These issues were in a different world from that of *Politics and Dependency*. The present book does not provide a full analysis of micro-authoritarianism — for example there is nothing on educational practices — but it does move towards a consideration of the symbolic aspect of politics. The future of democracy, and a future role for socialism, depend critically on the broadening of our analytical agenda to take up issues previously neglected, or at best not integrated within our political perspectives.

This book is about the southern cone of Latin America but its context is a much broader one. As I began to write it the students of China were pursuing their brave campaign for democracy under socialism. In South Africa the struggle for basic democratic rights against apartheid capitalism continued unabated. In Western Europe, vigorous struggles by women, peace campaigners and national minorities were all in their way challenging the threats to democracy posed by late capitalism. In all areas of the globe — in the advanced capitalist societies, under the bureaucratic socialist systems and in the so-called Third World — the struggle for democracy is vital and predominant. The left, in its various guises, has often in the past sneered at democracy for being merely 'formal', and the struggles on its behalf misguided 'reformism'. This smugness was nowhere more dangerous than in the southern cone of Latin America, and the long night of military dictatorship has led to a fundamental revaluation of democracy. This book reflects this tendency and contributes hopefully to the continuing debate on the nature and contradictions of democracy and its relationship with socialism, to which many erstwhile revolutionaries in the region are now saying farewell.

The organization and topics covered by this book are as follows: Chapter 1 carries out a broad reassessment of the 'question of democracy' in the Marxist tradition, from the legacy of Marx and Engels, to Lenin's famous formulation that is was 'the best possible shell' for capitalism, to the present. The Marxist paradigm has been particularly influential in intellectual circles in Latin America, and it is thus appropriate to understand its thinking about the question of democracy. The contemporary debates considered include that surrounding the attempt of Ernesto Laclau and Chantal Mouffe to define a new 'radical democratic' alternative for the left. We also consider the interrelationship of democracy and development, including the contentious position of Bill Warren, for whom they were as Siamese twins. For others, of course, dependent capitalist development must by its very nature be authoritarian. Chapter 2 relates these broad concerns to the concrete politics of Latin America. We examine the experience of populism and the so-called compromise state, and the bitter roads to dictatorship which followed in the late 1960s. This chapter also examines the dilemmas of the left during this earlier period, including the guerrilla experience and the general absence of a serious, sustained democratic practice. The left in Latin America (particularly in the southern cone after the dictatorships) is rethinking its views on democracy and socialism in a vital and far-reaching debate.

Chapters 3 and 4 consider respectively the modern dictatorships we are now seeing the back of and the transitions to democracy in a broad framework. We examine the new economic models implemented by the military regimes, their attempt at carrying out a radical transformation of politics, and the all-pervasive 'culture of authoritarianism' of these years. The following chapter turns to the internal and external causation of the transition to democracy, the renewed importance of political parties in this process, and the controversial question of the role played by social movements in the collapse of military rule. Both chapters examine the trends and differences unifying and distinguishing the cases of Argentina, Brazil, Chile and Uruguay. There is an attempt to strike a balance here between formalistic models which indicate various factors in splendid isolation from real history, and the detailed empirical account which gets lost in a mass of particulars.

Chapters 5, 6 and 7 examine in turn various aspects of the new democracies in Argentina, Brazil and Uruguay. For each country we consider the nature of the transition to democracy, the economic projects of the democratic governments, and the role of social movements in the new period, and we attempt some kind of political balance-sheet, albeit provisional. These chapters flow out of and build on Chapter 4 (on the transitions to democracy in general) to consider the concrete experience of the three southern cone countries that have commenced a new democratic era. They each followed quite a different path out of dictatorship, they each tackled an economic crisis of varied proportions and they each saw an increased role for labour and other social movements as democracy became consolidated. Each country in its way provides valuable lessons on how democracy is reborn, how the military is dealt with, and how social movements can find a place in the sun. They all show that the future for democracy in Latin America is a fragile one, and that the economic and social problems of the people are far from being resolved.

Finally, Chapter 8 turns to the prospects and limits of the 'new politics' in Latin America. We consider the 'actually existing democracies' of the southern cone within a broader historical context, relating back to the general theoretical concerns reconsidering democracy, articulated in Chapter 1. For many, a new democratic ideology is now in gestation which will fundamentally restrict a resurgence of military authoritarianism in the future. Such apparently exotic cases (from the Latin American point of view) as Austria are being closely examined for lessons by Latin American democrats. For the left, having learned the habits of democracy there is now a tendency to 'bend the stick in the other direction' and say farewell to socialism. Here too we return to the debates raised in Chapter 1 and consider whether socialism has a future in Latin America, or whether democracy has a future without the struggle for socialism again being placed on the agenda. On this lofty, but we hope not too abstract, note the text closes, with a general and country-by-country bibliography for further reading.

1.   Democracy Reconsidered

There has in recent years been a profound rethinking and re-evaluation of democracy by the left, due in part to the post-1968 ferment within Marxism, but due also to the onslaught of the new right in ideological and practical terms. The 'question of democracy' has joined gender, race and nation, once neglected by Marxism but now centre-stage. This chapter reviews the treatment of democracy in the classical Marxist tradition, and some of the major contemporary debates. We consider whether democracy is a means to an end (socialism) or whether it is an objective in its own right for socialists. Is democracy the 'best possible shell' for capitalism or is it, rather, profoundly contradictory to the objectives of late capitalism? What do we mean by 'bourgeois democracy' and how is it distinguished from the duly patented socialist version? These are some of the questions we ask in considering the general move towards a re-evaluation of democracy in recent years. The other strand of the debate we consider is the relationship between democracy and development in the so-called Third World. In reply to the over-optimistic views of orthodox modernization theory, the left developed a conception of development as necessarily authoritarian. Yet for others, who would also claim to be Marxists, there is a profoundly complementary relation between capitalism and democracy, even on the periphery. A broad review of this debate in both theoretical and comparative historical terms sets the scene for the second chapter which moves on to consider in more concrete terms major aspects of politics (both state and opposition) in contemporary Latin America.

The Marxist tradition

In *The German Ideology* of 1846, Marx and Engels commented that: 'all struggles within the state, the struggle between democracy, aristocracy and monarchy, the struggle for the franchise, etc, etc, are merely the illusory forms in which the real struggles of the different classes are fought out among one another'.[1] This statement sets the tone for subsequent Marxist treatments of democracy: there is a 'real' class struggle going on at the socio-economic level of nations and a 'superficial' political battle played out by other forces. This is a form of essentialism that seeks the underlying essence beneath phenomena or processes which may well have their own autonomy. This does not mean that Marx somehow neglected the importance of democratic political forms, or reduced all political forms to an undifferentiated bourgeois state. In *The Class Struggles in France* of 1850, Marx wrote that: 'the most comprehensive contradiction in the Constitution [of 1848] consists in the fact that it gives political power to the classes whose social slavery it is intended to perpetuate: proletariat, peasantry, petty bourgeoisie. And it deprives the bourgeoisie, the class whose old social power it sanctions, of the political guarantees of this power.'[2] Republican institutions, for Marx, force the bourgeoisie to rule through democracy and thus 'endanger the very basis of bourgeois society'.[3] In turn, democratic conditions depend on, and anticipate, the oppressed classes moving forward from political to social emancipation. Thus the constitution of the bourgeois democratic republic can be seen to express the contradictions between the social classes which coexist in capitalist society, and to provide the terrain for their ongoing struggle.

It was during the Paris Commune of 1871 and its aftermath that Marx and Engels developed their ideas of what a socialist democracy might look like. The Commune 'was not one of those dwarfish struggles between the executive and the parliamentary forms of class domination, but a revolt against both these forms'.[4] The Commune was nothing less than '*the political form of the social emancipation*, of the liberation of labour . . .'[5] In this revolt against the state in all its manifestations, be they democratic or monarchic, the division between the members of civil society and their political representatives begins to close up. This was, for Engels, the 'dictatorship of the proletariat'. The councillors of the Commune were to be elected by universal suffrage and subject to recall at short notice. This use of democratic procedures by the communes is contrasted with its abuse hitherto 'either for the parliamentary sanction of the Holy State Power, or a play in the hands of the ruling classes, only employed by the people to sanction (choose the instruments of) parliamentary class rule once in many years . . .'[6] But now general suffrage had been 'adapted to its real purpose'. No longer were the people to accept 'the delusion [that] administration and political governing were mysteries, transcendent functions only to be trusted to the hands of a trained caste . . .'[7] One of the most far-reaching conclusions that Marx and Engels would draw from this early 'republic of labour' in 1871 was that the working class could not simply seize the state and use it for its own purposes. Rather, this was a revolution against the state itself, the start of a transition to socialism and the process whereby the reunification of political and civil society would occur.

Marx and Engels were not bedevilled by the later concern with the either/or of reform/revolution in considering the socialist attitude towards democracy. Marx did have his flashes of 'ultraleftism', as when in *The Class Struggles in France* he argued, in relation to the proletariat's defeat in the 1848 Constitution, that 'Only its defeat convinced it of the truth that the smallest improvement in its position remains a utopia which becomes a crime as soon as it aspires to become reality.'[8] This attack on reform struggles — only the revolution matters — was out of character, and overshadowed by Marx's arguments in *Capital* and elsewhere that workers could gain reforms under capitalist democracy. A related issue is whether 'true' democracy or socialism could be achieved through peaceful or democratic means. Marx himself always maintained that universal suffrage was 'not the miracle-working magic wand which the republican worthies had assumed' and warned repeatedly about the dangers of 'parliamentary cretinism'. Engels, however, in the oft debated 1895 introduction to *The Class Struggles in France*, which became known as his political testament, seemed to make a plea for a peaceful road to socialism: 'The franchise has been, in the words of the French Marxist Programme, *transformé, de moyen de duperie qu'il a été jusqu'ici, en instrument d'émancipation* — transformed by them from a means of deception, which it had been before, into an instrument of emancipation . . . Rebellion in the old style, street fighting with barricades, which decided the issue everywhere up to 1848 was to a considerable extent obsolete.'[9] Arguably, Engels was calling for a revision of Marxist tactics rather than a wholesale change of strategy, but he, nevertheless, opened the door to a more positive Marxist attitude towards the ballot box and firmly rejected the mistaken conception of revolution as a 'revolution of the minority'.

The revisionists
After the death of Engels in 1895, some theorists of the Second International developed a 'revisionist' interpretation of Marxism which included a re-evaluation of democracy. Taking up the ambiguity of Engels's 'political testament' cited above, they developed a systematically reformist reading of Marx's legacy. For Eduard Bernstein, democracy was simply the political form of liberalism, and the transformation of capitalism into socialism would be a smooth process: 'the liberal organisations of modern society . . . are flexible, and capable of change and development. They do not need to be destroyed, but only to be further developed.'[10] The working class should not seek power through revolution but simply to effect the progressive democratization of the state. Bernstein assumed an inherent contradiction between political democracy and social inequality, and from this disharmony concluded that any extension of democracy is automatically a threat to continued capitalist rule. In Bernstein's reformist optic, the dividing line between democracy and socialism gradually fades away: 'Democracy is at the same time means and end. It is the means of the struggle for socialism and it is the form socialism will take once it has been realised.'[11] Kautsky's polemic against the victorious Russian Revolution after 1917 took as its starting point the logic of this statement. Though maintaining the verbal call for political revolution, Kautsky saw the whole process occurring within the framework set by democracy, so that the working class could pursue its aims through strictly legal methods alone, a gradualist class struggle based on what Kautsky saw as the revolutionary advocacy of reforms.

Leninism
While the Second International turned towards social democracy as we know it

today, Lenin was polemicizing against 'the renegade Kautsky' and developing what has become known as the Leninist conception of democracy and socialism. Lenin's position is expressed most clearly in his famous *The State and Revolution* of 1917, where he argues forcibly that 'fully consistent democracy is impossible under capitalism, and under socialism all democracy *will wither away*'.[12] Democracy is, above all, for Lenin, a *state* and thus represents the systematic use of *force* by one class against another. Even under the most favourable conditions for the development of a democratic republic 'this democracy is always hemmed in by the narrow limits set by capitalist exploitation, and consequently always remains, in effect, a democracy for the minority, only for the propertied classes, only for the rich'.[13] Freedom under capitalism, as in ancient Greece, is for the slave-owners only. The equality of citizens under capitalism is merely formal. In relation to the Paris Commune of 1871, Lenin saw it as a case of: '"quantity being transformed into quality": democracy, introduced as fully and consistently as is at all conceivable, is transformed from bourgeois into proletarian democracy . . .'[14] Such a degree of democracy entails overstepping the bounds of the democratic republic and commencing its socialist reorganization. Thus the fundamental Marxist–Leninist distinction between bourgeois and socialist democracy was born, the latter sometimes being seen as *more* democratic than the first but later becoming codified in the 'dictatorship of the proletariat', a category which became the subject of fierce controversy.

One of the more famous passages in *The State and Revolution* declares that: 'A democratic republic is the best possible shell for capitalism, and, therefore, once capital has gained possession of this very best shell, . . . it establishes its power so securely, so firmly, that *no* change of persons, institutions or parties in the bourgeois–democratic republic can shake it.'[15] Bourgeois law, resting as it does on the merely 'formal' equality of citizens, provides an ideological smoke-screen and encourages the fetishism of the political relations pertaining to the democratic state form. Universal suffrage, for Lenin, following Engels, can thus be seen as an instrument of bourgeois rule: it cannot be 'really capable of revealing the will of the majority of the working people and of securing its realisation'.[16] The bourgeoisie exercises its power all the more surely when it is indirect: it may often rule but not govern. Lenin implies that the democratic state is 'sewn up' to such an extent by the dominant classes that no change of personnel or even ruling political party, can shake its rule. Indeed, Lenin stresses that the omnipotence of wealth is more certain in a democratic republic. Of course in practice, particularly in the so-called Third World, the bourgeoisie has availed itself of other political forms to achieve its objectives. We can posit two sets of circumstances which lead to this: firstly, the inherent contradictions of bourgeois democracy in so far as it allows the dominated classes to organize and express themselves, and secondly, the inability of the capitalist class to achieve a full hegemony over society and thus avail itself of the benefits (albeit contradictory) of the bourgeois democratic republic.

In spite of the air of dogmatism which permeates the Marxist–Leninist discourse, Lenin himself was by no means simple-minded in his assessment of democracy. While stressing that democracy is a form of the state, Lenin does admit that 'on the other hand, it signifies the formal recognition of equality of citizens, the equal right of all to determine the structure of, and to administer, the state. This, in turn, results in the fact that, at a certain stage in the development of democracy, it first welds together the class that wages a revolutionary struggle against capitalism . . .'[17] For this class, democratic tasks are of primary importance. Lenin's analysis certainly suffers from essentialism in reducing 'bourgeois democracy' to the rule of capital and in counterposing it to 'socialist democracy'. Thus he argued that 'Only the soviet organisation of the state can really effect the immediate break-up and total destruction of the old, i.e. bourgeois, bureaucratic and judicial machinery . . . which is the greatest obstacle to the practical implementation of democracy for the workers and working people generally.'[18] Today we cannot afford to be so sanguine on the prospects for 'proletarian democracy', nor can we afford the certainty which rules out any continued role for formal democratic procedures under the transition to socialism. By not providing a viable model for socialist democracy Leninism led inevitably to abuses of democracy every bit as severe as those caused by the 'old bourgeois, bureaucratic and judicial machinery' which had administered the merely 'formal' democracy of the bourgeois republics.

Leon Trotsky, for his part, never developed an independent or consistent conception of democracy of his own. The young Trotsky was a sharp critic of Leninism, denouncing the methods of centralism within the party which led to 'substitutionism' (a dictatorship over the proletariat) and called for inner-party democracy and increased mass participation. Trotsky the post-1917 Bolshevik was to dub this early critique of Lenin's 'immature and erroneous' while he became a fervent supporter of the dictatorship of (over) the proletariat. In the struggle against Stalin, despite the later claims of his supporters, one of his biographers finds that 'Nothing could be further from the truth than to present Trotsky . . . as the voice of freedom and democracy striking out against the forces of darkness.'[19] Trotsky retained a deeply sceptical view of democracy, as in his denunciation of 'parliamentary fetishism' in a polemic with Kautsky.[20] Certainly, as in his later attack on the 'ultra-left' Third International line of 1928–35, Trotsky stressed the centrality of democratic *tasks*, but formal democratic institutions were still derided. Typical of Trotsky's view of democracy are his statements regarding the Paris Commune of 1871. Kautsky had compared favourably the Commune's respect for the principles of democracy with Soviet revolutionary practice. Trotsky replied that the Commune was in fact 'the living negation of formal democracy, for in its development it signified the dictatorship of working class Paris over the peasant country'[21] and that it was precisely its humanitarian considerations which led to its final demise. This was a rather one-sided interpretation of Marx's views on the Commune and a poor basis on which to elaborate a principled practice of democratic socialism.

Rosa Luxemburg

It is to Rosa Luxemburg that we must turn for a consistent critique of the

Leninist interpretation of democracy and socialism. She outlined her conception of democratic socialism in a sustained polemic with the leaders of post-revolutionary Russia. For Luxemburg, socialist democracy was not a pipe dream which could be put off till the promised land was reached, but a matter of daily practice in the struggle against capitalism and for the construction of socialism. She was quick to dismiss the sophistry in Trotsky's statement that 'As Marxists we have never been idol worshippers of formal democracy.'[22] Luxemburg questions Lenin's and Trotsky's counterposing of the soviets to 'the representative bodies created by general popular elections'.[23] As Luxemburg wrote of the post-October Soviet Union: 'Without general elections, without unrestricted freedom of press and assembly, without a free struggle of opinion, life dies out in every public institution, becomes a mere semblance of life, in which only the bureaucracy remains as the active element.'[24] The revolution becomes a 'clique affair' and the dictatorship of the proletariat the dictatorship of a handful of politicians; furthermore, 'such conditions must inevitably cause a brutalization of public life: attempted assassinations, shooting of hostages, etc'.[25] Luxemburg was herself to die at an assassin's hand in 1919, so she was not to witness the full degeneration of the Soviet revolution under Stalin, but she certainly warned of 'socialist dictators'. Socialism could not be constructed by decrees and the exclusion of democracy could only lead to corruption, mass apathy and, ultimately, terror.

Rosa Luxemburg had already advanced her views on democracy generally in *Reform or Revolution* of 1899. She begins by refusing any false counterposition between the two terms:

> the daily struggle for reforms, for the amelioration of the condition of the workers within the framework of the existing social order, and for democratic institutions, offers to the social democracy the only means of engaging in the proletarian class war and working in the direction of the final goal — the conquest of political power and the suppression of wage labour.[26]

She refuses, however, Bernstein's revisionist attempt to portray democracy as some inevitable stage in the development of society, as some type of historical law. Nor did Luxemburg accept the oft-made plea for labour to moderate its demands in the interests of democracy and argues that, on the contrary, 'democracy acquires greater chances of survival as the socialist movement becomes sufficiently strong to struggle against the reactionary consequences of world politics and the bourgeois desertion of democracy'.[27] In an era when labour is the only consistent supporter of democracy, the strengthening of democracy depends on the strengthening, not the weakening, of socialism. Democracy, finally, 'is indispensable to the working class, because only through the exercise of its democratic rights, in its struggle for democracy, can the proletariat become aware of its class interest and its historic task'.[28] Luxemburg retains a certain instrumentalist vision of democracy and a somewhat shaky distinction between the 'political form' of democracy and its 'hard kernel' of social inequality. Nevertheless, Luxemburg's political vision dictated a quite inseparable link between socialism and democracy both before and after the overthrow of capitalism.

Antonio Gramsci

Today it is Antonio Gramsci who occupies pride of place in the Marxist pantheon when it comes to developing a critical post-modern conception of politics. Surprisingly, however, his conception of democracy has received very little attention, usually being subsumed under the concept of hegemony. Gramsci's critique of liberal democracy in 1919 starts with the separation of economics and politics under capitalism. Workers can only participate as individuals or citizens in the arena of the democratic–parliamentary state, but 'The liberal experience is not worthless and can only be transcended after it has been experienced.'[29] Gramsci believed it was 'inane and ridiculous' to attempt to remove oneself from the sphere of operation of the democratic–parliamentary state. He did, however, believe that the proletariat would need to develop its own distinct forms of socialist democracy even before the overthrow of capitalism. This network of proletarian institutions generated by its associative experience is essential: 'Otherwise all our enthusiasm, all the faith of the working masses, will not succeed in preventing the revolution from degenerating pathetically into a new parliament of schemers, talkers and irresponsibles . . . '[30] The revolutionary party, of course, plays a key element in this process. Democratic centralism, the Leninist key to party organization, was, for Gramsci, 'an elastic formula, which can be embodied in many diverse forms; it comes alive in so far as it is interpreted and continually adapted to necessity'.[31] In fact, Gramsci's views on a new concept of democracy, which would surpass corporative demands, and his stress on diversity, show the distance he took from the bureaucratic centralism the Soviet party adopted in practice.

Gramsci's views on democracy, however, cannot be separated from his broader concept of hegemony, and its various interpretations. As Gramsci notes in one of his prison notebooks: '*Hegemony and Democracy*: Among the many meanings of democracy, it seems to me that the most concrete and realistic one must be connected with the concept of "hegemony".'[32] For Gramsci, the creation of socialism is not a thaumaturgical act but a process of development, and the modern development of capitalism leads to the 'war of position' taking precedence over the 'war of manoeuvre' of the Bolsheviks in the proletariat's strategic armoury. The democratic practice of hegemony in this sense represents a radical break with the vanguardism of orthodox Leninism and the corporatism of social democracy alike. Now that we live in the era of 'Gramscianism', the interpretation of the sometimes cryptic, always elusive, prison writings is a key task. For some, Gramsci simply represents the 'Leninism of the West', adapted to the more complex societies and conditions of democracy. On the other hand, in Ernesto Laclau's enterprise (see below), the Gramscian concept of hegemony serves as a springboard for a radical deconstruction of the whole Marxist tradition and a certain randomization of politics. Neither extreme seems persuasive in claiming the 'real' Gramscian imprimatur to itself. In conclusion, as Anne Sassoon argues, the building of hegemony, the gaining of widespread consent, and a democratisation of the practice of politics is an integral part of the socialist revolution in Gramsci's conception. He therefore provides an argument which can help to serve as a basis on which to develop the concept of the link between democracy and socialism.[33]

To conclude this all too brief survey of the Marxist tradition's concern with democracy we could, with some simplification, distinguish three currents of interpretations within Marxism:

revisionist or liberal: with a focus on 'citizenship', a radical democracy akin to that of Rousseau;
Leninist: with an emphasis on seizing power and a 'pragmatic' view of democracy;
libertarian: stressing the interrelationship of democracy and socialism, as a means and as an end.

In the field of political practice it is the Leninist variant of Marxism which has undoubtedly had the upper hand, particularly in the so-called Third World where its emphasis on organization and modernization have granted it an undoubted efficacy. As to the 'liberal' Marxist reading of democracy we could say that it is now regaining popularity (as we see in the next section) with an emphasis on socialist pluralism, the rights of the individual, the critique of 'statism', and other beliefs of the new post-Marxism. Altogether less developed is the libertarian Marxist reading of democracy and socialism which we could trace back to Rosa Luxemburg, Council Communism and the experience of the Soviets so rudely interrupted by Leninism in power. To some extent this discourse has been materialized in the new social movements with their emphasis on grass-roots democracy and the necessary congruence of means and ends. If the new liberal reading of Marxism is rapidly leading it beyond socialism to accept radical democracy as its objective, and Leninism is losing favour even in its homeland with *glasnost*, it remains for the new social movements to drag the old into a revitalized libertarian Marxist conception of democracy as integral to the socialist project, even while the latter retains its specificity and transcends 'bourgeois democracy' as we know it.

Contemporary debates

Marxism and liberalism
Out of the 'crisis of Marxism' in the 1970s has been born a renewed concern with democracy and its role in the overall socialist project. In England, we find E. P. Thompson asserting with bold confidence that Marxism must abandon before it is too late its tendency to dismiss all law as merely an instrument for class rule.[34] As civil liberties are being eroded under late capitalism, so we must refuse any conception of 'bourgeois democracy' as mere illusion, and the dropping of its mask as a glorious clarification of the battle between classes.

For Thompson, the left should make its own the liberal concern with upholding 'the rule of law' not as state-dictated system but as reassertion of the moral economy of the 'free-born Englishman'. From another political culture, Norberto Bobbio, leading intellectual of the Italian Socialist Party, bids us reassess the traditional hostility between Marxism and liberalism. He also argues that 'democracy is the rule of law *par excellence*'.[35] Bobbio argues that not only are the formal liberal civil and political rights essential for democracy, but the whole constitutional and institutional framework of liberal democracies as well. No facile critique of Thompson's and Bobbio's concern with the rule of law should be attempted, but undoubtedly they 'bend the stick too far', in compensating for Marxism's previous legal nihilism, by adopting a conception of the liberal democratic state quite devoid of class content. That the left in newly democratic Brazil is avidly debating the work of Bobbio testifies, however, to the importance of his challenge.

There has of course been previous critical discussion within Marxism which took seriously questions of law, order, social contract and political obligation — in the work of C. B. Macpherson for example. More recently, Carole Pateman has taken up Rousseau's theory of participatory political association as grounded in the free creation of political obligation by a society's citizens.[36] For Rousseau, the liberal social contract was a deliberate political contrivance by the rich to secure their socio-economic dominance through politics. Thus, for Rousseau, the social contract cannot be abstracted from the conditions under which it is made and its real underlying aims. Against the tenets of liberal theory, freedom and equality are integrally related to one another in Rousseau's political philosophy. Political obligation cannot thus be based on a formal equality under the law which disregards social inequality, but rather, as Pateman puts it, 'a substantive equality of active citizens who are political decision-makers, or the Sovereign, in a participatory political association'.[37] However, Rousseau did not extend his arguments to women, or grant the right of dissent or disobedience to the minority, which, Pateman argues, should be implicit in the practice of self-assumed political obligation. After decades in which the rule of Hobbes — where conflicts of interest and the struggle for power define the human condition — has reigned supreme in Latin America there is now a serious reconsideration of the work of Rousseau and that of Locke, who in rejecting the Hobbesian argument, anticipated the whole tradition of protective democracy.

Marxism and democracy

In 1980 the British Communist Party published a book entitled *Marxism and Democracy*, edited by Alan Hunt, which bravely opened the doors for a renewal of Marxist debate on the issue. The editor entitled his contribution 'Taking Democracy Seriously' and bid us recognize that 'What is absent from Lenin is any recognition of the contradictory character of bourgeois democracy'.[38] For the socialist movement the expansion of the sphere of democracy under capitalism should be an integral and even central task. To counterpose bourgeois and proletarian democracy in the tradition of Lenin is seen as an obstacle to this task. One of the contributors to this volume, Bob Jessop, developed this theme in trying to demonstrate the 'political indeterminacy' of democracy.[39] By this he meant that democratic institutions do not necessarily pertain to or reflect the interests of the capitalist class; other forces must intervene to ensure that the democratic republic functions on behalf of capital. It is this relative indeterminacy of democracy which provides the space for struggles over hegemony in the field of what Jessop calls popular–democratic as against class politics. Stuart Hall, for his part, shows how the right also knows how to 'take democracy seriously' and has seized the democratic–popular initiative in many advanced capitalist countries.[40] He also sounds a salutary note in stressing that the overcoming of the essentialism implicit in the 'reform–revolution' formula does not mean that the political problem of reformism has disappeared.

In the United States, meanwhile, socialist concern with democracy had progressed considerably, not surprisingly when we consider the abject failure of traditional socialism in that country. Bowles and Gintis, for example, stressed the contradiction between liberal democracy and capitalism and went on to argue that: 'Demands posed as universal rights and movements constituted by the universal discourse of liberal democracy are prone to become class demands and class movements . . .'[41] Because capitalism in crisis can no longer afford to make concessions, universal rights become a class struggle. Liberal democracy may, according to Bowles and Gintis, either turn into a corporate authoritarianism or, against all the evidence, 'toward an instrument, however imperfect, of popular power'.[42] It is not surprising that the new-found enthusiasm for liberal democracy on the part of the left coincides with a conservative onslaught by the likes of the Trilateral Commission on the problems of 'ungovernability' under capitalist democracy. It is also ironic that they both start from the assumption, not entirely demonstrated, that there is a basic contradiction between liberal democracy and capitalism. Meanwhile, George Novack had been reasserting the traditional American Marxist view of democracy in a broad restatement — *Democracy and Revolution*. Not surprisingly, he argued that: 'The bourgeois–democratic ideology has been permeated with mysticism from its birth, owing to the glaring discrepancies between its pretensions of equality and the persistence of inequalities on all levels of social life'.[43] However, these views were in a minority by the 1980s.

Clearly, few Marxists would dispute that socialism entails an extension of democratic control through all levels of society. Even when Lenin was speaking of 'smashing' the bourgeois state he was clear on this. What is new in the British and US debates on democracy is a conviction that democracy can be extended steadily, without fundamental ruptures, until it blends into socialism. Yet even if we accept the relative indeterminacy of democracy there are still social forces which will interpret differently what is meant by democracy and prevent — 'democratically' or forcefully — the full flowering of this utopian project. The new Marxist reading of democracy stresses the very ambiguity of the term in challenging the assumption that it 'belongs' to any specific class. In a sense this only reinforces the need to draw some distinction between various democratic projects, even if the original Leninist formulation of bourgeois and socialist democracy is too simplistic. To confuse the democracy of late capitalism, under Thatcherite/Reaganite administrations, with socialist democracy, is to fail to recognize the fetishism of bourgeois politics which makes us perceive as 'natural' — bourgeois parliamentary politics — precisely that which is not. Certainly, one can recognize the ambiguity of democracy as we know it — it is no mere 'sham' — and exploit those contradictions. No socialist project, however, is possible if it obscures, or even refuses to recognize, the process whereby the ruling class, however democratic or 'liberal' it may appear, will prevent a smooth and painless transition to socialism.

The Latin American dimension

In Latin America it was different factors, principally the bleak experience of military rule (as we shall see in Chapter 2), that helped to develop a concern with democracy in the late 1970s. The change in political thinking was a profound one. Juan Carlos Portantiero, one-time Maoist intellectual in Argentina, was now arguing that 'democracy as an objective is independent from the socio-economic order which contains it'.[44] Portantiero takes on board the conservative concern with the 'crisis of governability' in Latin America, and argues that the popular movement should enter a 'democratic pact', where social conflict can be conducted within an agreed institutional framework. Democracy is not seen as an end state which will usher in a reign of transparent social relations, as in Marx's communism, but rather as a permanent and difficult practice based on the principle of reciprocity. Other writers, including Chilean political scientists Norbert Lechner and Angel Flisfisch (whose work is considered in more detail in Chapters 2 and 8) have moved to a broader reformulation of what socialist politics means in Latin America today. To consolidate the fragile democracies of the 1980s it is seen as necessary to construct order rather than simply oppose, and to respect parliamentary institutions. Denying the possibility of total consensus, democracy is seen as a system where dissent is institutionalized. Against all previous instrumentalist conceptions of democracy (as merely a means to an end) these thinkers stress the merits of democracy in the socialization of power after the dictatorships, in redefining the identity of social actors so long submerged, and in the recovery of civil society from the military authoritarians.

One of the most interesting lines of enquiry of the new democratic Latin American left is that which calls for a socio-economic pact between labour and the new (or forthcoming) democratic governments. The key term in this discourse is *concertación*, which implies a more organic form of harmonization than that implied by the term compromise. Rather than engage in a zero-sum struggle between capital and labour we are bid to search for means to make compatible their divergent aspirations. Wage earners, in this political philosphy, are assumed to have a selfish orientation whereby they are 'free riders' in a system where others co-operate and compromise. This idea extends to workers Marx's dictum that capitalists wish to see their competitors' wages rise so that more can consume their commodities, produced under low-wage conditions. The democratic pact being proposed is, of course, much broader than a simple wages agreement: it implies an acceptance of the rules of democracy within which an ambitious programme of social and economic reconstruction can begin. As much of this book sets out to consider the prospects of the new democratic pacts, we need not develop a theoretical critique at this stage. However, I will simply register my agreement with Guillermo O'Donnell's troubled 'yes and no'[45] in response to the pacts: a facile rejection of them as simply class collaboration, reformist cul-de-sac or whatever must be followed by a more mature reflection which considers carefully their role after decades of military rule.

Ernesto Laclau

It is a Latin American writer, but one living in Europe and informed by the Eurocommunist debate — Ernesto Laclau — who developed the new conception of democracy to its fullest extent. A critical prerequisite for this project is the rejection of 'class reductionism' whereby ideologies (be they democracy or socialism) are reduced or subsumed by a particular social class. Thus democracy is not the sole prerogative of the bourgeoisie, and the working class is not the sole, or even main, agent of socialism. We cannot deduce the historical interest of this or that social group from their class position in contemporary society. In a somewhat obscure expression Laclau, and co-author Chantal Mouffe, write that 'Unfixity has become the condition of every social identity'.[46] There are a multiplicity of social interests which cannot be reduced to a simple class struggle. Against all forms of essentialism the authors reject self-defined totalities as a terrain of analysis: '"Society" is not a valid object of discourse'.[47] There is no single mechanism producing *the* working class or creating women's oppression, rather there are multiple social and cultural forms whereby these categories are constructed. There is, to use terms borrowed from psychoanalysis, 'a dispersion of subject positions'.[48] To some extent, in the so-called Third World, imperialist exploitation endows the popular struggle with a clearly defined enemy, and the diversity of democratic struggles is thereby reduced. Nevertheless, in the post-modern era we are now entering, antagonisms cut across societies in ways which cannot be reduced to two simple antagonistic camps.

It is difficult to deny this irreducible plurality of the social and replace the concept of 'autonomy' with outmoded calls for determination 'in the last instance' by the economic. In accepting the plurality of political spaces we are implying the centrality of democratic struggles. Laclau and Mouffe actually have as the subtitle of their book: 'Towards a Radical Democratic Politics'. Two hundred years ago, according to these authors, 'the democratic principle of liberty and equality [imposed] itself as the new matrix of the social imaginary'.[49] This 'democratic revolution' is today being renewed with the new antagonisms created by the so-called new social movements of sexual minorities, women, ethnic minorities and ecological struggle. This expansion and generalization of the democratic revolution is what marks out the present era. With the anti-democratic offensive of the neo-liberals that stalked its way from Chile 1973 to the imperialist heartlands, 'The task of the left . . . cannot be to renounce liberal–democratic ideology, but on the contrary, to deepen and expand it in the direction of a radical and plural democracy'.[50] Against all forms of classism (the idea that workers are privileged agents for social change), statism (that the state is the necessary platform for social change) and economism (that politics has an essentially economic root) we must accept the pluralism proper to a radical democracy, where the diverse elements and levels of struggle can no longer be expressed in a totality which transcends them.

In an earlier article Laclau expressed somewhat clearer, if less 'extreme', political guidelines for the left, taking up the analysis of Umberto Cerroni for whom 'Political democracy tends towards socialism, and socialism towards political democracy'.[51] Given the contradictory nature of bourgeois democracy (at once elitist and revolutionary) and the idea that the defence of democracy is an anti-capitalist task (under the authoritarianism of late capitalism) this conclusion is inevitable. Laclau then coins the expression 'democratic equivalent' to refer to the connections drawn between diverse symbols of oppression and expressed through a general equivalent. The confrontation with colonialism may unify and express diverse democratic struggles by workers, peasants, women and intellectuals, for example. The class struggle today takes place on a terrain increasingly dominated by democratic antagonisms, but Laclau also recognizes that 'the fundamental antagonism which reproduces the system continues to be class exploitation'.[52] The main problem for Marxist theory and practice today is to seek a new form of politics that can articulate class and democratic antagonisms. The key is to find a general democratic equivalent as a condition for the struggle for direct democracy and the withering away of the state, and the precondition for this, according to Laclau, 'is the generalisation of democratic antagonisms, and their unification with the struggle of the working class'.[53] Such a formulation would be acceptable to much of the old as well as the 'new' democratic left in Latin America.

Such an iconoclastic project as Laclau's could not fail to elicit a counter-attack from the bastions of traditional Marxism. Ellen Wood expressed an intelligent defence of orthodoxy most eloquently against all those she dubbed the new 'true' socialists, arguing that in the Laclau and Mouffe book they have 'taken the final step not only by detaching ideology from social determinations but by dissolving the social altogether into ideology or "discourse"'.[54] We now have detachable, class-neutral popular-democratic 'interpellations' up for grabs by the highest bidder. So democracy, as we saw above, can, for Laclau, be detached from its bourgeois interpellations and taken up by the socialist movement. For Wood this argument 'is calculated to bridge the gap between bourgeois and socialist democracy and to conceptualize away the radical break between them'.[55] This is reasserting the Leninist position (see above) but it does not actually get us much further. When Wood goes on to say that we should reclaim democracy for socialism by challenging the limits of bourgeois democracy with alternative socialist forms, we are moving on to a more con-crete terrain, one animated by the debates of the new social movements. We cannot subsume socialism as a mere moment of 'the democratic revolution' which Laclau and Mouffe stress so much. Though democracy cannot be reduced to a clever mask for capital's rule, it is not either a classless ethereal ideology. To ask what democracy actually means for Laclau and Mouffe helps clarify their 'discourse'.

The birth of democracy is conventionally reckoned to have happened in classical Greece, where the Athenian republic was based on direct participation by citizens, a category which excluded slaves, women and foreigners. Will Durant has defined Athenian democracy as 'the narrowest and fullest in history; narrowest in the number of those who share its principles, fullest in directness and equality with which all citizens control legislation, and administer public affairs'.[56] It is, of course, the French Revolution which gives birth to the modern conception of democracy based on *Liberté, Egalité, Fraternité*. This marks for Laclau 'the invention of the democratic culture' and, henceforth, there would be no clear antagonistic limits between two forms of society as presented in the people/*ancien regime* opposition. Marx was to seek out the basis of a new principle of social division based on the confrontation of classes, but this was illusory. Yet 'the democratic revolution' of the late 18th century has little basis in history. The great American Revolution regarded 'democracy' with horror, as rule by the *plebs* or, to use a more familiar term, mob rule. Democracy can certainly refer to popular power but it was gradually subsumed under the practice of liberal democracy where it symbolized the procedural forms and civil liberties with which we are now familiar. As Ellen Wood points out: 'Indeed, by the new standards, the direct exercise of popular power might be perceived as "anti-democratic".'[57] In conclusion, we should accept the relative indeterminacy of the democratic discourse, its importance as a site of struggle for the left, without dissolving socialist objectives and socialist forms of organization into a vacuous, tasteless, classless and ultimately ahistorical stew.

Before closing this section it would be well to remember the sensitive yet realistic approach to socialism and democracy taken by Nicos Poulantzas in his last book, *State, Power, Socialism*. Poulantzas argues that both social democracy and Stalinism are marked by their statism, distrust of mass initiatives, 'in short by suspicion of democratic demands'.[58] This does not, however, lead him to embrace the doctrine of direct democracy and endorse the self-management political current. The sweeping substitution of rank-and-file democracy for representative democracy is seen as, to some extent, responsible for the failure of Soviet democracy after 1917 and the rise of centralizing and statist Leninism. The Marxist tradition must, for Poulantzas, shake off its basic distrust of the institutions of representative democracy and of political freedoms, mistakenly demeaned by the term 'bourgeois democracy'. Democratic socialism is the only kind possible and we cannot conceive of 'the transition', as though politics will be transformed overnight. The democratic road to socialism implies, for Poulantzas, 'a real permanence and continuity of the institutions of representative democracy — not as unfortunate relics to be tolerated for as long as necessary, but as an essential condition of democratic socialism'.[59] Facile appeals to the failure of the 'peaceful road to socialism' in Chile in 1973 cannot prevent us from recognizing the importance of so-called formal liberties, such as universal suffrage and political and ideological pluralism, within the democratic socialist project. Nor does the Sandinista victory in 1979 provide a simple counterpoint to Chile and prove 'armed road, only road'.

Democracy and development

Modernization approach
Neither the Marxist tradition nor contemporary debates within the Marxist field of influence have been over-concerned with the relationship between democracy and development. To trace the debates which do exist we must first turn to the orthodox sociology of modernization of the 1950s and its super-optimistic view of democracy and capitalist development. James Coleman, in the conclusion to a 1960 volume, *The Politics of the Developing Areas*, which examined various regions, concluded that 'with certain striking deviations', there was statistical support for the view that social and economic development was associated with increasing democracy.[60] In the language of Max Weber, there was an 'elective affinity' between capitalism and democracy. In a second wave of 'revisionist' modernization studies Samuel Huntingdon recognized that economic development could also have the unfortunate (for the US) effect of increasing social mobilization and the demand for 'political participation'.[61] The key issue for Huntingdon then was political institutionalization which could absorb the demands placed on the state, or, as he put in the famous opening sentence to his book *Political Order in Changing Societies*: 'The most important political distinction among countries concerns not their form of government but their degree of government'.[62] The difference between democratic Western forms of government and those in the communist East were, for Huntingdon, less than the difference between both of these and those of the Third World where 'governments simply do not govern'. From classical modernization we go to a cynical modernization theory which says that the Third World is not ready for democracy. Rather, it is not convenient for the dominant powers.

One of the most cogent critiques of the politics of modernization theory was developed by Guillermo O'Donnell, all the more interesting because it was operating at least partly within the framework of mainstream political science. In his *Modernization and Bureaucratic Authoritarianism*, published in 1973, O'Donnell questioned S. M. Lipset's formula that 'More socio-economic development = More likelihood of political democracy' and replaced it with his own dictum that: More socio-economic development = More political pluralization $\neq$ More likelihood of political democracy'.[63] By political pluralization O'Donnell meant the emergence of more political units interrelated in more complex ways. Pursuing this argument he took up Robert Dahl's model of the emergence of political democracy as a function of decreasing costs of tolerance and increasing costs of suppression. That is, social differentiation leads to the emergence of more autonomous groups which cannot be suppressed by government or each other. O'Donnell extends this model to argue that in Latin America, while the social differentiation caused by modernization has increased the costs of suppression, social integration has lagged and praetorianism has resulted, such that the costs of toleration have risen even more rapidly.[64] This accounts for the higher costs of suppression each time it is resorted to again. The overall conclusion proffered by O'Donnell in this early work is that political authoritarianism and not political democracy is the more likely concomitant of increased modernization. Rather than between democracy and development, we find an 'elective affinity' between the most advanced dependent capitalist countries and dictatorial rule.

Milton Friedman

Though the 'political development' school faded in the 1970s, a similar theme was revived by Milton Friedman, whose theories inspired Chilean generals and leaders of 'Western liberal democracies' alike. Friedman's main line of argument in *Capitalism and Freedom* was strikingly simple: 'The kind of economic organization that provides economic freedom directly, namely, competitive capitalism, also promotes political freedom because it separates economic power from political power and in this enables the one to offset the other'.[65] In other words, democracy thrives under competitive capitalism and is incompatible with any other form of economic system. The familiar litany then ensues that 'political freedom', defined purely in terms of individual choice, depends on reducing the overbearing role of the state, in particular the economic intervention of the state. The trade unions, as corporatist organizations, affecting the free play of market forces by allowing workers to combine, are seen as one of the main threats to democracy. For Milton Friedman, 'The story of the United States is the story of an economic miracle and a political miracle that were made possible by the translation into practice of two sets of ideas'.[66] These were respectively Adam Smith's view of the market system as free exchange which benefits all, and John Stuart Mill's stress on the individual as sovereign. Since the 19th century, governments have, for Friedman, steadily displaced the invisible hand of the market in regulating economic affairs, and eroded the sovereign rights of the individual. Writing in 1980, however, Friedman could take heart and note that: 'Fortunately the tide is turning'.[67] We will all soon again be 'Free to Choose'.

The critique of Friedman's conception of democracy through the market place has taken diverse forms. There are, of course, sound technical objections to his quantity theory of money and its better known offspring, 'monetarism'. On the other hand, writers such as André Gunder Frank have said that:

> As far as Chile is concerned, it [the Friedmanite doctrine] can, should and must be termed economic genocide; a calculated and massive policy of genocide through hunger and unemployment which is perhaps unknown in the recent or even distant history of the world in peacetime.[68]

Along this vein many have argued that Friedman's unrestricted freedom for the individual/market is at the cost of poverty for the many. The charge of 'inhumanity' is one which Friedman is, in the abstract, well able to counter, showing the benefits of his system to all.[69] We can go beyond moralism and expose the myth of 'bourgeois freedom' which socialism will do away with in the name of the 'dictatorship of the proletariat'. This is hardly a persuasive argument even for the 'person in the street' in Santiago; neither would turning to the experience of 'actually existing socialism' be persuasive in this regard. While recognizing that Friedman's conception of economic and political freedom bears little relation to history, we cannot brush away so easily the ideological challenge it represents. Much of the economic, political and social discourse of the South American dictatorships in the 1970s was couched in terms which derived from Friedman's onslaught on bourgeois orthodoxy. It is only more recently that a similar challenge has led to a rethinking of socialism and a rejection of debilitating orthodoxies.

Radical responses

For radical social science in the 1970s it became an accepted fact that dependent development was incompatible with political democracy. André Gunder Frank, who mounted one of the most effective rebuttals of the 1960s political modernization perspective, pursued this theme as the new authoritarian regimes of the 1970s came to power and, in some Third World countries, conducted vigorous industrialization programmes. Gunder Frank saw the growing repression by military governments in the 1970s as 'not accidental or merely ideologically motivated. Rather it is a necessary concomitant of economic exploitation . . .'[70] Whether the case in question be South Korea, Thailand, Pakistan, Ghana or Uruguay, for Gunder Frank the evidence points clearly to the conclusion that political repression is absolutely essential to impose increased economic exploitation on the masses. In other words, capitalist development in the conditions prevailing in the Third World is incompatible with political democracy. Gunder Frank makes much of a leading Japanese business magazine's 'league table' of countries according to investment risk, arguing that it shows a clear correlation with repressive socio-political measures.[71] Yet *Nikkei Business* was deriving its investment climate on the basis of perceived 'political stability' and at the top of the list were countries such as Sweden, the Netherlands, and Belgium, hardly prime examples of terrorist states. The point is that one cannot *a priori* declare that this or that political system is essential to capitalist development. There are efficient and thriving democratic and dictatorial capitalist regimes and, equally, unstable and faltering examples of both. Sketchy, impressionistic tours of capitalist 'horror stories' do not make an automatic case for socialism.

Another author who pursued this theme was James Petras, particularly in an article (with Edward Herman) on the rhetoric and reality of the resurgent democracies in Latin America during the 1980s. Unimpressed by the democratization process in the southern cone, Petras insists that 'the political–economic constraints accepted by [the] newly elected regimes . . . in Latin

America allow them few opportunities for consolidating a democratic consensus'.[72] In the text which follows we will certainly emphasize the economic and political constraints on the new democracies, but it seems wrong to assume that some 'authoritarian imperative' will subvert these regimes. Petras doubts there will be any shift in power because 'the menu of candidates is restricted to an official list approved by a behind-the-scenes elite'.[73] Against the evidence, he argues that the military have 'proven to be largely beyond prosecution for horrendous crimes' and that, furthermore, they 'hold the resurgent democracies hostage against any incursion on their rights or any departure from what they regard as sound principles'.[74] He finally suggests that it is 'possible that the new civilian rulers are "fall guys" whose alloted task is to take primary responsibility for assured economic failures'.[75] This is an implausible scenario where a far-sighted imperialism works fiendish plots with 'behind-the-scenes elites', the military are all-powerful even when defeated, and the economic prospects for capitalism are so hopeless that the new democracies are simply 'fall guys' to hold the store until more appropriate conditions emerge for the natural military state of capital to take the reins once again.

From within the Marxist camp (although some would dispute this) Bill Warren launched a fierce attack against what he saw as the revolutionary romanticism of the dependency approach to politics.[76] For Warren, the left had wrongly forsaken Marx's emphasis on the progressive nature of capitalist development, even in the periphery. He believed Lenin had committed an about-turn on the question of imperialism, from his early writings where it was judged progressive, to his later 'classical' statement which, of course, forms the background to dependency theory. Warren argues that:

> There is an important connection between capitalism and parliamentary (bourgeois) democracy; the latter provides the best political environment for the socialist movement and creates conditions that favour a genuine learning process by the working class.[77]

This is a reformulated version of the argument that democracy provides the 'best possible shell' for capitalism, now saying that it does so for the socialist movement. The connection between capitalism and democracy will be explored shortly, but the other part of Warren's argument — that democracy is better than dictatorship or feudalism for the advance of labour — is unanswerable. Warren does, however, go further than this and actually says at one point that 'Capitalism and democracy are, I would argue, linked virtually as Siamese twins'.[78] A footnote qualifies this argument by noting that 'it relates specifically to Western Europe' but, nevertheless, it seems excessive. Certainly, as Warren argues, the conditions which led to political democracy for the bourgeoisie did not lead to democracy 'for everybody'. The statement is, of course, even less true for the areas of the globe conquered by colonial capitalist expansion.

At one time the accepted orthodoxy on the left was that democracy and development were incompatible in the Third World. Now, positions derived from that of Bill Warren are much more common. Thus Gavin Kitching starts from the assumption that only capitalism can create the general prosperity which is a precondition for socialism and thus argues logically that 'the central task of the Left in the current situation is to help restore boom conditions as quickly as possible . . .'[79] The clear lesson is that socialists should promote capitalist development and replace the narrow interests of class by a concern with the general interest. Kitching goes on to say that he wants 'to remarry socialist ideals with the much older concepts of *civitas*, or republican "virtue", of the duties and powers as well as the passive rights of the citizen . . .'[80] The struggle for economic survival under conditions of dependent capitalist development provides a poor basis for democratic socialism. The appeal to 'citizens' thus strives to restore more forcefully the relationship between democracy and socialism. In a sense, Kitching draws out the political implications of Bill Warren's analysis, albeit more pessimistically because Warren tended to see an inexorable advance of capitalism producing a working class which would then march on to socialism. What both authors are saying is that the Third World is at present not ripe for socialism, that capitalist development is a progressive task to be accomplished, and that the struggle for democratic virtues should replace the narrow self-interest of social classes.

We have, up to this point, examined several starkly counterposed positions on the relationship between democracy and development. For the political development school the two are inextricably linked and the best prospects for democracy come from capitalist development. The military dictatorships of the 1960s are 1970s soon put paid to this illusion. On the other hand, a 'hard line' Marxist analysis simply restated that democracy and dependent development were incompatible. Without underestimating the fragile nature of the new democracies in the 1980s, this position seems equally untenable. Both positions argue on the basis of lists of countries where democracy and development have, or have not, coexisted. Such crass empiricism is no substitute for a careful historical examination of the essentially contradictory relationship between capitalism and development as put forward by Marx himself among others. Then we came to Huntingdon, who constructs a Leninism of the bourgeoisie in his report to the Trilateral Commission, which argues that 'threats to democracy arise ineluctably from the inherent workings of the system itself'.[81] From this position springs the concern with the 'crisis of governability' which has now spread to the left in Latin America coming out of the military dictatorships. On the left, following Bill Warren, we can construct a renewed Marxist orthodoxy which stresses the positive aspects of capitalist development in creating the conditions for democracy and, ultimately, for socialism. Yet this position also neglects the stress on the contradictions of capitalism in Marx himself, and downplays the imperatives of survival in the peripheral areas of capitalism.

The historical record
In a broad sweep of the rise of capital Goran Therborn found that 'Bourgeois democracy has been attained by such diverse and tortuous routes that any

straightforward derivation from the basic characteristics of capitalism would be impossible, or at best seriously misleading'.[82] Quite simply we cannot deduce that capitalist development will lead ineluctably either to democracy or to dictatorship. What we have is a particular historical constellation of social and national forces. Nevertheless, the historical record does show that democracy has usually followed the struggles of the subaltern classes (to use Gramsci's terminology) albeit not always as a direct or immediate result. This conclusion lends credence to Rosa Luxemburg's argument that true democrats should favour, and not restrain, the advance of the working class. Another of Therborn's conclusions is that 'none of the great bourgeois revolutions actually established bourgeois democracy'.[83] Friedman's reconstruction of the American Republic notwithstanding, this was a state of white propertied gentlemen with a genuine fear of democracy as rule of the *demos* (people). The other feature Therborn finds striking by its absence 'is that of a steady, peaceful process accompanying the development of wealth, literacy and urbanization'.[84] Indeed, democracy has been characterized by severe reverses and by its uneven spatial distribution across the globe. We should not be surprised by the uneven development of democracy across and within nations, in so far as this is one of the basic principles of capitalist expansion. That, and its essentially contradictory nature which can mean that democracy can be at once its 'best possible shell' and profoundly inimical to its inherent tendencies, and thus subversive.

Under conditions of dependent or dominated capitalism the advance of democracy is even more halting and problematic. External constraints on the development of capitalism have prevented the full and unfettered expansion of market relations. The lack of a powerful industrial bourgeoisie subject to the contradictions of capitalism (the need to incorporate the subaltern classes) has made democracy less of a pressing concern. Therborn, in a survey of the original democratization of Latin America, finds that 'Democracy in Latin America presents no clear trends or evolution, either in chronological time or in stages of "development".'[85] There are certain international political conjunctures which created the conditions for a move towards democratization but the timing and outcome of such a move were determined by local relations of forces. As to the working class, it did play an important role where its weight was significant, even if this was not determinant. With due regard to the different context in which it was made, Engels's remark that in Britain the bourgeoisie 'had not yet succeeded in driving the landed aristocracy completely from political power when another competitor, the working class, appeared on the stage',[86] is of considerable relevance. With the bourgeois democratic revolution not having been completed (in some countries it had not even commenced) the threat of a new socialist revolution loomed on the horizon, particularly after the declaration of socialism in Cuba in 1961. It is, indeed, hard to overestimate the influence of the Cuban revolution on Latin American politics, in far more ways than those immediately obvious.

Citizenship and capitalism

In seeking an understanding of the relationship between citizenship and capitalism we could do worse than turn to the contribution of T. H. Marshall, the well known theorist of the British welfare state. Marshall begins by distinguishing three elements or aspects of citizenship: civil, such as freedom of speech, the right to justice, and other prerequisites for individual freedom; political, involving the right to participate in the exercise of political power through local government and parliament; and social citizenship, by which he meant a whole range of things, from 'the right to a modicum of economic welfare and security to the right to share to the full in the social heritage and to live the life of a civilized being according to the standards prevailing in the society'.[87] In pre-capitalist times these various strands of citizenship were fused, but under capitalism they became separated. Many of the political struggles of the 20th century focused around these three moments of citizenship. We have here a broader notion of citizenship than one restrained by juridical definitions. Civil rights were in origin intensely individual and, as Marshall notes, 'they harmonized with the individualistic phase of capitalism'.[88] A purely political definition of citizenship, on the other hand, neglects the essential contradiction between personal freedoms and the coercive role of the state. By introducing the social element of citizenship, Marshall recognized that civil and political citizenship under capitalism was at best partial without the essential rights to social and economic welfare.

Marshall has been criticized for advancing an evolutionary view of the development of citizenship as some inherent characteristic of capitalism.[89] Yet this neglects the considerable fluidity of Marshall's conception with its emphasis on the contradictory relationship between parliamentary democracy and the free market of capitalism. The status of citizenship, with its implicit egalitarian principles, is in conflict with the essentially unequal system of capitalism. Perhaps Marshall overestimated the capacity of citizenship to override class, and underplayed the ambiguous aspect of freedom/control inherent in bodies such as the welfare state. Nevertheless, as S. M. Lipset notes in his introduction to Marshall's book, *Class, Citizenship, and Social Development*:

> In stressing the revolutionary character of citizenship, the creation of a status in which all men are equal, Marshall has revived an idea common among nineteenth-century thinkers, leftists and rightists alike, that equal suffrage and hereditary class privilege are incompatible.[90]

Such a debate on citizenship is now beginning in the new democracies of Latin America. The idea of a 'civic culture', once the preserve of the conservative political modernization discourse, is assiduously debated by the left. Certainly, these are cultures where civic instruction lessons at school preach a formal democracy while outside the tanks are rumbling. These inconsistencies are widely recognized as is the need to extend the concept of citizenship from its civil and political connotations to a full social citizenship with all the rights which that implies.

Notes

1. K. Marx and F. Engels, *The German Ideology* Part 1 (Lawrence and Wishart, London, 1970), p. 54.
2. K. Marx, *Surveys From Exile*: Political Writings Vol. 2 (Penguin Books, Harmondsworth, 1973), p. 71.
3. Ibid, p. 71.
4. K. Marx, *The First International and After*. Political Writings Vol. 3. (Penguin Books, Harmondsworth, 1974), p. 249.
5. Ibid, p. 252.
6. Ibid, p. 251.
7. Ibid.
8. K. Marx, *Surveys From Exile*, p. 60.
9. K. Marx and F. Engels, *Selected Works* Vol. 1 (Lawrence and Wishart, London, 1970), p. 650.
10. E. Bernstein, *Evolutionary Socialism* (Schoken Books, New York, 1961), p. 1631.
11. Cited in P. Gay, *The Dilemma of Democratic Socialism* (Octagon, New York, 1952), p. 244.
12. V. I. Lenin, *Selected Works* Vol. 2 (Progress Publishers, Moscow, 1970), p. 343.
13. Ibid, p. 349.
14. Ibid, p. 317.
15. Ibid, p. 296.
16. Ibid.
17. Ibid, p. 360.
18. Ibid.
19. B. Knei-Paz, *The Social and Political Thought of Leon Trotsky* (Clarendon Press, Oxford, 1970), p. 371.
20. L. Trotsky, *Terrorism and Communism* (Ann Arbor Paperbacks, USA) p. 972.
21. Ibid, p. 84.
22. M. A. Waters (ed.) *Rosa Luxemburg Speaks* (Pathfinder Press, New York, 1970), p. 393.
23. Ibid, p. 391.
24. Ibid.
25. Ibid.
26. Ibid, p. 36.
27. Ibid, p. 76.
28. Ibid, p. 81.
29. A. Gramsci, *Selections from Political Writings, 1910–1920* (Lawrence and Wishart, London, 1967), p. 74.
30. Ibid, p. 78.
31. A. Gramsci, *Selections from the Prison Notebooks* (Lawrence and Wishart, London, 1971), p. 189.
32. Cited in A. S. Sassoon, 'Gramsci: A New Concept of Politics and the Expansion of Democracy', in A. Hunt (ed.) *Marxism and Democracy* (Lawrence and Wishart, London, 1980), p. 98.
33. A. S. Sassoon, *Gramsci's Politics* (Croom Helm, London, 1980), p. 223.
34. See E. P. Thompson, *Writing by Candlelight* (Merlin, London, 1980).
35. N. Bobbio, *The Future of Democracy* (Polity Press, Oxford, 1987), p. 156.
36. C. Pateman, *The Problem of Political Obligation* (John Wiley, New York, 1979), p. 154.
37. Ibid, pp. 151–2.
38. A. Hunt (ed.) *Marxism and Democracy*, p. 13.
39. B. Jessop, 'The Political Indeterminacy of Democracy' in A. Hunt (ed.) *Marxism and Democracy*.
40. S. Hall, 'Popular–Democratic vs Authoritarian Populism: Two Ways of "Taking Democracy Seriously"', in A. Hunt (ed.) *Marxism and Democracy*.
41. S. Bowles and H. Gintos, 'The Crisis of Liberal Democratic Capitalism: The Case of the United States', *Politics and Society* No. 11, 1982, p. 92.

42. Ibid, p. 93.

43. G. Novack, *Democracy and Revolution* (Pathfinder Press, New York, 1971), p. 124.

44. J. C. Portantiero, *La Democratización del Estado* (CLAEH, Montevideo, 1986), p. 39.

45. G. O'Donnell, 'Pactos Políticos y Pactos Económico-Sociales. Por que si y por que no', draft paper, São Paulo, 1985.

46. E. Laclau and C. Mouffe, *Hegemony and Socialist Strategy* (Verso, London, 1985), p. 85.

47. Ibid, p. 111.

48. Ibid, p. 117.

49. Ibid, pp. 154–5.

50. Ibid, p. 176.

51. E. Laclau, 'Democratic Antagonisms and the Capitalist State', in M. Freeman and D. Robertson (eds) *The Frontiers of Political Theory* (Harvester Press, Brighton, 1979) p. 105.

52. Ibid, p. 138.

53. Ibid.

54. E. M. Wood, *The Retreat From Class: A New 'True' Socialism* (Verso, London, 1981), p. 47.

55. Ibid, p. 52.

56. Cited in G. Novack, *Democracy and Revolution*, p. 31.

57. E. M. Wood, *The Retreat From Class*, p. 67.

58. N. Poulantzas, *State, Power, Socialism* (Verso, London, 1980), p. 251.

59. Ibid, p. 261.

60. G. Almond and J. Coleman (eds) *The Politics of the Developing Areas* (Princeton University Press, New Jersey, 1960), p. 538.

61. S. Huntingdon, *Political Order in Changing Societies* (Yale University, New Haven, 1968).

62. Ibid.

63. G. O'Donnell, *Modernization and Bureaucratic–Authoritarianism* (Institute of International Studies, University of California, Berkeley, 1973), p. 4, p. 8.

64. Ibid, p. 89.

65. M. Friedman, *Capitalism and Freedom* (University of Chicago Press, Chicago, 1962), p. 8.

66. M. and R. Friedman, *Free to Choose* (Penguin, Harmondsworth, 1983), p. 19.

67. Ibid, p. 26.

68. A. G. Frank, *Critique and Anti-Critique* (Macmillan, London, 1984), p. 127.

69. M. and R. Friedman, *Free to Choose*, pp. 15–16.

70. A. G. Frank, *Crisis: In The Third World* (Heinemann, London, 1981), p. 188.

71. Ibid, p. 228.

72. E. Herman and J. Petras, 'Resurgent Democracy: Rhetoric and Reality', *New Left Review* No. 154, 1985, p. 96.

73. Ibid, p. 87.

74. Ibid, p. 91.

75. Ibid.

76. B. Warren, *Imperialism: Pioneer of Capitalism* (Verso, London, 1980).

77. Ibid, p. 7.

78. Ibid, p. 28.

79. G. Kitching, *Rethinking Socialism* (Methuen, London, 1983), p. 29.

80. Ibid, p. 131.

81. M. Crozier, S. Huntingdon and S. Watanaki, *The Crisis of Democracy* (New York University Press, New York, 1975), p. 8.

82. G. Therborn, 'The Rule of Capital and the Rise of Democracy', *New Left Review* No. 103, 1977, p. 28.

83. Ibid, p. 17.

84. Ibid, p. 19.

85. G. Therborn, 'The Travail of Latin American Democracy', *New Left Review* No. 113–14, 1979, p. 85.

86. K. Marx and F. Engels, *Selected Works*, p. 391.

87. T. H. Marshall, *Class, Citizenship, and Social Development* (Greenwood Press, Westport, 1973), p. 72.

88. Ibid, p. 93.

89. See A. Giddens, 'Class Division, Class Conflict and Citizenship Rights', in his *Profiles and Critiques in Social Theory* (Macmillan, London, 1972).

90. T. H. Marshall, *Class, Citizenship, and Social Development*, p. x.

2. Politics in Latin America

The nation-states of Latin America emerged from the struggles for independence from Spain and Portugal in the early 19th century. Decades of internal strife were followed by acts of consolidation which took various forms but which established the foundations of the bourgeois republic. In Argentina, the federal constitution of 1853 sealed the political unity of the country and set it on course for a prolonged period of economic expansion. In Brazil, it was not until the aboliton of slavery in 1888 and the fall of the Empire in 1889 that a stable alliance of the coffee growers and the traditional urban middle class was formed. Meanwhile, Chile's victory in the War of the Pacific (1879–83) and its acquisition of the northern territories helped establish an early alliance of landowners and mine-owners centred around Valparaíso. In the case of Uruguay, the military government of Latorre had achieved a certain level of political stability by 1880, while the rise to power of Batlle in 1903 led to a prolonged period of social stability. At different paces and with different modalities the various nation-states of the southern cone and Brazil were to experience a prolonged period of agro-export-based modernization under the aegis of economic liberalism for some forty years, until the catastrophe of 1929 overtook the world system. The economic, political, social and ideological consequences of the great slump and the associated traumas of the 1930s, were to lead to a fundamental reorganization of these nation-states and the beginning of a new cycle of modernization involving industrialization, urbanization and the replacement of liberalism as the ideology of modernization.

Populism and the compromise state

The crisis of 1929
The relative stability and coherence of the agro-export-based states of the southern cone was shattered by the international capitalist crisis of 1929 and subsequent upheavals of the global order. There was a sharp reduction in the demand for primary goods in the industrialized nations of Western Europe and North America, which had a devastating effect in most of Latin America. On top of losing around half of their purchasing power owing to this, the Latin

American economies were also faced with an increase in the proportion of resources which had to be allocated to servicing the foreign debts contracted prior to 1929. Imports also dropped dramatically, which led to increased prices and a reduced capacity for the state to raise funds through the taxation of foreign trade. The reduction of exports also led, of course, to an increase in unemployment, to a dramatic extent in enclave economies such as Chile, which saw copper production decline from 321,000 tons in 1929 to 103,000 tons in 1932. The export price of wheat dropped by over 50% between 1929 and 1930, which led to a similar contraction of Argentina's and Uruguay's power to purchase. Unlike other fluctuations and crises in the world economy, that of 1929 had a generalized and simultaneous effect across Latin America. Owing to its impact on trade, finances, production and employment, the crisis of the 1930s led to drastic transformations within the Latin American political economies, which may have commenced as short-term policy changes but which resulted in profound structural changes.

The agrarian-based 'oligarchic' political regimes had already begun to lose their hegemony before 1930. As Cardoso and Faletto note, 'the way in which the socio-political system was reorganized at this point depended on whether the socio-economic order was of the enclave type or of the type in which the local financial-agro-exporting bourgeoisie controlled production'.[1] In Chile the enclaves of copper and nitrates gave immense political power to a small local elite in association with foreign interests. However, since the First World War, this political economy had suffered severe setbacks, accentuated by the impact of 1929. Following the depression, the sizeable urban middle class was gradually incorporated into the power structures, in particular through the state bureaucracy. In Argentina and Uruguay production was under national control, and even prior to 1929 there had been moves to incorporate the urban middle class into the power structures. In Argentina the impact of the 1930s allowed a temporary reaffirmation of oligarchic rule, but economic policies nevertheless shifted towards industrialization. In Uruguay a complex system of social alliances and political settlements led to a relatively stable compromise state. In Brazil, the breakdown of the regional pattern of oligarchic–capitalist domination was most severe, with the 1930 Revolution and subsequent changes in economic and political policies most far-reaching. To conclude, in the words of Cardoso and Faletto, 'development changed fundamentally in character after the 1929 depression as a result of pressure on the political system by new social groups and of the reaction by groups linked to the export sector'.[2]

Developmentalism

The new post-1930 political regimes in the southern cone and Brazil were not of a type but certain general underlying trends can be noted. The state as night-watchman (an overseer but not an actor) gives way to the interventionist state which foments industrialization and, with varying effectiveness, strives to implement policies of social integration. The working class generated by industrialization posed a potential problem for the dominant classes, and this encouraged moves towards political institutionalization. The social differentiation which resulted from industrialization and urbanization moved the centre of gravity of society away from the *hacienda*, the plantation and the mine. Liberalism ceased to play a historically progressive role and became an ideology of containment and defence. A *laissez-faire* attitude towards the state had little purchase in the new era, with the agro-export phase basically exhausted and the popular classes seeking a place in the sun. The new dominant ideology of developmentalism combined Keynesian economic policies, a pronounced statism and varying degrees of populism. According to Flisfisch and Lechner, this new ideology possessed a vision of history as progress, the idea that social development depended on industrialization, and valued the state not only as generator of order but as agent of social integration.[3] A new social force came into being to implement this programme, as the landowners were joined in a hegemonic class alliance by industrialists, and financial and commercial interests, constituting a broad bourgeois front.

Industrialization had begun in most countries of the southern cone around the turn of the century, but it was clearly subsidiary to the dominant agro-export sector. The prolonged period of crises in the world economy from the First World War to the Second — through the Bolshevik Revolution, the depression of the 1930s and the rise of fascism — had created the need for further and more systematic industrialization. Class structures became more diversified, the relationship between the city and rural areas changed, as did the role of the state, and new ideologies surfaced. This was, nevertheless, a process of incomplete modernization, in so far as the traditional oligarchic sectors retained considerable economic (and even political) power. It was this incomplete nature of Latin American modernization which was to mark much of its subsequent political history. The lack of a stable system of political mediations led frequently to military takeovers, and shaped the experience of the national–populist regimes of Perón and Vargas, as we shall see. The representative democracy which prevailed in Chile and Uruguay until 1973 reflected a higher degree of political institutionalization but shared most of the tenets of the developmentalism espoused by the national–popular regimes. We shall now examine both paths through modernization, to evaluate the implementation of democracy in practice and its relationship with industrialization. Though later both paths led to military dictatorships, as we shall see in the next section, this should not preclude our emphasis on previous differences.

Peronism

The most clear-cut populist 'compromise state' was Perón's regime in Argentina from 1946 to 1955. Perón emerged as Gramsci's proverbial Caesar: 'a great personality entrusted with the task of "arbitration" over a historico-political situation characterised by an equilibrium of forces heading towards catastrophe . . .'[4] Since 1930 a series of fraudulent regimes had attempted to maintain a semblance of oligarchic rule. Yet to deal with the effects of the world depression, industrialization policies were put into effect and the working class was greatly enlarged. On the international plane, the once hegemonic power in the region, Britain, had been weakened by the world wars and was now in decline, while the United States had still not imposed its own hegemony over the area. Peronism came into this national and international stalemate with a project of independent capitalist development which at the same time was based on, and controlled, the organized working class. It was neither '*criollo* fascism' nor the 'Argentine road to socialism' as its more fervent detractors and admirers professed to believe. It was simply a form of populism in which the myth of the providential person comes to substitute for the ideological relationship on which social consensus is usually based. Peronism represented a compromise state, which reflected the social reality of an unstable equilibrium between, on the one hand, a defensive class alliance of the petty bourgeoisie linked to the internal market, and, on the other, the dominant class front of landowners, financiers and 'internationalized' bourgeoisie which could not impose its own hegemony over society.

Peronism's relationship with democracy was, of course, ambiguous. Perón himself could claim in 1946, with some justification: 'I am much more democratic than my adversaries, because I seek a real democracy, while they defend the appearance of democracy, the external form of democracy . . .'[5] Certainly, Perón created something akin to social democracy in Argentina but his adhesion to political democracy was itself 'formal'. Continuing in the tradition of Yrigoyen's popular movement prior to 1930, Peronism was a movement more than a party. It thus perpetuated a tradition of weak political parties, unable to mediate between social interests and the state. In fact with Peronism party and state were practically indistinguishable. Political parties in Argentina were not apt to negotiate in an open competitive arena; they became exclusivist, claiming to represent the whole of society, and of course 'the nation'. Following the overthrow of Perón by the military in 1955, a period of 'black parliamentarianism' began in which a semblance of democratic politics continued, with Peronism retaining its social power to veto any solution to the chronic political crises Argentina suffered. When Perón was finally allowed back to Argentina by the military in 1973, there was an attempt to create an 'organized democracy', but in fact this degenerated under the presidency of his widow into a virtual civil war within the Peronist movement, which could no longer contain its corporatist/statist elements in the same framework as the revolutionary tendency.

Brazil

A political process broadly parallel to Argentina's can be discerned in Brazil under the aegis of Getulio Vargas, who first came to power through the Revolution of 1930. His authoritarian *Estado Nôvo* from 1937 to 1945 laid the basis for a dynamic phase of conservative modernization in which the working class was firmly subjected to corporatist controls. A prominent politician, Antonio Carlos, said in 1930: 'We must make the Revolution before the people do it'. In a policy of pre-emptive co-option the capital/wage-labour reaction came directly under the sway of the state, moulded into a class-collaborationist structure and subordinated to nationalist ideology. On this secure basis the state promoted a vigorous strategy of industrialization, providing the essential infrastructure and finance for private capitalist initiative. In this period, the capital accumulation process in Brazil acquired its own endogenous dynamic, with the previous, unplanned 'horizontal' pattern of investment giving way in 1955 to a new mode based on a block of complementary investment which completely transformed the structure of production. This latter move was carried out under President Kubitschek's (1956–60) ambitious *Plano de Metas*. Vargas himself had been re-elected democratically in 1950 and set the subsequent 'populist' tone of Brazilian policies which would last until 1964. The key themes were nationalism, developmentalism and populism, including the personalization of power in the 'charismatic' leader. Vargas was able to pose as '*Pai dos pobres*' — Father of the Poor — until his death in 1954. His successors, particularly his direct ideological heir, João Goûlart, who succeeded Kubitschek, was to find his workers rather less saintly.

Brazilian political parties since Vargas have been relatively weak compared to the state. So much so that Vargas himself had to create not only the party of order, the Partido Social Democrático (Social Democratic Party), but also the oppositional Partido Trabalhista Brasileiro (Brazilian Labour Party). Vargas was thus personally expressing the difficult equilibrium which existed between the old pre-1930 Brazil and the new. In the rural areas traditional political bosses (the *coroneles*) maintained a base through clientelism while in the urban areas a more 'democratic' populism prevailed. The state was the only central authority, and the Brazilian political classes were unable to create true national-level political parties. The precarious balance between the conservative and the revolutionary operated by Vargas was broken under Goûlart, but without an alternative political formula emerging. There was a grave political fragmentation which reflected a lack of articulation between social relations and political action. As Liliana de Riz argues:

> While in Argentina the fragility of political society took the form of a direct politicization of interest groups, in Brazil the defensive movements were not able to consolidate organizations and identities capable of challenging state omnipotence and converting the state into the arena of political conflict, as occurred in Argentina.[6]

The overwhelming role of the state and the weakness of political parties is still something which Argentina and Brazil have in common, compared to the highly developed political party system of Chile and Uruguay.

Chile

In Chile, meanwhile, a political process markedly different from those of Argentina and Brazil had taken shape. In brief, political parties had become the axis around which Chilean society was articulated; they were effective intermediaries between the state and civil society. Since the 1930s there had been a systematic opening of the political system to wider social layers, and a consequent legitimization of parliament as an arena for resolving or mediating social conflict. Political parties tended to represent social classes or their fractions following a 'European' pattern, with little evidence of national 'movements' along the lines of Peronism. None of this automatically precludes an analysis in terms of populism and the compromise state, however. For example, the Popular Front (1938–1947) saw the working class parties in government making the central axis of their work industrial development led by the state. This was not so different from what was happening at the same time under the *Estado Nôvo* of Vargas. Second International Marxism had an ideology similar to the 'developmentalism' advocated by their conservative counterparts. Nor was Chile immune to populist 'explosions' as shown by the sudden eruption on to the political scene of ex-dictator Ibañez in 1952: he was elected without having the support of any of the major parties on the basis of his 'charismatic' personality and the discontent of those marginalized by the political system. Populism was thus far from irrelevant in Chile; the construction of a compromise state was the objective of right and left alike.

The Christian Democrats, who came to power through Eduardo Frei in 1964, had a clear project of conservative modernization to overcome the chronic economic and political crises Chile had been going through. With Christian Democracy the peasantry came into politics for the first time, and the party's technocrats were not unaware of the potentially revolutionary role of that class, even if in far-off lands. The 'Revolution in Liberty' proposed by the Christian Democrats was of course ambivalent, and according to critics: '"communitarianism" was a cover for a modernizing, reformist, pro-capitalist and pro-imperialist party whose leadership hoped that by emphasizing community participation as a solution to social injustice, could create for itself a mass base'.[7] Whether proposed in good faith or as a 'cover' for something else, this populist ideology led to a far-reaching process of radicalization. The failure of the right in power under Alessandri (1958–1964) further legitimized a turn to the left by the more centrist Christian Democrats. Under this regime the process of extending political democracy to all classes and sectors was completed and the agrarian reform (taboo under the old 'compromise state') was launched. Nevertheless, by vacating the centre ground, the Christian Democrats opened up a crisis which could only be resolved by a new capitalist revolution or a more decisive democratization, which would inevitably question prevailing property relations. Thus a minority coalition of left-wing parties, Popular Unity, came to power in 1970.

Uruguay

Finally, in Uruguay we find a political pattern with certain similarities to that of Chile, but with its own particular features. As already mentioned above, there was a relatively early political stabilization in Uruguay under José Batlle y Ordoñez, which gave rise to the term *batllismo*. The two main political parties in Uruguay, the *Blancos* and *Colorados*, were born out of the civil wars following the struggle for independence, and reflected respectively the interior of the country and Montevideo. To this day these parties maintain their regional and personalist characteristics, although they are in a way political fronts with clear-cut tendencies within them. As for *batllismo*, it was an ideology centred around the notion of national reconciliation, and has helped create a representative democratic regime with full participation from an early date. It is crucial in this respect that the political incorporation of the working classes into the democratic system actually preceded industrialization. Workers were thus citizens before they were fully fledged proletarians. This in part accounts for why two clearly bourgeois parties regularly obtained 90 per cent of the vote. The compromise state in Uruguay was based on a solid two-party system where the rules of the game were agreed and adhered to. As de Riz points out: 'The institutionalization of compromise ensured political stability'.[8] It was the political parties which took over and dominated the state, unlike Brazil where the state created the parties. As in Chile, the political parties were strong, but they shared some of the characteristics of Argentina's parties as multi-class movements, with a quite diffuse ideology.

Around 1955 the first signs of malfunction appeared in this quite unique Latin American nation-state. Essentially, since that date, there has been a period of prolonged economic stagnation, in marked contrast to the pre-1930 agrarian expansive phase and the post-Second World War industrialization drive. From 1955 onwards, by contrast, agrarian production has remained stationary and industrial investment, production and employment have barely grown at all. At the same time, as in the rest of Latin America, foreign investment increased and the state ceased to play its role as vigorous defender of national industry. The electoral triumph of the *Blancos* in 1948, over the *batllista colorados*, set the seal on this new turn, and the economic crisis reduced the space for political compromise. In the 1960s the general economic deterioration was matched by a growing social mobilization, which in turn met with an unprecedented (for Uruguay) level of state repression. The growing inadequacy of traditional channels for the political representation of social interests compounded the growing lack of legitimacy of the government. This process of degeneration of a bourgeois regime reached its peak with the Pacheco Areco regime which, between 1968 and 1972, systematically closed the whole *batllista* cycle in Uruguay. A bourgeois political class, brought up on a 'spoils system' of politics along the lines of the USA, found itself confronted by an exacerbated class struggle which was overflowing the boundaries of the system, and which it was incapable of dealing with by itself.

It would be futile to sum up diverse national histories in terms of a common underlying pattern, if that were done in a reductionist manner. Nevertheless, the theme of 'passive revolution', as elaborated by Gramsci, does provide certain clues to understanding the unity within the diversity of Latin American history from 1930 to the mid-1960s. Passive revolution or 'transformism' is, for Gramsci, a strategy for the bourgeoisie which combines revolution and restoration. It involves 'molecular changes which in fact progressively modify the pre-existing composition of forces, and hence become the matrix of new changes'.[9] The history of the southern cone political economies following 1929 can be interpreted along those lines. Gramsci specifically relates the concept to situations, as in Latin America, where 'the impetus of progress is not tightly linked to a vast local economic development which is artificially limited and repressed, but is instead the reflection of international developments which transmit their ideological currents to the periphery . . .'[10] The strength of the analogy with the European 'passive revolution' to outflank the French Revolution, is greatest however in its dual political effect of revolution/ restoration. Gramsci refers to the way in which

> the demands which in France found a Jacobin–Napoleonic expression were satisfied by small doses, legally, in a reformist manner — in such a way that it was possible to preserve the political and economic position of the old feudal classes, to avoid agrarian reform, and, especially, to avoid the popular masses going through a period of political experience such as occurred in France in the years of Jacobinism . . .[11]

Transformism in Latin America incorporated industrialists and the urban middle class into the power structures, but was only partially successful with the working classes.

The road to dictatorship

Latin America has known dictatorships of various types from the colonial period to the present, but the 'new' dictatorships of the 1970s (see Chapter 3) were quite specific in their origins and subsequent evolution. The question addressed in this section is the transition — often abrupt and violent — from the populist semi-democracies to the new military dictatorships. Undoubtedly the most coherent and encompassing approach to this theme is that advanced by Guillermo O'Donnell in his writings on the bureaucratic–authoritarian state.[12] In its basis the argument is as follows: by the early 1960s import-substitution industrialization under populist regimes had lost its dynamism and there was an increased political activation of the popular sector, which led to the 'deepening' of industrialization under authoritarian regimes after the necessary defeat of the popular sectors. The delayed, dependent industrialization since 1929 had reached an impasse with chronic inflation and instability, a decline in local and foreign investment, and a fiscal crisis of the state. To this potential crisis of accumulation one can add the equally threatening crisis of political hegemony which was caused by, and, in turn, led to, increased political activity by the hitherto quiescent urban and rural working people. The context for this crisis is set by the growing internationalization of the Latin American economies since the mid-1950s, which was to lead to a transnationalizing 'overflowing' (*desborde*) of society, as a new economic elite and its technocratic advisors sought to take direct control of the state.

Economic aspects
The first element in this theoretical framework to receive sustained criticism was the notion of import-substitution industrialization becoming 'exhausted', and the need for 'deepening', or vertical integration, of the economy. In a

detailed study of the paradigmatic Brazilian case, José Serra finds no evidence for this hypothesis: the deepening process had advanced considerably under the pre-coup democratic regimes, deepening was not the crucial problem facing Brazilian capitalism before the coup, nor was it the core of economic policies after the military regime was implanted.[13] Beyond the specific account of Brazilian development, Serra is arguing against an analytic framework in which 'these regimes [bureaucratic–authoritarian] allegedly arise as a result of the implacable logic of the underdevelopment and dependency that characterize the economy of this region'.[14] Clearly this criticism is correct, but it should not preclude the careful examination of the complex set of mediations between economic variables and political outcomes — as carried out, for example, in O'Donnell's own concrete analysis of the rise of dictatorship in Argentina. We are seeking to uncover not the 'economic determinants' of authoritarian rule, but the interplay between the economic and other dimensions of life under capitalism. While accepting that only one cycle of import-substitution industrialization had become 'exhausted' by the mid-1960s, it does seem clear that military intervention did respond to a perceived lack of continued stable and dynamic expansion of capitalism under prevailing political forms.

Political aspects

The political aspects of O'Donnell's original formulations have also been questioned. Thus Paul Cammack argues, for example, that 'such coherence as the model had arose directly from its focus upon a crisis in populism, and was shattered by its extension to the cases of Chile and Uruguay'.[15] We may question whether the emergence of dictatorships in Uruguay and Chile in 1973 (see below) undermined O'Donnell's whole problematic so conclusively. Clearly the national-popular regimes of Argentina and Brazil (O'Donnell's main focus of interest) followed a distinct path to dictatorship compared to the representative democracies of Chile and Uruguay. There was still a similar crisis of developmentalism as the hegemonic ideology under which modernization took place. There was an even more pronounced 'activation of the popular sectors', an aspect of the rise of dictatorships that O'Donnell stresses and develops much more in his later writings than the 'elective affinity' between dependent capitalism and dictatorship. Perhaps the real problem springs from the early tendency to focus, in the bureaucratic–authoritarian state debates, on 'models' as though it was an ingenious jigsaw into which diverse histories could be fitted: did the 'model' extend to Mexico? Was Peru's not a progressive variant of the bureaucratic–authoritarian? And so on. O'Donnell may have suggested a rather rigid identification between the military regimes and a particular social base, but Cammack does seem to exaggerate in suggesting on this basis that 'the model rules out any sustained consideration of the "relative autonomy" of the state'.[16]

When all is said and done, O'Donnell's analysis of the bureaucratic–authoritarian state retains considerable theoretical and political pertinence. Like Cardoso and Faletto's analysis of the social and political forces operating in situations of dependency, in spite of subsequent theoretical inflation and formalization, so O'Donnell's *methodology* repays attention today, even after severe critiques. Its main inherent weakness is its economism — the temptation (in spite of self-administered injunctions) to seek the 'economic roots' of political processes, and a certain reductionism which looks always for social forces behind this or that political tendency. Its strength lies in its continuation of Cardoso and Faletto's historical–structural approach which, following O'Donnell, 'investigates interrelationships through time between a system of forces and social relationships — capitalism — and its mutually consistent political domination patterns'.[17] This approach is analytical, yet its referents are historically grounded. Though complex ahistorical models of dependency and the bureaucratic–authoritarian state have been derived, in the original studies there is a rich interplay between structure and history, economics and politics. Certainly we cannot 'explain' specific national histories by appealing to simple overarching theories, but we can derive categories of analysis. That is because as O'Donnell writes about Cardoso and Faletto,

> the initial *problématique* leads to the selection of some aspects or factors (development of productive forces, class formation and articulation, insertions in the international context, formation and enforcement of political alliances and of the national state) that operate as conceptual promontories around which both the data and other, less central, concepts can be managed.[18]

Brazil 1964

It was the 1964 military coup in Brazil that led to the first of the 'new' military dictatorships and, arguably, set a trend for the whole southern cone. A preliminary phase of an economic crisis opened up in 1960, with a slowing of accumulation in certain key industries. Then, in 1963, the crisis became sharper with a violent acceleration of inflation. By this stage, inflation had ceased to play a stimulating role for production, in so far as it led to massive wage claims which disrupted production, favoured speculation, and generally disorganized the state apparatus. International credit organizations made all aid conditional on the adoption of rigid monetary and political stabilization measures that had become practically impossible to implement by this stage. The exacerbation of labour struggles sharpened the deterioration of profitability and led to a further contraction of capital investment. At another level, the pact between industrial and agrarian interests established during the *Estado Novo* was now being openly called into question by a dynamic industrial sector that had been consolidated during the Kubitschek years. More specifically, the model of highly concentrated capital accumulation, based on foreign capital and an 'internationalized' fraction of the national capitalist class, had become incompatible with the populist mode of political domination. It was a situation of asymmetry, or dislocation, where the economic rearticulation of society had proceeded more rapidly than the political.

In retrospect — looking back from after the Chilean coup of 1973, for example — the Brazilian coup of 1964 does not appear to have been a response to any serious threat from the dominated classes. However, a careful examination of the political turmoil just preceding 1964 reveals a considerable *perceived* prior threat. The peasantry was organizing in rural trade unions and the famous *Ligas Camponesas*; urban workers had organized a series of massive 'political' general strikes; students were in an activist political phase; even sections of the military had organized small-scale yet potentially dangerous radical actions. There was a general radicalization of the mass movement and, additionally, the populist manipulation of labour was breaking down in the face of mass pressure and actions. General strikes were able to impose a virtual labour veto over crucial questions in the political arena. Thus, over a crisis of capital accumulation was overlaid at least a potential crisis of capitalist hegemony. The Brazilian power elites were, for their part, profoundly worried by what they saw as the radicalism of the Goulart government itself. Thus it came about that populism and the compromise state was threatened on both sides; the people it was designed to co-opt and pacify were no longer the passive poor who Vargas professed to love. On the other hand, the newly dominant economic sectors began to feel, along with a lucid military and technocratic elite, that they could seize political power directly to launch a new phase of the Brazilian bourgeois revolution.

Argentina

Argentina suffered a succession of increasingly repressive military takeovers in 1955, 1966 and 1976. In terms of O'Donnell's variable of 'prior threat level', there is some evidence that it increased each time, and consequently repression was more severe and the military project more far-reaching and decisive. Certainly the level of polarization in society and the degree of popular radicalization was greater in 1976 than in 1966. It is probably futile to construct a comparative cross-national table of 'prior threat levels' because there is no easy objective criterion by which to measure what is after all a threat perceived by the dominant classes. In 1955, the armed forces united to overthrow the Peronist regime in order to counter the perceived radicalization of the working class and the threat of disorder posed in spite of Perón's avowed anti-communism. As always populism may be designed to co-opt the masses, but the masses might be encouraged by the rhetoric to surpass the limits set from above. However, repression of Peronism was not in itself a coherent political programme, and the bourgeoisie as a whole opted for a civilian government in 1958. Having broken the power of the unions — at least temporarily — the military would withdraw to their traditional role of ultimate guarantors.

During the civilian government of Arturo Frondizi (1958–62), there was a marked expansion of monopoly capitalism in Argentina and a consolidation of the economic position of the 'internationalized' fraction of the bourgeoisie. This was not, however, translated into a clear-cut political hegemony by this sector. When a Peronist candidate won the Buenos Aires provincial elections in 1962, the armed forces again intervened to install a 'caretaker' regime. Following a period of severe in-fighting within the armed forces, a new civilian government came to power in 1963. President Arturo Illia was unable to deal effectively with the severe social and economic conflicts which dominated Argentina. The military were soon preparing a new coup, this time with the active support of a sophisticated technocratic element. Following a series of set-piece confrontations with the Peronist trade unions (agitating for Perón's return), the military seized power in 1966. This was the most coherent attempt so far to break the particular class stalemate that had characterized Argentina since 1955. In ways similar to the 1964 coup in Brazil, this event was, in Gramscian terms, a move by the internationalized bourgeoisie to resolve in its favour the situation of organic crisis, and transform its economic *predominance* into political *hegemony*. The strategic aims of the dictatorship were not, however, achieved, largely owing to the insurrectional mobilization of industrial workers, office workers and students in the uprising in Córdoba in 1969 (known as the *Cordobazo*) and its subsequent repercussions. An attempt to revive Peronist populism in office between 1973 and 1976 failed abysmally, from the point of view both of the dominant classes and of the popular classes. This led, inevitably, to a further military coup, in 1976, which will be the subject of Chapter 3. Suffice it to say that it was more decisive, more far-reaching, and, even, partly, more successful (in its own terms) than earlier coups.

Chile 1973
In Chile, in September 1973, the democratically elected socialist government of Salvador Allende was overthrown by the military, which installed a regime widely described as 'fascist'. On the face of it, this military intervention to terminate a unique 'parliamentary road to socialism' seemed far removed from actions against populist governments by the military in Brazil and Argentina. One was a clear-cut move, backed by the USA, to thwart the 'encroaching communist menace', whereas the others merely dealt with the inefficiency of populism. Certainly we should not ignore the much higher 'prior threat level' felt by the Chilean dominant classes in 1973, which virtually threw the whole political centre behind the rightist conspiracy with the military. Socialism is ultimately a more threatening ideology for the bourgeoisie than is populism. Yet if we delve beneath surface events and take a longer view of Chilean political history, the 1973 coup was more than a move against socialism. As Manuel Garretón has written:

> The military regime which commenced in September 1973 and which resolved the political crisis in favour of the interests of the capitalist bloc, put an end not only to the democratic system and processes of 'substantive democratization', but attempted in some way to construct a new social and political order, based on a model of development profoundly contradictory with that which had prevailed until then in the country.[19]

It was not just Allende that was being overthrown but a whole political system constructed over decades. What was being questioned was the very ability of the bourgeoisie to maintain capitalism under democratic conditions.

The Popular Unity experience was, over and beyond its own project with all its problems and ambiguities, the culmination of a process of decomposition of bourgeois rule in Chile. The tragedy was that this government was not able to offer a coherent alternative that could attract the support of the majority of the population. As under the populist regimes of Brazil or Argentina, there was intense social and political radicalization and polarization in the Popular Unity years, not only in the popular sectors, but among the middle classes and white-collar workers as well. The political mechanisms for the resolution of conflict were losing legitimacy and effectiveness — in short, there was a growing social and political disarticulation of Chilean society. There was a growing gap between social pressures and the capacity of the political system to absorb and disperse them. In the past, as Liliana de Riz writes, 'The opposition of strong ideological identities had been functional for the stability of the political system, because it coexisted with the integrative and defensive practice of the left wing parties in parliament'.[20] However, the ideological radicalization that occurred between 1964 and 1973 surpassed the boundaries established by the political order and created a situation which could not be contained within the traditional pattern of party politics. Political democracy had achieved a certain stability in Chile with a genuine, competitive party political space. Nevertheless, the long-term failure of the bourgeoisie to create a stable bourgeois economic and political order, as much as the failure of the left to present an alternative, created the conditions for the 1973 coup.

Uruguay 1973
Finally, 1973 was also marked by a military takeover in Uruguay, albeit a more gradual one which, furthermore, the traditional political parties acquiesced in. As with the Chilean case, the perceived prior threat level was high, with the extremely proficient Tupamaro guerrilla movement complementing the mobilization of a politicized, if not massive, working class. In the 1971 elections, the leftist Frente Amplio had achieved 20 per cent of the vote, thus apparently breaking the two-party mould. Batllismo, as a way of conducting politics, now appeared to have been superseded by events. The traditional party politicians thus voted in 1972, in their own parliamentary arena, to declare a 'state of internal war', and thus call the armed forces to the centre of the political stage in Uruguay. Already, Pacheco Areco had installed what has been called a 'constitutional dictatorship'; now his successor Bordaberry was to call for an end to party politics, and to remain as titular head of a military regime until the end of his mandate in 1976. Through a slow-motion takeover, the military had seized control of the state and put paid to Batlle's dream of a 'model country'. From economic stagnation to political crisis, the traditional bourgeois political elite found itself gradually losing hegemony, not only over the masses, but over the various layers of the dominant classes themselves. An alienated middle class (long since driven out of its favoured role in the power scheme) and an alliance of thoroughly disenchanted workers, students and urban poor were threatening the very stability of the economic and political system.

Uruguay, like Chile, shares many aspects of its recent political history with its larger neighbours, Argentina and Brazil. Since 1955 the general condition of dependency had imposed an even more severe distortion of the economy. An earlier political settlement between the fundamental social classes did not prevent an exacerbation of the class struggle, as the legitimacy of the old order began to crumble. Even Uruguay's revolutionary movement — the Tupamaros — while following a continent-wide turn towards armed struggle, also reflected Uruguay's particular political history. For many observers it was the Tupamaros — and the considerable sympathy they evoked in wide social layers — that led to the decisive weakening of the political system and the rise of the military state. In fact, the Tupamaros appeared, in the symbolic nature of many of their actions, to share many of the illusions about Uruguay as it had been prior to 1955. It was the organized labour movement that in fact seemed to be a more deep-seated menace to the orderly reproductions of the capitalist order, however much the Tupamaros' war with the military may have contributed to the precipitation of the military takeover. Uruguay's military, interestingly enough, defined their coup in terms of the struggle against 'all forms of subversion', but also against 'politicians' as such, who were accused of weakness, corruption and even complicity with 'subversion' (i.e. guerrillas).

Again we are faced with the task of summing up natural diversity within a common social and political pattern. In the case of the rise of the military dictatorships in the southern cone and Brazil after 1964, Gramsci's concept of 'caesarism' may prove illuminating. By 'caesarism', Gramsci referred to 'a historico-political situation characterised by an equilibrium of forces heading towards catastrophe'.[21] In the dialectic 'revolution/restoration', one or other may prevail. There are certain phases of the class struggle, marked by unstable equilibrium, in which either revolutionary advances will occur or there will be, in Gramsci's words, 'a tremendous reaction on the part of the propertied classes and governing caste'.[22] In the southern cone of Latin America and Brazil, there was, as we saw above, just such an unstable balance between the social forces in conflict. National–populist and representative democratic regimes had not altered the basis of capital accumulation, but had opened the doors to social and political participation by the masses. Following Gramsci, 'the catastrophic phase [of equilibrium] may be brought about by a "momentary" political deficiency of the traditional dominant force . . . such as to make possible the advance of the rival force B (progressive) in a precocious form. . . .'[23] The historically premature advance of the working class and the left on the basis of the exhaustion of populism and representative democracy as a stable form of bourgeois rule, ignored the fact that (as Gramsci showed for a quite distinct but nevertheless relevant historical situation) 'the existing social form had not yet exhausted its possibilities for development, as subsequent history abundantly demonstrated'.[24]

Dilemmas of the left

Having examined in broad outline the populist phase of Latin American politics and the rise of the dictatorships, we may now turn to the politics of opposition, the mode of insertion of the left into Latin American politics, and its past and current strategic dilemmas. The 'crisis of Marxism' is a reality recognized by all on the left except a few hidebound conservative cliques. The old certainties are no more, and the experience of exile has brought an important comparative element to bear. Before examining the current situation, we must turn briefly to some of its main historical co-ordinates.

Marx and Latin America

Marx and Engels looked at South America from 'the outside', as a land without history, except that imposed by successive invaders. The formation of nations in the area appeared to them as mere state constructions, with the absence of any manifestation of social will. It would seem that, in keeping with Hegel's view of America as an empty territory where all was an echo or reflection of the Old World, Marx was simply reading South American history as a pale imitation of European history. Thus Simon Bolívar, hero of the early 19th century independence movement, was reduced to a caricature of Napoleon III by Marx. This failure by Marx to grasp the specificity of Latin America was due in part to Eurocentrism, and in part to a rather mechanical faith in the advance of capitalism. Nevertheless, there were elements in the continent's political history that were difficult for a focus on the capital/wage-labour relation to apprehend. The European form of emergence of the nation-state was inverted in Latin America, where the nation was not a starting point but only slowly constructed. It was the role of the state in this nation-building process — what Gramsci was to call the 'passive revolution' — that Marx failed to grasp. The nation was reduced to the state, and social classes did not seem to articulate any coherent project of 'social regeneration'. For Marx, a basic principle was the denial of the Hegelian notion of the state as the production agent of civil society. Yet in Latin America, national formations appeared as mere state constructions with the apparent absence of any manifestation of social will.

Following Marx's singular 'misreading' of Latin America, the revolutionary currents of the continent tended to divide into an authoritarian, statist 'American' tendency and a liberal 'European' strand. Marx had, for example, seen in Bolívar only his incipient personality cult and his penchant for pomp and ceremony, missing his concern to prevent the 'balkanization' of the region and his broad pan-American project. But the misplacement of Marx's polemic against Bolívar should not be allowed to mask its rational kernel, which was a fervent opposition to authoritarianism. When much of the left in Latin America is rediscovering the importance of democracy, this is perhaps a timely reminder. The point to make here is with regard to the peculiar mode of insertion of Marxism into the region's politics. While one revolutionary strand developed a nationalist, statist, populist and authoritarian ideology, the Marxists stressed the universality of capitalist development, and worked with analytical categories that were inadequate with regard to the economic and political phenomena they were designed to analyse. Only with the Cuban Revolution would these two strands merge to produce the powerful blend of Castroism and Guevarism, at once Marxist and nationalist.

In the meantime, for a whole historical period, the 'national left' and the 'European left' remained quite separate. As Régis Debray writes:

> Whatever the reasons for this split between nationalism and socialism . . . its effects distorted both. On the one hand it kept socialism apart from the mass of the people, and on the other it gave a certain fascist tinge to all the nationalist and anti-imperialist movments: in fact the two effects are inseparable.[25]

The social democrats of the Second International in Latin America pursued a line no different from that of their German counterparts, stressing the benefits of capitalist development and the efficacy of peaceful reformist politics. The communists of the Third International after 1919 followed the international turns of their movements, viewing nationalist forces favourably or unfavourably according to international conjuncture. Even the minuscule body of Trotskyists of the Fourth International found themselves, after 1940, constantly torn between an anti-imperialist and a classist orientation. Yet in all these debates, in all the different brands of Marxism, we note an increasingly impoverished political vocabulary. Marx himself left no legacy of writing that could be appealed to directly for strategic initiatives in Latin America. Lenin, and the Communist International after him, did not see the region as particularly important, and did not devote much analysis to it, partly on the basis that, realistically, it was and would remain the 'backyard' of US imperialism.

As we saw above, Marx's own categories of analysis could not account for the historically specific development of nation-states in Latin America. The Second International, for its part, developed a harmless 'left-wing' version of bourgeois liberal evolutionism. Leninism contributed the vocabulary of imperialism, which, though imperfect, did point to some genuine features of the situation. From fervent opposition to the 'fascism' of some nationalist movements in the 1930s, this current could swing to uncritical adhesion to their successors in the 1950s. The revolution in Latin America would be anti-imperialist, anti-feudal, national and democratic. Following a tradition of Marx himself, national political developments were usually subordinated to the perceived needs of the 'world revolution', which, of course, rapidly came to mean the national interests of the USSR. Bouts of sectarian politics would be followed by the most unabashed opportunism. All social forces were neatly placed into class boxes and these slotted into 'progressive', 'democratic' and other shelves by dictate of the central committee. Socialist and communist forces could reflect very real social and political aspirations — of different layers of urban workers, occasionally of peasants, of some military officers, of office workers and, of course, of intellectuals. Yet their terminology, reflecting as it did an impoverished political imagination, never really grasped the complexity of national, ethnic, regional, class, cultural and gender politics in the area. When the Cuban revolutionaries 'stormed the heavens' in 1959, like the Paris Communards before them, there was a widespread feeling that this could 'clear the decks' for the renewal of a critical socialist theory and practice.

The impact of Cuba

Cuba meant, above all, that socialism was a real possibility and not just a pipe-dream. It entered the political imagination of Latin America in a way comparable to that of the Bolshevik revolution in Europe in the 1920s. There was no doubt that the revolution was to be socialist and not contained within a supposed bourgeois–democratic 'stage' of the long-term orthodox Leninist project. Ernesto 'Che' Guevara did indicate that democratic conditions should lead to different methods of struggle, but the overall tone was that an immediate armed frontal assault on the state was the order of the day. The OLAS (Latin American Solidarity Organization) declaration of 1967 stated that the main 'lesson of the Cuban Revolution' was that guerrilla warfare 'is the most effective and the most adequate form of waging and developing revolutionary war in our countries . . .'.[26] War 'on a continental scale' was being foisted on countries with diverse political trajectories and unevenly developed class struggles, usually bypassing existing mass organizations of the oppressed. The metropolitan left encouraged these excesses in its post-1968 euphoria, its critique of everyday life under late capitalism leading them to seek an outlet for violence, struggle and death in the exotic 'Third World', while they stayed at home practising 'solidarity'. In the meantime, in many countries of Latin America, a good part of a whole political generation entered a bloody and unequal conflict, which many did not survive. As to the Cuban state, the first free territory in America, its penchant for exporting revolution was to decline in the mid-1970s.

Cuba was a model for the left, but not one that was known closely. The rhetoric of revolution took precedence over the cold light of critical analysis. The road to exile took many through Cuba, and even sympathetic observers regained their critical faculties. This is not the place for an analysis of Cuban politics, but it can be accepted that the system is not a model of socialist democracy. In the mid-1970s, two tendencies came together: the internal evolution of Cuban society towards 'Sovietization', and the crushing defeats in the southern cone. This forced a redefinition of political alliances, with sometimes bitter hostility between the old Leninist left and the new Castroist left coming together, as Cuba itself became a much more orthodox Soviet type state. The Sandinista victory in 1979 did, for a while, bring back some of the old sparkle into revolutionary rhetoric. As time went by, however, Nicaragua became bogged down in a bitter defensive struggle against US-backed counterrevolutionaries, and its early commitment to pluralism and democracy gave way to 'dictatorship of the central committee'. What these experiences have created is a new political realism on the left, a refusal of totally uncritical support for every revolutionary process, and a desire to think through local problems without importing models and ready-made paths to the promised land. The appeal of immediate revolution gives way to the recognition that political processes develop at an uneven pace across nations, regions and social groups, and that every 'victory' comes at a price.

The overthrow of Popular Unity in Chile in 1973, along with the slow coup in Uruguay of the same year, and the renewed military takeover in Argentina in 1976, led to a process of rethinking by sectors of the left. Some, of course, merely reaffirmed old orthodoxies, as happened in Brazil after the 1964 coup, but, particularly in Chile, the blows were so severe as to lead to a complete collapse of traditional political categories. Eugenio Tironi writes of the Chilean left how the Pinochet coup, 'for the generation of the 1960s signified the pulverization of their image of the world, of their reference points, of their deepest personal beliefs'.[27] The break was such, and the political vacuum so total, that the left was thrown into perplexity and crisis. In Argentina and Uruguay, it was the crisis of the 'armed-struggle' left, in its nationalist and Castroist variants, that was most marked after the coups. In Brazil, as the long night of the dictatorship began to lift in the late 1970s, a renewed labour movement caused the left to rethink its categories and strategies. In all the cases, questions were asked about orthodox Marxism and traditional and 'new' post-Cuban revolutionary strategies. With some inevitably arbitrary classification, we will attempt to follow these debates in the following pages.

What is socialism?
The first question to be asked was 'What is socialism?'. The experience of exile, particularly for Chileans, brought up in an orthodox Leninist tradition, was a revealing one. What they saw of 'actually existing socialism' was not encouraging. What they saw of advanced capitalist societies brought home the drama of underdevelopment and the historically progressive role of capitalism in the spirit of the *Communist Manifesto*. The idea of a single, clearly identified, socialist model, following a historically proven path, was irreversibly destroyed. The experience of the 'new politics' of feminism, pacifism, ecology and so on, broke into the rather wooden discourse of Latin American marxism. The over-politicized left now realizes that there are other dimensions to human life, including the social, cultural and even religious aspects. The undisguisable fact of political failure has brought home the danger of self-proclaimed political elites acting as though they alone have 'the word' on socialism as it should be. A new political pluralism has crept into the marxist discourse in Latin America. Short term insurrectional perspectives have given way to the long-haul perspective, the 'war of position', to use Gramsci's term. The distance between the rhetoric of socialism and the aspirations of the people has become patent to many, along with the arcane language in which the politics of socialism is expressed. Of course, secure orthodoxies have a habit of becoming re-established, owing either to people's insecurity or to their sheer dogmatism, but the door has been opened for a reconsideration of what socialism means.

Means and ends

The second question to address is the adequacy of means to ends in the struggle for socialism. Traditionally, the political party was seen as the correct instrument by which the proletariat was to achieve its objectives. Yet the Chilean and Uruguayan cases, in particular, saw a wide dispersion of the political scene and the multiplication of new social conflicts not mediated by political parties. The divorce between the main political parties of the left and the social movements (both old and new) was patent, as was the strong will for autonomy by forces in struggle against the dictatorships. In the Chilean case, as Tironi argues, 'the reduction of social change to politics — the *imperialism* of politics — has totalitarian implications if that conception achieves control of the state'.[28] The depreciation of politics in general, and political parties in particular, is truer for Chile than for Argentina, where, on the contrary, political parties (as opposed to movements such as Peronism) were espoused by the new democratic intelligentsia. Nevertheless, the idea of the single revolutionary party, the professional revolutionary of Leninist mythology, and their attendant pathologies, have taken a serious blow.

The other post-Cuban means for achieving socialism was seen to be the armed vanguard. The bitter collapse of armed struggle in Argentina, Brazil and Uruguay led inevitably to the drawing-up of a self-critical balance-sheet of these experiences. Some turned to a more orthodox, party political Marxism, while others adopted a vague 'basism', which looked to spontaneous grass-roots movements. There were a few sectors, indeed, which advocated an unreconstructed guerrilla war strategy in the 1980s. The critique of *guerrillismo* was of varying degrees of sophistication. Some movements admitted defeat but not that they had been wrong in their strategy and tactics. Others carried out some of the most far-reaching re-evaluations of democracy, as though compensating for previous gross underestimations of its importance. The other lesson learned was in relation to what is cumbersomely known as 'substitutionism' — the attempt by small, self-appointed vanguards to substitute themselves for the organized mass activity of the working classes.

Statism

The third recurring theme in these political debates is the problem of 'statism', a politics that looks always to the state. The left would appeal for the economic intervention of the state to restrain private power, be it local or foreign; it also wanted to 'seize' the state as a platform from which to launch its own economic model; but it also (sometimes) wanted to 'smash' the state. Quite apart from the logical inconsistencies, we should be aware of the effects of such an overbearing orientation towards the state. This is a Napoleonic conception of state and politics, where scientific and rational change by technical and bureaucratic means is seen as the agent of change. Milton Friedman is not just tilting at windmills when he attacks the growing intervention of the state in people's lives. The left seems to have accepted the concentration of power in the hands of the state and the legitimacy of the 'expert' as the source of all authority. In the struggle against the military dictatorships there was a concerted bid for the revaluation of civil society and the growth of considerable anti-statist sentiment. Theoretically, the left had learned some time before — from Poulantzas — that the instrumentalist conception of the state was wrong, that it expressed a power relation and was not a 'thing' to be seized. Now, political practice has led many on the left to break out of their blinkered focus on the state as the main enemy and the favoured springboard for a new system. The experience of the state socialism of the East was also a powerful incentive for rethinking the traditional Napoleonic orientation of the Latin American left.

Social movements

From the critique of political parties, armed vanguardism and a statist conception of politics, comes a renewed interest in the role of social movements, which is our fourth point. As we shall see in the chapters which follow, social movements, including labour but also squatters, citizens, women and human rights movements, were instrumental in the overthrow of authoritarian rule. These movements often arose beyond the control of the organized left, were diffuse rather than centralized, mistrusted politics in general, and practised a genuine democracy. These movements strove to maintain their autonomy from political parties, and the latter proved unable to mediate the social demands they expressed. The new social movements rejected the linear, organicist conception of politics of the traditional left. There was a partial redefinition of the relationships between the social and the political to the detriment of the latter. The privileged role of the working class in the socialist project was questioned, especially since the monetarist projects of the dictatorships had dramatically reduced the weight of industrial workers within the working class. The new social movements, not finding an adequate (or possible) means of representation in the world of party politics, often turned to the world of the church. What the left has been unable to do, as Tironi argues, is to

> make the social movement the starting point and daily reference of the political business of the opposition; with the task of globalizing and integrating its demands to project them on a national scale within a historical project which interprets the majority of workers and the majority of the country.[29]

Democracy reassessed

Running through all the above debates, like a red thread, is the so-called question of democracy, our fifth and last point. The long experience of authoritarian rule led inevitably to a reaffirmation of democracy. So did the experience of bureaucratic socialist parties and states, and so did the example of genuinely democratic new social movements. Democracy is seen as something to be valued in its own right, here and now, and defended assiduously even in its formal 'bourgeois' variant. Inner-party democracy and a pluralism of the left have replaced democratic centralism and sterile political sectarianism and elitism. The human rights movement introduced a new ethical component into the discourse of the left and promoted the new-found sensibility towards democracy. Inevitably the distinction between democracy and authoritarianism began to take precedence over that between socialism and democracy (see Chapter 8). Socialism began to be thought of in terms of a democratic transformation of society. This was partly in reaction to the previous belief in a radical and violent rupture which would usher in the new dawn overnight. Clearly, the new democratic ideology which emerged in the late 1970s has its limits (see Chapter 8), but at the same time we must recognize its origins in the profoundly authoritarian, statist, and instrumentalist attitude of the left towards democracy hitherto. At the very least it is promoting a renewal of socialist thought and an honest confrontation of unavoidable dilemmas.

What we must retain from these discussions is the call by a section of the Latin American left for a democratic renewal of socialism and a break with 'theological' Marxism. The new secular Marxism is less prone to accept questionable dogmas at face value and allow certain themes to become 'sacred cows', beyond rational discussion. Politics and culture are no longer reduced to an economic base; political ideologies are no longer tied inexorably to particular social classes; and a socialism that is not democratic is no longer recognized as socialism. From the politics of total opposition, the left is now talking about a 'politics of order' under the new democracies, in which all parties would accept certain constitutional rules. The idea that society is cut across by one univocal contradiction, between labour and capital, or nation and imperialism, is no longer accepted, as we recognize the multiplicity of antagonisms in late capitalist society. The notion that socialism is inscribed in the immutable laws of history has scarcely any credibility. The tendency to view socialism as a reign of transparency where conflicts would simply fade away can no longer be sustained. As we shall see in Chapter 8, this renewal of the left has led many to say 'Farewell to Socialism'. This is not, of course, necessary if one returns to basics, to make out what socialism is and seek a realist approach to the capitalism of today which could lead to a viable hegemonic project of the left.

Notes

1. F. Cardoso and E. Faletto, *Dependency and Development in Latin America* (University of California Press, Berkeley, 1971), p. 76.
2. Ibid, p. 100.
3. A. Flisfisch, N. Lechner, T. Moulián, *Problemas de la Democracia y la Política Democrática en América Latina*, Documentos de Trabajo No. 240, FLACSO, Santiago, 1985.
4. A. Gramsci, *Selections from the Prison Notebooks* (Lawrence and Wishart, London, 1973), p. 219.
5. M. Peña, *El Peronismo* (Peña Lilo, Buenos Aires, 1972), p. 72.
6. L. de Riz, 'Política y Partidos. Ejercicio de Análisis Comparado: Argentina, Chile, Brasil y Uruguay', *Desarrollo Económico*, Vol. 25, No 100, 1986, p. 678.

7. I. Roxborough, P. O'Brien, J. Roddick, *Chile: State and Revolution* (Macmillan, London, 1979), p. 40.

8. L. De Riz, 'Política y Partidos', p. 668.

9. A. Gramsci, *Selections from the Prison Notebooks*, p. 109.

10. Ibid, p. 116.

11. Ibid, p. 119.

12. On O'Donnell's work see D. Collier (ed.) *The New Authoritarianism in Latin America* (Princeton University Press, Princeton, 1978).

13. J. Serra, 'Three Mistaken Theses Regarding the Connection Between Industrialization and Authoritarian Regimes', in D. Collier (ed.) *The New Authoritarianism in Latin America*, p. 117.

14. Ibid, p. 99.

15. P. Cammack, 'The political economy of contemporary military regimes in Latin America: from bureaucratic authoritarianism to restructuring', in P. O'Brien and P. Cammack (eds) *Generals in Retreat: The crisis of military rule in Latin America* (Manchester University Press, Manchester, 1985), p. 8.

16. Ibid, p. 11.

17. G. O'Donnell, 'Reflections on the Patterns of Change in the Bureaucratic-Authoritarian State', *Latin American Research Review*, Vol. XIII, No. 1, 1978, p. 5.

18. Ibid.

19. M. A. Garretón, *Chile: En Busca de la Democracia Perdida*, Documentos de Trabajo No. 263, Santiago, 1985, p. 19.

20. L. de Riz, 'Politica y Partidos', p. 672.

21. A. Gramsci, *Selections from the Prison Notebooks* (Lawrence and Wishart, London, 1973), p. 219.

22. Ibid, p. 94.

23. Ibid, p. 221.

24. Ibid, pp. 221-2.

25. R. Debray, *A Critique of Arms: Vol 2. The Revolution On Trial* (Penguin, Harmondsworth, 1978), p. 235.

26. OLAS General Declaration, reprinted in *International Socialist Review* 28:6 (Nov–Dec 1967), p. 58.

27. E. Tironi, *La Torre de Babel. Ensayos de Crítica y Renovación Política* (Ediciones Sur, Santiago, 1984), p. 13.

28. Ibid, p. 69.

29. Ibid, p. 108-9.

3. The Modern Dictatorships

In the previous chapter we saw how the polarization and collapse of the compromise state set the southern cone countries along the path to dictatorship. In this chapter we examine some of the major economic, political and social features of the resulting military regimes. This constitutes, of course, a necessary step in our endeavour to analyse the more recent collapse of these regimes and the subsequent transitions to democracy (see Chapter 4). A preliminary task is to examine briefly the various analytical frameworks deployed in the study of the military regimes. We have already mentioned in the previous chapter Guillermo O'Donnell's term, 'bureaucratic–authoritarian state', which attempts to capture the specificity of the new military regimes in the southern cone. My own feeling is that while it addresses many of the pertinent issues, the term itself is misleading: the regimes are more technocratic than bureaucratic; to call them authoritarian seriously underplays the level of repression; and they are forms of regime on the pre-existing basis of a capitalist state. Others (for example, Theotonio Dos Santos) have advanced the formulation of 'dependent fascism' to describe these regimes. Here we have an unjustified extension of a historically bound state form, based on the mobilization of the petty bourgeoisie and an unbridled expansionism, to regimes that share none of these characteristics bar repression. For my part, I would simply characterize these regimes as modern military dictatorships. 'Military dictatorship' seems the only possible term to describe the monopoly of political power by the armed forces, and we may call them 'modern' to distinguish them from the personalist rule by military *caudillos* of an earlier era, and to account for their essential characteristic of fomenting an accelerated rhythm of capital accumulation, based on further integration with the world economy.

Terminology, however, is not as important as the analytical approach taken to uncover the dynamic of the new military dictatorships. The bureaucratic–authoritarianism model tends towards a certain economism, in which it is tempting to detect a correlation between infrastructural and political processes where that may not exist. The term 'dependent fascism' suffers from a rather simplistic notion that socialism or fascism are the only political choices which 'dependent capitalism' is inexorably driven towards. To avoid both problems we can turn to the literature produced by political scientists (for example Juan

Linz) which focuses on the nature of the regimes produced by the military takeovers. We should examine the concrete political institutions and mechanisms characteristic of each case: Brazil is quite different from Chile, for example, in this respect. The problem here is that political actors are granted perhaps an undue level of autonomy from structural constraints. The opposite of a structural determinism, which sees a regime as the inexorable result of economic changes, is a form of voluntarism. There is a third line of analysis which focuses almost entirely on the military as an institution to explain the rise of the new military dictatorships. For example, there are detailed accounts of how the so-called National Security Doctrine was shaped in the various military academies, and of its role in the military regimes. While some Marxist accounts saw the military as simply the 'armed party of the bourgeoisie', and did not bother with specificities, these accounts tend to inflate the importance of military ideology and fall into a conspiratorial approach to the rise of the new military regimes. It should be possible to integrate the best elements of all three modes of analysis — the structural dimension, the nature of the regime, and the importance of the military actors — in our account of the modern military dictatorships of the southern cone.

A new economic model

The importance of the economic plans implemented by the new military dictatorships can hardly be overestimated: in many ways they actually were the political project to be implemented. The political economy of monetarism was to take the place of the populist import-substitution industrialization policy with a Keynesian basis. Of course, monetarism as such was not new and had for long contested the sway held by the structuralism of the Economic Commission for Latin America (ECLA). In this earlier debate of the 1950s and 1960s, the structural approach of ECLA had argued that the roots of inflation were imbedded in the economic structure, and that stabilization policies had to recognize the various structural bottlenecks (around food supply, availability of foreign exchange, supply of imports, etc) that forced the economy into inflationary cycles. The early monetarists, on the contrary, according to Foxley, 'focused on the use of a few policy instruments: control of money supply; reduction of the government deficit; exchange rate devaluation; freeing of prices; and eliminating subsidies'.[1] Thus a short-term policy to deal with inflation took precedence over structural reform. Both these policies were applied in most of the southern cone countries at various points in the late 1950s and early 1960s without marked success. The new monetarists of the 1970s differed in three respects from the earlier versions:

1. the international context was, or was to become with the advent of Thatcherism and Reaganism, much more favourable to this approach;
2. there was the added 'advantage' of military dictatorships to impose the political conditions necessary for their full implementation;

3. the orthodox policies of the 1970s had a much stronger long-term component than their earlier counterparts which focused on short-term adjustment policies.

In brief, 1970s monetarism was to be a far more 'structural' economic policy.

Monetarism

The main tenets of monetarism are deceptively simple. The market should work unimpeded to allow the free determination of prices; thus the state should withdraw from its regulatory functions, the national economy should be opened up to international trade, and the capital and labour markets should be deregulated. The new economic liberalism argued that the market, functioning freely without state intervention, is the most efficient allocator of resources in society. The main source of economic difficulties in the southern cone was seen to be the 'bloated' public sector and the distortion of relative prices introduced by an 'artificial' industrialization policy. The undoubted failure of populist economic policies gave a certain superficial plausibility to this diagnosis. Through 'sound economic management', the confidence of the international financial community would be restored, so that loans and investments would once again flow into the southern cone. None of this was new (having been advocated by economic liberalism for decades), but the military regimes could deliver the one previously missing ingredient: labour discipline. Trade unions would not be allowed to alter the free determination by the market of the price of labour-power; labour courts and social security bodies would no longer provide any 'artificial' safeguards to workers; labour laws would not constrain the free mobility of labour. The technical measures advocated by monetarism to deal with inflation are debatable, but there was an undoubted coherence and ruthlessness in the liberal economic project to restructure the Latin American political economies and lay the basis for a stable hegemonic order.

In the various countries of the southern cone, economic management teams emerged to carry out these policies for (under) the military dictatorships: Martínez de Hoz in Argentina, Roberto Campos and later Delfim Neto in Brazil, the 'Chicago Boys' in Chile, and Vegh Villegas in Uruguay. They all had something in common, namely their close association with international financial centres. Jorge Schvarzer has written of how 'it became evident that Martínez de Hoz disposed of an enormous and practically unexplained political power during his stay at the Ministry of the Economy'.[2] Compared to previous ministers he remained in post for a long period of time and exercised an unrivalled control over key economic variables. The cohesion and power of the 'Chicago Boys' in Chile has become legendary. Philip O'Brien writes: 'They were thus able to act as a "vanguard party" of a sector of capital. Backed by leading sectors of the Chilean capitalist class, and international capitalist agencies and US business interests, they argued for a revolutionary overhaul of Chilean economy and society'.[3] The picture that emerges is of a lucid bourgeois technocracy, based on the internationalized sectors of the capitalist class with the strong backing of global capitalist agencies such as the International

Monetary Fund. There was a felicitous blend between global economic transformations — the era of financial capital hegemony was arriving — and the internal class struggle which had thrown up a decisive bourgeois leadership committed to ending the populist cycle and reasserting a new order to match the pre-1930 'golden era' of the agro-export based oligarchy.

The compromise state was, of course, shattered by the modernizing military dictatorships whose rise to power we examined briefly in the previous chapter. There is a history of class struggle in each country leading up to the date of each military intervention. We would not wish to portray the military coup as an event dictated by international financial or military agencies, however indirectly. What we do have is a particular 'fit' between shifts in the international arena and national trajectories. Sábato and Schvarzer note that: 'The new cycle has a moment of birth as clear-cut as 1929 was for the previous one. The changes were consolidated in a gradual manner and achieved their finished form from 1975 onwards'.[4] It was the transformed and increased role of international finance that set the scene for this new phase, with the spectacular rise in the debt of a selected group of Third World countries marking a new departure. International credit was not channelled chiefly through bodies such as the World Bank, but rather through large private banks operating on the Eurodollar market. Since the Second World War, the southern cone economies had become integrated into the international circuit of production, through direct foreign investment; now the internationalization of the circuit of money capital was opening up a new era. The integration of the southern cone economies into the international financial market in the 1970s was carried out at a pace and in a mode dictated by the internal class struggle and the rise of a new bourgeois leadership.

Wages down

The political economy of the modern military dictatorships of the southern cone was fundamentally restructured under the aegis of the monetarist economic teams. With the defeat of the popular classes, and the withdrawal of legislative safeguards, wages were driven down dramatically after the coups. Within a year of the respective military takeovers, wages had been reduced by between 20 per cent and 40 per cent in real terms in Brazil and the southern cone countries. There was a concomitant rise in unemployment rates as the 'shakeout' of industry continued apace. Income distribution became increasingly more concentrated. The other side of the coin was a deregulation of prices, but due to lower wages, there was a sharp drop in effective demand. This amounted to a demand-centred stabilization programme with the chief victims being the popular classes. As Foxley writes for the Chilean case,

> One of the most striking aspects of the economic experience from 1973 to 1980 was the simultaneous deterioration of employment, wages, per capita consumption, and other social indicators that measure the population's access to housing, education, and health, as well as the skewing of consumption by income strata.[5]

In Argentina and Uruguay a very similar pattern prevailed. In Brazil there was a spread of consumer durables to layers of the working class, but the overall distribution of income became still more retrogressive in the twenty years of military rule. Of course, the counterpart was a brief era of conspicious consumerism for parts of the middle class, as *plata dulce* (sweet money) became readily available through speculation.

Markets open

The opening of the southern cone economies to the world market was the next most important aspect of the military's monetarist policies. Protectionism in favour of internal industrial activities was held to be as obnoxious as the interference of trade unions in the free determination of wage rates. So, in Argentina, Chile and Uruguay, there was a systematic dismantling of tariff protection structures and an encouragement of imports to replace those sectors affected. Thus, earlier import substitution policies were turned on their head, and a process of deindustrialization occurred. Brazil, as in all the generalities about the monetarist model, only partly followed the trend of the southern cone countries. As Regis de Castro Andrade writes, 'Development in Brazil is by and large the manifestation and the consequence of the internationalisation of the Brazilian economy'.[6] But in this case, multinational corporations were integrated into the local productive structure, producing mainly for the internal market. The Brazilian model also depended on the conversion into international currency of locally generated profits for their realization. Thus, as Andrade notes, 'a continuous expansion of profits and external financing becomes imperative'.[7] The opening of the southern cone economies to the world market was also, of course, designed to attract foreign investment. Certainly bodies like the International Monetary Fund looked kindly on the new economic administration, but the hoped for wave of foreign investment never really materialized. More precisely, productive investment did not rise markedly (except in Brazil) but there was an influx of 'hot money' seeking to profit from the open financial markets.

Financial boom

The deregulation of the financial markets was another key component of the new economic policies, designed as it was to guarantee the free flow of capital. Financial reforms in the southern cone countries under military rule led to interest rates being determined solely by supply and demand, thus doing away with their regulation by the state, which had been used in the past to encourage industrialization. Rapidly, the financial sector became the sole growth sector as money poured in from home and abroad. In Argentina, for example, the number of banks doubled between 1976 and 1979. The financial reform was much worse than a means to make money fast and give a good 'shake-out' to the industrial sector, now faced with higher interest rates. Indeed, the financial reform was designed to make it impossible to return to the pre-coup political economy. As Schwarzer writes:

The most important change in the whole stage derived from the encouragement of a financial–speculative system whose impetuous action, from the start of 1976 had destroyed the last defensive barriers of the Peronist government. In June 1977 this displacement of economic power was sanctioned and organically structured.[8]

Due to the differential access of firms to credit, the financial reforms of the southern cone led to a severe concentration of assets in a few large conglomerates, a process encouraged by the concomitant privatization of many public enterprises. The *'patria financiera'* (financial nation), as it became known in Argentina, became a powerful social force, one which has continued its destabilizing influence under the new democracies.

The restructuring of the southern cone economies under the monetarist teams represented an ambitious attempt to generate a new hegemonic bloc. One of the early interpretations of the military coup in Argentina in 1976 argued that it represented an attempt to 'set the clock back' to the pre-1930 situation by reasserting the hegemony of the agrarian sector. If we examine more carefully who the beneficiaries of the new economic policies were, we find this interpretation is not borne out. In all the southern cone countries the agrarian sectors protested vigorously about aspects of the military economic policies. Nor were the subsidiaries of multinational corporations clear-cut beneficiaries of the new order. Sectors which did benefit were those linked to agro-industry, financial intermediation and key dynamic industrial sectors integrated into the world economy. Through economic leadership that was able to stand back from the immediate economic interest of this or that fraction of the bourgeoisie, the military states were able to lay the basis for the emergence of a new hegemonic bloc in which the financial sector would play a dominant role alongside the internationalized fractions of the industrial and agro-industrial sectors. A new regime of capital accumulation was being forged — most successfully in the case of Brazil — in a broad economic and political restructuring process which cannot be reduced to a simplistic return to pre-1930 conditions. What was being sought was a stable and profitable insertion into the international division of labour in the 1980s in a way that was characteristic of the region between 1880 and 1929.

The record

Today, some fifteen years after the monetarist economic policies began to be implemented in the southern cone, it is possible to draw up a balance-sheet of its successes and failures. Without doubt the policies were more far-reaching in their effects than the monetarist programmes of the late 1950s and 1960s. There have been fundamental changes in the structures of production, employment and financial intermediation which cannot be reversed in the short term. Much of the 'hidden agenda' of monetarism — to alter fundamentally the balance of class forces — has been achieved. If we assess its success or otherwise in its own terms, we find a mixed balance sheet. In Table 3.1 we can follow the evolution of the Gross Domestic Product per capita in the four countries.

Table 3.1
Southern cone: GDP per capita
(US$ 1986)

	1960	1970	1980	1987
Argentina	2,241	2,893	3,161	2,745
Brazil	941	1,292	2,348	2,428
Chile	1,712	2,075	2,272	2,213
Uruguay	2,182	2,300	2,990	2,733
Latin America (average)	1,274	1,675	2,340	2,223

Source: Inter-American Development Bank. *Economic and Social Progress in Latin America 1988.* (IDB, Washington. 1988).

These global figures show Argentina's relative stagnation and Brazil's 'great leap forward' in the last two decades, but very little else. Production grew in the 1960s under the Keynesian policies of ECLA and also in the 1970s, chiefly under monetarist management, although it is significant that in the 1980s, GDP per capita declined noticeably in Argentina, Chile and Uruguay — hardly a measure of success. If, however, we examine, in Table 3.2, the evolution of average annual growth rates in per capita GDP we obtain a uniformly more negative picture, even for Brazil.

Table 3.2
GDP per capita, average annual growth rates
(%)

	1960–2 to 1971–3	1971–3 to 1979–81	1979–81 to 1982–4
Argentina	2.5	0.3	−3.7
Brazil	4.1	4.8	−1.8
Chile	1.8	0.7	−4.1
Uruguay	0.4	3.3	−4.3

Source: United Nations Economic Commission for Latin America. *Statistical Yearbook for Latin America 1986.* (UN. Geneva. 1987).

In brief, Brazil and Uruguay saw some expansion in the first phase of military rule, but since 1980 there have been negative growth rates.

If inflation was deemed the main enemy of monetarist policies, we should expect some results on this score. In Table 3.3 we can examine the evolution of inflation between 1960 and 1986 in Brazil and the southern cone countries.

The first obvious conclusion to draw from this data is that the military regimes were able to reduce considerably the inflation rates inherited from the civilian regimes. However, as Thorp and Whitehead argue, 'the gains from any such reduction must be weighed against the damage to development prospects that has frequently accompanied anti-inflation packages'.[9] The prospect of 'stagflation' — inflation with stagnation — seems a real one. Certainly, we note a certain resilience of the inflation rate despite sustained stabilization policies: in Argentina it was four years after the coup before inflation was reduced to

Table 3.3
Annual variation in Consumer Price Index
(%)

	1961–70	1971–80	1987
Argentina	21.4	141.5	131.3
Brazil	46.2	36.6	231.7
Chile	27.1	174.3	19.8
Uruguay	47.8	64.0	63.6

Source: Inter-American Development Bank, *Economic and Social Progress in Latin America. 1988 Report.* (IDB, Washington, 1988).

under 100 per cent, and Brazil, the one 'success story', has seen a dramatic increase in inflation in the 1980s. At best, the open economy monetarism of the 1970s has had a partial success in terms of its main stated objective.

In terms of opening the economy to the world market there is a mixed balance sheet. On the positive side we can note a marked increase in the level of non-traditional exports from all four countries. Previous reliance on coffee, grains, meat or copper is not so marked as semi-manufactured and light manufacturing goods are sold increasingly abroad. This diversification of the economic base must, however, be set alongside the dramatic increase in the foreign debt over the same period, as traced in Table 3.4.

Table 3.4
External public debt outstanding
(US$m)

	1960	1970	1975	1980	1986
Argentina	1,275	2,455	5,249	12,350	40,903
Brazil	2,407	4,706	17,897	50,922	88,331
Chile	562	2,543	4,389	5,163	16,605
Uruguay	132	356	1,034	1,646	3,262
Latin America	7,205	20,800	59,426	160,193	330,826

Source: Inter-American Development Bank, Economic and Social Progress in Latin America. 1987 report. (IDB, Washington, 1987).

The massive foreign debt is, undoubtedly, the heaviest legacy that the modern military dictatorships bequeathed to their civilian successors. Whereas between 1975 and 1981 Latin America received an inflow of US$171 billion and paid out US$89.3 billion in profits and remittances (net transfer: +US$81.7 billion), between 1982 and 1985 only US$38 billion came in, against a transfer of resources out of the region of US$144 billion (net transfer: –US$106 billion).[10] Behind the bare economic data lies a potential social crisis of enormous proportions. Inflation is creeping up steadily, growth rates are sluggish and the international conditions are far from favourable. The new democratic states are being called on to resolve the debt crisis by imposing on the people stringent austerity measures equal to, if not harsher than, those of their military predecessors. As one cynical banker declared in the newly democratic Argentina: 'We foreign bankers are for the free-market system when we are out to make a buck and believe in the state when we're about to lose a buck. This thing will come down to a matter of muscle'.[11] At the moment the situation in Latin America shows close parallels to that of Germany following the war reparations settlement imposed by the Versailles Treaty in 1919, and not lifted until the Hoover Moratorium of 1931 (without which Germany would still be paying reparations in the 1980s). Neither spectacular defaulting dramas nor a concerted debtors' cartel seem likely; meanwhile each of the new democracies has to pick up the bill for the years of indulgence by the *patria financiera*.

Political reformation

The new military dictatorships went through two clearly distinguishable phases, one of reaction towards the old order, and a second where they sought a virtual political reformation. Their first task is one of repression and containment, but later they must seek some form of institutionalization if they are not to become permanent emergency regimes. The first phase is well documented and relatively familiar. It involves the forcible seizure of the state by the armed forces, led by an intellectual elite or a strong figure such as Pinochet, and the assumption of *de facto* governmental power. This self-assumed political task is usually justified in terms of 'cleaning out the stables' of the old regime, or 'cutting out the cancer' of populism or Marxism. It is usually presented as an emergency regime, with no political ambitions of its own other than to restore peace and stability in the land. It carries out this task through a systematic dismantling of the constitutional order, although some continuity may be allowed for the juridical realm and even, as in Brazil, for the legislative arena itself. What the armed forces inevitably must do is take unto themselves the political control of force: to defeat any 'subversive' movement, whether it take political, trade union, social or guerrilla form. The first phase of military rule can thus be characterized as one of containment: trying to repair the burst dams of the capitalist order and return things to normal.

Containment
Normality and order are established by the deliberate cultivation of fear, passivity and conformity. The presence of fascist ideologies in the ranks of the military does not lead these to adopt Nazi-style mobilization techniques. These regimes do not seek to exacerbate the class struggle, as occurred in the rise to power of European fascism, but rather to dampen it so as to quell all mobilizing impulses. Order is induced through a dismantling of the old order: political parties are banned or suspended, censorship is imposed and insurgents are eradicated. Within a year of coming to power the military dictatorships of Chile (1973), Uruguay (1973) and Argentina (1976) had successfully dealt with all the open manifestations of opposition, including, in the latter two, powerful urban guerrilla movements. In Brazil, an armed challenge to the state did not

occur until 1969, five years after the coup, and this was dealt with quickly and efficiently. A panoply of repressive measures dealt systematically with all forms of resistance to military rule, including in the cultural domain. Yet, as we saw in Chapter 2, the modern military dictatorships saw themselves as ending broad political cycles — populism, socialism, welfarism, etc. — and not just dealing with a political emergency. Having coped successfully with the immediate task at hand, they inevitably looked towards the deeper roots of the malaise which had formed their nations into 'sick societies'.

The armed forces themselves were well aware of the temporal limits of this first stage of containment. In a book justifying the military intervention in Uruguay, we learn that:

> It took no more than seven months to destroy the seditious apparatus, armed branch of subversion, through a military action of sufficient energy and cohesion to reestablish the confidence which the State, in years of indolence and politicking, had progressively been losing as an instrument of order, peace and progress.[12]

What emerges from this statement is the distinction drawn in the military mind between sedition — illegal armed action against the established order — and subversion, which is given a much broader meaning as anything which, in any way, threatens the 'Western and Christian way of life'. That is why Argentine generals would declare after their coup that they would deal first with armed rebels, then with people who sympathized with them, and, finally, those not sufficiently behind the established order. Repression was not reserved for those who, outside the law, confronted the state, but was directed at all those who created the conditions for that challenge to emerge. To deal with this more deep-rooted problem the military would need to launch a veritable political reformation. From repression and containment, the military regimes passed to a stage of institutionalization and, in different ways, they launched what Garretón has called a 'refoundation project'.[13] After dismantling an old order they would now seek to build a new one, based on monetarist economics (as we saw above) and a militarist conception of politics.

Renewal
The modern dictatorships did not seek simply to return to the *status quo ante*, but rather to found a new order based on distinctive development models and political foundations. They were counter-revolutionary regimes, stemming as they did the threat by the dominated classes to overflow the bounds of bourgeois legality, but they also sought to build. As Garretón argues:

> Both dimensions, the reactive and the foundational, are complementary and cannot be separated. And even though they are more or less important, depending on the situation through which the regime is passing . . . elements of both are present in all phases and mutually condition each other.[14]

In the installation phase of the new military regimes, the reactive or defensive element prevails and the military discourse centres on its role in re-establishing order in the face of the 'chaos and anarchy' of the old regime. In Brazil in 1964, Argentina in 1966 and especially in 1976 and in Chile and Uruguay in 1973, this element prevailed, but then, if to differing degrees, the various military regimes set about constructing a new order. In this consolidation phase of the military regime there could be a return to the reactive: Brazil in 1969; Chile at various stages when the regime has thwarted moves towards liberalization. In other cases, such as Uruguay especially, the military began to return to the role of caretaker until bourgeois hegemony had been re-established, whereas in Argentina they continued as weary managers of a permanent political crisis.

As the logic of war gave way to a political logic, so the various military regimes set about establishing some form of legitimacy for themselves. In Brazil, a new constitution adopted in 1967 was aimed at just such an institutionalization of the military regime, in the shape of the national security state. Whereas, traditionally national security had been defined in terms of the defence of national territory against foreign aggression, it was now broadened to include the defence of ideological frontiers. Constitutional guarantees concerning industrial rights took on even less meaning with the (in)famous Institutional Act No. 5 of 1968 which, as Moreira Alves notes, 'repeated provisions contained in the first two institutional acts, but there was a major difference: there was no time limit on its validity. The controls and suspension of constitutional guarantees were permanent'.[15] Yet even as the new military states were being institutionalized — i.e. 'legalized' — from above, there was often recourse to the old democratic referent. Thus in Uruguay, as the generals began their retreat in 1984, one of their number could declare how

> the Armed Forces legitimately entered the national political life in 1973, supporting a constitutional president to fill a power vacuum which had left the Republic sailing without a course, in a netting of disorder, violence, demagogy and misgovernment. *It was at no moment a movement of force opposed to democracy*. On the contrary, it was in defense of democracy.[16]

The rhetoric of national security was only a fragile basis for legitimacy, and democracy (however interpreted) often figured in the foundational military discourse.

Chile

In Chile, the phase of institutionalization was consolidated with the Constitution of 1981. Already in 1974, the military regime's Declaration of Principles had affirmed that theirs would not be a mere transitional regime, but did not set out anything beyond a vague, Catholic-based corporatism, and called merely for democracy 'purged of its vices'. The 1977 Plan de Chacarillas advanced a clearer version of a severely restricted and exclusionary democracy, where representation would be matched by nominations by the military authorities. After a plebiscite in 1980 (of which more in Chapter 4), a new constitution — the 'Constitution of Liberty' — was finally brought in in 1981. A long-term timetable for redemocratization was effectively negated by the severe curtailment of democratic norms and the creation of a new Council of

National Security which joined the trinity of executive, legislature and judiciary in the new 'organic democracy'. In Argentina, the military coup of 1976 was justified not in terms of the illegality or lack of legitimacy of the decaying Peronist regime; rather, the military, long used to intervention in politics (unlike their counterparts in Chile and Uruguay) took it upon themselves to define the needs of the nation: 'The Armed Forces, in keeping with an obligation they cannot shirk, have assumed control (*conducción*) of the State . . . it is a decision for the nation (*Patria*)'.[17] With considerable insight, the military did not (as in 1966) proclaim a new era of uninterrupted military rule, but actually claimed that this should be the last military intervention and that it would end, in the words of General Videla, 'the cycle of weak civilian regimes and strong military regimes'.[18]

Brazil

In Brazil, the coup was most clearly linked to a lucid bourgeois reformation (revolution being a bit strong) project, generated in discussions between military and business sectors prior to 1964. As Moreira Alves analyses it:

> The Doctrine of National Security and Development, as taught in the Escola Superior de Guerra and other military schools, must be understood in its entirety. As it was constructed in Brazil, it is an integrated body of thought that includes a theory of war, and theory of internal subversion and revolution, a theory of Brazil's role in world politics and its geopolitical potential as world power, and a particular model of associated-dependent economic development that combines Keynesian economics and state capitalism.[19]

This last element is crucial, because the Brazilian military and their technocratic allies specifically rejected *laissez-faire* capitalism, even though monetarist techniques would, of course, be deployed against inflation. On the crucial economic front, as in the continued space allowed to a restricted practice of normal party politics, the Brazilian modernizing military displayed the pragmatism which goes a long way to accounting for their twenty and more years in power and their ability largely to dictate the terms of the democratization process, as we shall see in Chapter 4.

In Chile, the Pinochet regime also articulated a foundational discourse, centred around the concepts of 'security' and 'market'. José Brunner develops this theme:

> if we represent these axes as chains of signifiers, then the first links the thematic universe of order (or repression) and the second, the universe of progress (or satisfaction). One is dictated by the principle of necessity, the other ushers in the reign of liberty.[20]

Between them, the concepts of security and the market construct the symbolic space for authoritarian social integration. These two components of the military discursive matrix follow each other in time: the doctrine of national security aims to generate a moral solidarity, followed by the neo-liberal ideology of the market designed to foment an organic solidarity. The resulting military or authoritarian discourse both expresses and reproduces a specific conception of the world that creates a level of collective identity for the regime and its social base. As Brunner notes, 'Bourgeois consciousness, cowed by the depressing history of statism, was now being invited to flower and create its own revolutionary utopia'.[21] This line of interpretation takes us far from simplistic analysis of the 'mad dictator Pinochet' which reduces social domination to repression or false consciousness, and thus ignores the powerful social practices generated by the militarist discourse and the attraction of a new safe bourgeois world in which the market ensures its automatic reproduction.

Argentina

In Argentina, however, the 1976 military coup manifested much more a discourse of exception. As Sigal and Santi explain: 'The differences in terms of the construction of a legitimate position cannot be explained without taking into account the *pre-existing discursive material* in both countries'.[22] Thus the 1976 putschists did not need to portray the regime being overthrown as illegal or illegitimate (as their counterparts in Chile did) nor sanction their move by appeal to higher authority. Since 1930 the armed forces had assumed a political role and maintained the 'right' to seize political power. In 1976 they sought only to differentiate that coup from previous ones by saying it would break the cycle of imitability. Once the immediate task at hand — the disarticulation of guerrilla and radical labour movements — had been accomplished, the armed forces would move back to a dialogue with traditional politicians rather than attempt a Franco-style long-term project. Barely a year after the coup, General/President Videla was declaring: 'We believe that today, having overcome the fundamental stage of establishing order, it is possible and necessary for us to open a dialogue with the whole community, a dialogue which will only exclude the corrupt, the economic criminal and the subversive criminal . . .'[23] At this stage the military were probably only seeking to establish credible civilian allies to construct political parties capable of founding a 'stable democracy'. Nevertheless the appeal to an Other — the 'honest and representative' politicians — represented the first crack in the military discourse.

Uruguay

In Uruguay, finally, there is a first period (1973–76), in which the regime displayed a clear discourse of exception, followed by what Gonzalez has called a 'foundational attempt' (*ensayo*) to distinguish it from Chile's more clear-cut foundational project.[24] In the first phase it was the re-establishment of order which prevailed and the military showed no evidence of a clear political project of their own. In 1976, a crisis precipitated by the moves towards a corporatist state by the civilian president led to a new situation, in which the military took on constitutional power (as against merely establishing legislative norms). New constitutional bodies were created, such as the National Council (*Consejo de la Nación*), and the political role of the armed forces was institutionalized through the Council of National Security (*Consejo de Seguridad Nacional*). As in Chile, a plebiscite was called in 1980 to sanction the new constitutional arrangements, but the *de facto* government lost and thus set the country on the road to democratization (see Chapter 4). This failed foundational attempt was a hybrid, combining a Brazilian-style 'national security' doctrine, Chilean-style corporation, and an Argentine-style role to political parties in recognition of their considerable weight and, indeed, conservative role in the past. The Uruguayan military discourse combined development and security in a concept of 'organic democracy' with a certain reformist tinge, but which essentially sought parallels with the 'Roman peace conquered by arms and stabilized by law'.[25]

Social recomposition

Social transformations do not operate purely at the level of discourse (although this is a crucial and neglected element), so we must also examine the process of political restructuring accomplished by the modern military dictatorships. Essentially, we cannot separate the aspect of capital restructuring managed by the monetarist technocrats and the profound social recomposition which occurred under military rule. The free-market ideology and all its social consequences operated a shake-out of the various capitalist sectors and led to a partial decomposition of the working class. The social basis for a resurgent populism (and Keynesianism) was severely curtailed. The political space for a socialist project was dramatically reduced. Yet, the new military regimes had set out to do more than just inflict a severe defeat on the dominated classes so as to launch a new cycle of capital accumulation. With varying degrees of lucidity, the generals and their technocratic advisors (and co-conspirators) sought a more fundamental reordering of society to prevent any further crises of bourgeois hegemony. The strong military states stood above the particular interests of this or that fraction of the bourgeoisie and were thus able to implement policies which were often against the immediate interests of individual capitalists, as against capitalism as a whole and in the long term. It is still probably too early to assess whether the modernizing military were able to create the conditions for stable bourgeois rule with at least semi-democratic forms.

The political transformation of the military state can be seen in terms of a dialectic between initiatives from above and pressure from below. This must be said because the pages above describe a social process in abstraction from that key element of resistance to domination. In Brazil, after a brief guerrilla and labour outburst in 1968–69, there was a distinct lull in the class struggle until around 1978. A decade of 'social peace' provides, of course, an essential breathing space for the military to restructure capital and social relations. In Argentina, on the other hand, the military state was faced by an unremitting, if at first inchoate, rebellion in factories and working-class neighbourhoods, through human rights associations and general cultural resistance, which impeded the smooth imposition of military rule. In Chile, the 'silence of the cemeteries' was imposed for nearly a decade after the ostentatious brutality attendant on the 1973 coup, but when resistance did commence, it was the main factor in a complex process of liberalization and subsequent hardening by the regime. In Chapter 4 we examine in some detail the role of social movements in determining the pace and extent of democratization: at this stage we are just laying a marker which should dispel any notion that the military states operated in a social vacuum on which they could simply imprint their reformation projects.

The culture of authoritarianism

The modern military dictatorships imposed their rule over society in the first place through naked terror. The management of terror can take various forms, from the ordinary prison cell, exile, and the systematic use of torture to the dreaded 'disappearances' (*desaparecidos*). The latter technique of terror, as described by a report for the Independent Commission on International Humanitarian Issues, is particularly effective: 'Disappearances are a doubly lethal form of torture, for the victims who are kept ignorant of their fate, and for family members who wait and wonder, and may never receive any news'.[26] The personal nightmare of the detained/disappeared is matched by a ripple of terror which spreads out from the immediate family, relatives, friends, neighbours, to society at large. Society is kept hostage for the (remote) possibility that the prisoner may be released. There are no prisons for international bodies to inspect, no torture to denounce — at least none visible. A further beauty of this system for its perpetrators was that it is deniable: it could be passed off as the work of 'paramilitary groups' outside the control of the legitimate state forces. As in all counter-revolutionary wars, the state has learned from its guerrilla enemy to act with stealth, unpredictability and ruthlessness. The Latin American dictatorships, particularly that of Argentina, pioneered the *desaparecido* technique of terror and deployed it to considerable effect to create a true culture of authoritarianism.

Torture
Torture is, of course, a better established terror technique. It may be simply a means to extract information from captured members of insurgent organiza-tions. In this mode, torture techniques are refined as a means to an end: to obtain the 'co-operation' of the victim as quickly and as easily as possible. Torture has moved on since then to acquire a much wider role in cowing a defeated civil society. As Foucault writes:

> The term 'penal torture' does not cover any corporal punishment: it is a differentiated production of pain, an organized ritual for the marking of victims and the expression of the power that punishes; not the expression of a legal system driven to exasperation and, forgetting the principles, losing all restraints . . .[27]

In the 'excesses' of torture a whole economy of power is invested. Torture must be seen as a technique rather than an expression of blind pathological fury. It is calculated, not irrational. Torture is a ritual that plays a key role in generating a culture of fear. It marks the victim and civil society alike. A not inconsiderable side effect is the *camaraderie* it creates amongst its perpetrators and collaborators: the (in)famous 'blood pact' (*pacto de sangre*) which bound the torturers and executioners of the military dictatorships. The punishment of the individual body through the regulated production of pain is also a punishment of a rebellious social body that dared to confront the established order.

After torture, if lucky enough not to be 'disappeared', the detained person ended up in prison. Confinement in prison of the political detainee is designed to destroy the prisoner as an individual and obtain collaboration. Torture continued as a routine form of punishment. In many cases, prisoners were held as hostages and executed if their colleagues outside took action against the state. New techniques of discipline were tried out and the agents of the state were trained in the exercise of these disciplines. Most important of all, however, was the 'demonstration effect' which the prison was designed to have on the rest of society. Prisons created fear in all layers of society. As Juan Rial notes for the case of Uruguay, through the relatives of prisoners wider social layers were reached and 'with that the spiral of terror was extended and diffused through the rest of society from the centres of repression'.[28] The prison establishment allowed news to filter out from the political hostages and stressed the damaging psychiatric effect of prison: the spectre of madness joined that of confinement. At the same time the authorities would allow relatives and support groups to collect food and clothes for prisoners, thus spreading fear among the layer of sympathizers and reinforcing the feeling of running a risk. In the culture of fear, created and disseminated by the military dictatorships, prison played a pivotal role. Exile, of course, was another form of prison, and there was also the prison of the wider society.

A mainstream Uruguayan politician, in an interview after the fall of the military regime in that country, spoke of how:

> The traditionally open and polemical style of life which always characterized our society began to change. Neither in the offices, nor the clubs, schools, factories or workshops were sincere and unprejudiced dialogues continued, and everything was limited to the inconsequential and non-compromising . . . Perhaps for the first time in the modern history of Uruguay were their people conscious of having lost the very right of intimacy. As ironically remarked, we were prisoners in our country.[29]

'Prisoners in our own country' is a phrase that keeps recurring in the literature of resistance to emerge from the southern cone dictatorships. It marks a brutal shattering of the traditional separation between the public and the private. The all-seeing eye of the state penetrated the deepest recesses of civil society, or at least people believed it did. The culture of fear generated the culture of the tout, the informer and the *kapo*, that dreaded agent of repression to emerge from the ranks of the repressed in these authoritarian situations, as in the Nazi concentration camps. We cannot avoid the theme of complicity and collaboration, and whatever theoretical criticisms the notion of 'authoritarian personality' may have received, it helps us account for many of the seemingly pathological characteristics of the dictatorships.

Discipline
O'Donnell has, in this respect, usefully distinguished between the macro and the micro aspects of authoritarianism. A sociology of everyday life under the southern cone dictatorships has yet to be written, but several aspects can be mentioned. The usual emphasis on the regressive social and economic policies of the military regimes should not blind us to the equally important, if less spectacular, regimentation of daily life. O'Donnell refers in this respect to

> the systematic, continuous and profound attempt to penetrate the capillaries of society, so as to also there, in all the contexts which the long hand of the government reached, implant ORDER and AUTHORITY, both based on the radically authoritarian, vertical and paternalist vision which the government . . . had of itself.[30]

The military 'surgeons' would operate on a 'sick society' and exorcise the 'cancer of subversion' that had, in their view, infected the very fabric of society. The breakdown of authority relations had, again in their view, gone beyond the economic and political arena, and was reflected in the educational and cultural realm generally. Social non-conformity of the mildest sartorial type was to be condemned equally with the armed insurgent. Conformity and passivity were now shining virtues, and a general depoliticization of daily life, a reversal of 'the personal is political', was the most adequate means of defence against the authoritarian cultural onslaught.

Given the undoubted perception of chaos prior to the military interventions, there was a widespread *need* for 'order', which was not merely imposed from above. Order can mean stability as well as discipline and punishment. The capillary transmission of the authoritarian discourse throughout society should not be neglected. This has obvious implications for the discussion of democratization in Chapter 4, in so far as this must also operate at a macro and micro level. The cycle of mobilization at all levels of society under the pre-dictatorial regimes was followed by a cycle of privatization under the military. In the atmosphere of fear and uncertainty there was a certain receptiveness to the military message that

> the duty of all good citizens is to work hard, enjoy the benefits of the forthcoming 'economic modernization' of the country, and beware that the ever-present risk of politicization, and thus of subversion, did not re-surface again in the family, school, work place or even in the streets.[31]

The self-rationalization that went on to deny torture, disappearances and daily arbitrariness was a natural consequence of the virtually hegemonic authoritarian discourse. Developing this line of interpretation, with uncomfortable echoes of self-repression, betrayal and wilful ignorance, is not in any way to minimize the enormity of the military crimes, but better to understand the context in which they were committed.

Of course, macro-level policies can have effects at the micro level. Thus, censorship is imposed in the military dictatorships as much for the mind-management of the masses, as for the necessary management of the news. As Moreira Alves notes: 'The control of the press, of radio, and of television has been extremely important in the overall logic of the national security state'.[32] Silence prevents organization but it also creates isolation and increases fear. As in other cases, the exercise of power has 'positive' effects and not merely negative ones. Censorship before publication — *censura previa* — is the most insidious because it inculcates values of self-repression. There was not often the need for gross censorship in the form of seizures or arrest. Disciplined media allowed the dictatorships to maintain a democratic facade, at least publicly. As Joan Dassin notes, again for the Brazilian regime, a paradigm in such matters, censorship operates at two levels: at a psychological level, it contributed to the prevailing fear culture by creating a climate of uncertainty and intimidation but, of course, the resistance to arbitrary authority, self-criticism and the reaffirmation of critical standards were also side effects of censorship.[33] The creation of small opposition papers, the growth of a people's theatre, and, above all, the spectacular rise of musical resistance forms showed a people ready to combat state censorship with bravery, imagination and wit.

The final, and most Orwellian, technique of repression we must mention is the Uruguayan practice of citizen categories. Through Institutional Act No. 7 of 1977, the military dictatorship set mechanisms whereby citizens would be classified and those considered a 'security threat' could be dismissed from work, be prevented from obtaining a passport, etc. A 'Category A' citizen had no history of leftist or trade union political involvement, and had not participated in strikes or other dissident activity. A 'Category B' citizen would be one who could be allowed to work under supervision, tolerating certain slips they may have committed in the past. A 'Category C' citizen was politically dead and was barred from holding any public office. It was the military and police authorities who handed out these certificates of democratic good conduct or, on the other hand, sacked or blacklisted people for real or imaginary crimes against democracy. Uruguayan writer Eduardo Galeano tells of how:

> In the computer of the Joint Chiefs of Staff Headquarters all Uruguayan citizens were classified in three categories, A, B and C according to the degree of dangerousness from the point of view of the military rulers. We could not obtain work, or keep it without the Certificate of Democratic Faith which that computer emitted and handed to the police — specialized in Democracy through courses given by Dan Mitrione, US professor of Torture Technique. Even to celebrate a birthday police authorization was indispensable. Every home was a cell; every factory, office or university department became a concentration camp.[34]

We can sum up this catalogue of terror techniques designed to create a culture of authoritarianism with the concept of 'disciplinary society', associated with the work of Michel Foucault. He begins by recalling Jeremy Bentham's panopticon, that singular architectural invention of the ideal prison, consisting of a circular building housing prisoners in cells at the periphery, with an inspection post at the centre. The effect of the panopticon was 'to induce on the inmate a state of conscious and permanent visibility that ensures the automatic functioning of power'.[35] Thus the panopticon is the architectural embodiment of exclusion and the disciplinary techniques. It is also a powerful image going to the essence of the southern cone military dictatorships. Foucault's image of the 'carceral society' as applied to Western Europe has been criticized for confusing bourgeois democracy, however repressive, and totalitarianism. However, as applied to Latin America it is a far better analogy than that of fascism. Panopticism is here generalized to embrace all in society who require normalizing, disciplining and excluding by the new regime. According to Foucault, the disciplinary modality of power does not replace all others: 'because it has infiltrated the others, sometimes undermining them, but serving as an intermediary between them, linking them together, extending them and above all making it possible to bring the effects of power to the most minute and distant elements'.[36] The disciplines reach parts of the social body that crude repression on its own cannot reach.

A more common response than resistance to the disciplinary societies of the southern cone was a social autism, a frozen conformist quietism. Despair after the coups led to a failure to maintain the previous counter-hegemonic projects, or even the counter-imaginary, faced with the powerful discourse of the free-market dictators. Nostalgia for past politics or a refusal to recognize present reality were, of course, other options. Silence was, as always, a strategy for survival in the disciplinary societies of the southern cone. In this respect, the regimes had considerable success in spite of the islands of resistance that remained or emerged in different areas of society. As O'Donnell writes:

> This success did not only consist of the fact that many of us submitted, were silenced or disguised ourselves in the face of this enormous pressure to appear as obedient, uniformed and silent children, prepared to allow those who 'knew' . . . to run things to the benefit of all . . . [but] for that to have occurred there was a society which patrolled itself . . .[37]

There was in all areas a flourishing of authoritarianism: informers, mini-despots, patriarchs, homophobics, and others of their repressive ilk took on the values of the new disciplinary societies, and applied them in full. The corrosive effect on the bonds of solidarity within society were considerable and no democratization project that ignores this domain can hope to be successful.

The effects of the disciplinary societies can be differentiated according to generations and it is always very important to distinguish the political experience of various generations when evaluating political trends and transformations. For example, young voters today who did not experience Peronism, the Tupamaros or Popular Unity are a world apart from those for whom it was a formative experience. For adults, socialized and politicized in the pre-dictatorial period, the experience of the *de facto* regimes was, following

Carina Perelli, 'only comparable with the experience of those suffering from shell shock'.[38] The trauma was such that there was a widespread retreat to the safer terrain of the family, and a meticulous dissociation from everything in the past, present and future associated with the ever-broadened concept of subversion. For a younger generation, however, brought up in the undoubted chaos of the collapse of the old populist or socialist regimes and movements, there was, according to Perelli, an even more conscious dissociation from everything considered political, but allied with the practice of prohibited rituals, even if these were often 'only' cultural. For the youngest generation, brought up in the aseptic atmosphere of the disciplinary societies, there was a complex mix of rejection of past myths, a certain retreat into hedonism but also the development of new resistance practices and a refusal simply to dissociate oneself from the new reality.

In conclusion, the military mode of domination operated a profound change in the means whereby society secures obedience, consent and legitimacy. They failed in their bid to construct a new stable hegemonic order but, nevertheless, their effect was profound. Joaquín Brunner argues in this respect that: 'The disciplining of social relations demands a privatization of power and the substitution of communicative influences by the operation of control techniques which are equally private'.[39] The very basis on which individuals become citizens and act collectively is undermined: the public person has no role in the disciplinary society. The public control of the powers that be becomes impossible. Communication gives way to control. That arena of the public in which historically the political integration of society took place, is now closed. Now, as Brunner describes, 'the market represents a mechanism of integration, through exchange, of individualized masses'.[40] The ideological effect of the market should not be neglected, with its whole meritocratic ethos, its hymn to individualism and its self-proclaimed technical efficiency. We have thus come round to our starting point — namely the new economic models of the southern cone military regimes — and seen how they, and the political reformation projects, influence, and in turn are deeply marked by, the culture of authoritarianism generated and reproduced by the dictatorships — with their own particular variants, as we shall now examine.

Trends and differences

Brazil

Brazil's was the first and the most durable of the modern military dictatorships. Taking a long view of the twenty years of military rule following 1964 the most striking element is the unprecedented acceleration of capital accumulation during that period. Regis de Castro Andrade writes that:

> In a metaphorical sense, Brazil is a frontier of the capitalist world. It is the empty lands to be conquered by the gun and turned into profitable business. In a more analytical sense it is a young industrialized country where capital

has spread in a blind rush, without developing the self-consciousness and institutions which could have attenuated its socially unacceptable effects. In any sense it is a case of savage capitalism.[41]

This unbridled capitalist expansion has some notable achievements, such as average growth rates between 1968 and 1973 of over 10 per cent. Critics of the 'economic miracle' point to the social cost of capital's gains from the point of view of the excluded and the oppressed. It is argued that super-exploitation is a necessary condition for capitalist development in countries such as Brazil, and that military dictatorship is its essential framework. This ignores the basic (Marxist) point that all socio-economic processes are contradictory, and that there is no implacable logic relating economic and political changes. The total transformation of Brazilian society by capitalist expansion and dynamism since 1964 cannot simply be explained away or negated by its social consequences.

The second most striking characteristic of the Brazilian dictatorship was the continued role of party politics under the regime. Paul Cammack hardly exaggerates when he claims that 'the continuity of electoral politics in Brazil, totally ignored by the BA [bureaucratic–authoritarian state] debate, is *the vital element which contains within it the specificity of the regime*'.[42] Unlike all the southern cone countries, the political space was not simply closed in Brazil but remoulded, orchestrated and controlled. Indeed, state-sponsored clientelistic politics was extended by the Brazilian generals to all levels of the administration. The attempt to create a pro-regime party, ARENA, was not unique, but its stability and relative success was. In the early debates around the nature of the Brazilian regime, great emphasis was laid on the organic link between the infrastructural context of late, dependent, state-led industrializa-tion and the repressive aspects of the military state. Juan Linz, drawing on his experience of the Francoist state, emphasized instead a political and institutional analysis which, early on, detected internal debates within the regime that would lead to liberalization.[43] In retrospect, the structural analysis marked strongly by a dependency framework provided less understanding of the Brazilian regime and its specificity than an analysis centred in the symbolic and ideological level, which sought out legitimation formulas available to the regimes and the associated forms of political institutionalization.

Finally, the Brazilian case shows a preponderant weight for the state both in economic and political affairs. Guillermo O'Donnell advances an interesting analysis of how 'statism' develops as an alternative to what he calls the bureaucratic state, if the level of threat from the working class is low and the 'normalizing' economic project can be implemented successfully and rapidly.[44] Brazil would seem to have been particularly successful in promoting an increased role for the state, while maintaining a mutually profitable alliance with international capital. During the 1967–73 boom period, some 60 per cent of all investment was carried out by the state, which now consolidated its role as a key economic actor. At the political level, the military regime effectively deployed the resources of the state to build up a pro-regime political apparatus.

Repression was deployed following the 1964 coup in a brief flare up of conflict in 1968–69, but nearly always in a carefully controlled and selective manner. We cannot understand the Brazilian regime purely in terms of coercion, ignoring what Cammack refers to as 'an increasingly explicit commitment to exploiting the monopoly power of the state in key areas and turning it to electoral advantage'.[45] Far from wishing to close the political arena, the Brazilian military have used the state to participate actively in it. If Mexico was the model for the Brazilian military, with its relatively stable statist and clientelistic politics, Argentina was the example to avoid.

Argentina

In Argentina, military interventions had a long political history when the 1976 coup occurred. A considerable part of the population either actively, or more likely passively, supported the military coup. The very real fear of civil war with rightist and leftist armed groups operating with seeming impunity was a strong incentive to at least 'give the military a chance'. If the ultimate threat to the established order was definitely greater in Chile, the perceived level of chaos and the general disaggregation of society was no less great. Had the crisis been seen merely as a political one — Isabel Perón's inability to govern — the elections due towards the end of 1976 could have provided a way out. Had the economic crisis been the only one — galloping inflation, lack of investment, growing foreign debt, and so on — then a new economics minister would have sufficed. But, as Francisco Delich writes, 'if there was a total social crisis, affecting the very fundamentals of the social order, then only a radical change in the state/society relations would suffice, so that the former might discipline the latter'.[46] More than in the other cases, the Argentine military believed that they were dealing with a fundamentally sick society, an ailment traceable back to the rise of Peronism or even 1930, with developmentalist economics and populist politics its main symptoms. Overlaid on this was a further belief that the Third World War between Western Christianity and atheistic (or Zionist) communism had already commenced, with Argentina its main battlefield.

The Argentine military regime is best known, and rightly so, for the scale and depth of repression it unleashed on civil society. A meticulously organized and ruthlessly exercised counter-revolutionary 'dirty war' was waged on the popular organizations and the popular 'sea' in which they swam. General Videla, the first *de facto* president, presented an ascetic, honest face to the public (so much so that the Communist Party supported him) and yet was the intellectual and operational author of massive crimes against humanity. As Juan Corradi writes,

> Argentina was ruled by both a visible and an invisible government; by dignified military chiefs and also by secret associations whose hidden executioners were agents from an unseen realm that intervened in ordinary life at certain moments, holding sway by virtue of the widespread fear of their strange powers and through the violence of their acts.[47]

Society was redefined as a war zone and a discourse of summary justice held sway. There were few rules, and safety could not be guaranteed to the non-combatants. The purpose of this unprecedented (in the southern cone) wave of repression was to break down the familiar interpellations of party or class, neighbourhood or friends. Each subject knew that his or her life, at the very least his or her liberty, was at stake and that obedience, self-imposed as much as everything else, was the order of the day. In this field, Argentina's military dictatorship was undoubtedly a paradigm for other regimes.

The other most striking aspect of the Argentine case was the unremitting resistance of the working class and the people generally to military rule. The accepted wisdom amongst Argentine social and political scientists is that this was a period of unprecedented labour quiescence. Certainly, in terms of strike indicators, 'days lost' and so on, there is a marked hiatus in the class struggle after 1976. Yet one finds active strike movements in spite of the arrest and disappearance of their leaders. More important, there was always in Argentina an official and an unofficial labour movement, and while the first was quite rigorously controlled and cowed, the latter burrowed away under the surface encouraging resistance to despotism in the plants and in the streets. In the working-class districts there was a dense social network of assistance and solidarity which provided unforeseen reservoirs of strength and resistance. A quite distinct resistance movement (of which more in the next chapter) was that waged by the relatives (especially mothers) of the disappeared. In a steady and persistent manner this campaign broke through the wall of silence and disinformation about the *desaparecidos*, and their role in the democratization process itself was not inconsiderable, If repression in Argentina was particularly severe and arbitrary, so the level of popular resistance was considerable, especially bearing in mind the dire circumstances in which it was waged.

Chile

Chile's 11 September 1973 is marked in the political consciousness of people across the globe: the dramatic bombing of the presidential palace, President Allende's heroic last stand with his Cuban machine gun, and the terrifying images of the torture and executions in Santiago's main stadium. The subsequent dictatorship under General Augusto Pinochet has been analysed with more passion than cold logic. For the left, it was a simple task to denounce the dictatorship, and the general feeling was that it was condemned to a rapid and inevitable collapse. As Tomás Moulián notes: 'In a traumatized society, in which an authoritarian power carries out transformations in the economic structure, the state, and culture, the parties act . . . as though they were survivors from the past'.[48] The mere achievement of survival under the new conditions was considerable, but it was at the price of a referral to past politics and past stories, which were no longer relevant. This lack of historical fit between the modernizing dictatorship and the traditional political parties (which in Chile includes the left) was at the root of the latter's failure to appreciate the new historical epoch. Even the label of 'fascism' deployed to characterize the new regime was a means of denunciation rather than analysis.

Moulián correctly argues that 'the left used the term fascism, but thinking that the regime was some type of momentary excrescence, resulting from a malign conspiracy, and not an attempt at an organic response to a state crisis'.

An example of a somewhat conspiratorial approach to the Chilean regime emphasized the importance of the Chicago school of economists. In O'Brien and Roddick's account of the making of the coup, there is an explicit denial that it was 'the product of a Machiavellian conspiracy directed by the CIA, ex-president Frei, or . . . General Pinochet'.[49] Nevertheless, the same authors go on to trace in great detail the personal, financial and political links of a series of individuals, down to an allegedly key group:

> One of their members called them 'the Monday Club' because they met every Monday for lunch in the offices of Hernan Cubillos, in Lord Cochrane Street. Cubillos had been left in charge of the Edwards' business empire when Doonie Edwards fled the country, and one of his most important responsibilities was *El Mercurio*. He was also widely assumed to be one of the CIA's key contacts in Chile.[50]

The left advocates a Leninist model of politics, the group of professional conspirators, bound by secrecy and possessed of a ruthlessness due to the certainty of their beliefs. Yet, if the bourgeoisie acts in a similar way it appears to be genuinely shocked and indignant. Whether Pinochet received the economic master plan for the new regime before or after 11 September is of little interest. The coup was produced by a broad social conflict and polarization, which led to a bourgeois backlash, and, let it not be forgotten, by the grievous mistakes and failures of the left in power. Far more relevant is to seek an understanding of the reasons behind the continuity of the Pinochet regime.

The considerable social support for a military coup in 1973 can hardly be denied. This was not because of allegiance to a doctrine of national security or neo-liberal economics, but because of a deep-rooted desire for order in the face of the perceived chaos of the Allende regime. As time went by, the illusions of the military regime's fragility and divisions faded, as it became clear that it represented a coherent and decisive move to restore bourgeois hegemony in Chile. The regime assigned considerable importance to the ideological domain and sought to alter the common sense of the era. As Norbert Lechner argues:

> The market has managed to undermine the organized interests which were the social base of the old political system, which thus loses its sociological and ideological referents. In this sense, the neo-liberal offensive obtains an important political victory. Thanks to commodity consumption, collective mobilization is replaced by individual ascent.[51]

The pattern of mass mobilization is replaced by the dream (reality for some) of individual upward mobility. There is an atomization of civil society, a passive conformism, and a radical depoliticization of the public domain. As the conservative *El Mercurio* editorialized in 1982,

Instead of spending energy in the struggle for the change of structures as a means of social ascent, the great revolution of this government consists in each person making decisions on an individual basis, taking that which is rightfully theirs, and understanding in practice the dynamic value of property.[52]

Uruguay

Last but not least, we turn to Uruguay, which has many parallels with Chile, in spite of its economy and polity being greatly affected by Brazil and Argentina. The role of the traditional political parties, and their roots in civil society, were such that the generals sought only to change their leaderships (held responsible for the rise of subversion), but not do away with them or create new parties. The strong liberal tradition in Uruguay even meant that the military accepted the negative verdict of the 1986 constitutional plebiscite, something unimaginable in Pinochet's Chile. Unlike the Chilean military, their counterparts in Uruguay operated on a collegial system, with the conscious avoidance of strong leaderships, and limited internal assemblies, where divisions within the military institution could be ironed out. Though it created a carceral society and suppressed democracy, the Uruguayan regime has been called a 'generals' democracy' because of these particular features. It was the civilian President, Bordaberry, who in 1976 sought the implantation of a corporatist state and a radical abolition of traditional political parties, and the military who rejected this project and began what they hoped was a controlled reinstitutionalization process. If we recall that it was the armed forces in Argentina who in 1966 sought to implement a corporatist project along Francoist lines, and Pinochet's ambitions in Chile, then the specificity of the Uruguayan case becomes clearer.

Repression in Uruguay took rather a different form from that in Argentina, but was no less effective. Compared to the tens of thousands of disappearances in Argentina, there were 'only' 20 or so physical eliminations in Uruguay, although around 200 Uruguayan political dissidents 'disappeared' in Argentina. There appears to have been a conscious decision to avoid the international opprobrium attracted by outright killings as in Chile and Argentina. Even though in 1981 the President of the Military Supreme Court could declare that there were '1600 problems because we do not have 1600 dead',[53] referring to the political prisoners, the option of physical elimination was not followed. However, there was probably a higher percentage of people tortured in Uruguay than in the other southern cone countries: it is estimated that one in 500 citizens passed through prison, and that one in 50 of these was tortured. The image of the whole country becoming a police cell and the economic devastation of the military economic policies also led to another 'record': some 300,000 people emigrated from Uruguay during the military regime, which represented 10 per cent of the population and fully 20 per cent of the economically active population. Society in Uruguay was dominated by an overarching terrorist apparatus, although it preferred the subtlety of driving prisoners mad to dumping them into the River Plate from helicopters.

Unlike Brazil, and more like Chile, the military-imposed economic policies were essentially a failure. The long-term economic decline of Uruguay since the mid-1950s was halted briefly under the liberal economic experiment imposed by the military, but this success was short-lived. Following 1982, as a group of Uruguayan economists note, 'the intensity and gravity of the crisis is not only expressed in the contraction of production and employment, but also in the high degree of disarticulation of the economic system it has led to'.[54] The opening of the economy to international capital flows created a speculative financial whirlwind which led inevitably to an increased susceptibility to the international fluctuations of the 1980s. The economic crisis represents the national problem in Uruguay and the relative consensus of the two big traditional parties in economic matters does not encourage radical alternatives to emerge. There is no iron law linking economic crisis and political authoritarianism, but clearly those military regimes which were able to deliver the economic goods — albeit to a relatively restricted social layer — were able to buy political space for their hegemonic project. It was the particular combination of economic crisis and the lingering influence of liberalism that was to lead to redemocratization in Uruguay. It is precisely this differential path to democracy in Brazil and the southern cone countries which is the subject of the next chapter.

Notes

1. A. Foxley, *Latin American Experiments in Neo-conservative Economics* (University of California Press, Berkeley, 1983), p. 12.

2. J. Schvarzer, *Martínez de Hoz: La lógica política de la política económica* (CISEA, Buenos Aires, 1983), p. 8.

3. P. O'Brien, 'Authoritarianism and the new economic orthodoxy: the political economy of the Chilean regime 1975–1983', in P. O'Brien and P. Cammack (eds) *Generals in Retreat. The crisis of military rule in Latin America*. (Manchester, Manchester University Press, 1985), p. 151.

4. J. Sábato, and J. Schvarzer, 'Funcionamiento de la economía y poder político en la Argentina: trabas para la democracia', in A. Rouquie and J. Schvarzer (eds) *¿Como Renacen las Democracias?* (Emece, Buenos Aires, 1985), p. 199.

5. A. Foxley, *Latin American Experiments*, p. 48.

6. R. Castro de Andrade, 'Brazil: the Economics of Savage Capitalism', in M. Bienefeld and M. Godfrey (eds) *The Struggle for Development: National Strategies in an International Context*, (John Wiley, Chichester, 1982), p. 78.

7. Ibid.

8. J. Schvarzer, *Martínez de Hoz*, p. 53.

9. R. Thorp, and L. Whitehead, 'Review and Conclusions', in R. Thorp and L. Whitehead (eds) *Latin American Debt and the Adjustment Crisis*. (Macmillan, Houndmills, 1987), p. 318.

10. Ibid., p. 346.

11. Cited in C. Diaz Alejandro, 'Some Aspects of the Development Crisis in Latin America', in R. Thorp and L. Whitehead (eds), *Latin American Debt*, p. 20.

12. Cited in J. Rial, *Las Fuerzas Armades*, (CIESU, Montevideo, 1986), p. 23.

13. See M. A. Garretón, 'Political Processes in an Authoritarian Regime: The Dynamics of Institutionalization and Opposition in Chile, 1973–1980', in J. Samuel Valenzuela and A. Valenzuela (eds), *Military Rule in Chile*, (Johns Hopkins University Press, Baltimore, 1986).

14. Ibid., p. 145–6.
15. M. H. Moreira Alves, *State and Opposition in Military Brazil.* (University of Texas Press, Austin, 1985), p. 95.
16. Cited in C. Perelli, *Someter o Convencer. El Discurso Militar* (CLADE, Montevideo, 1986), p. 39.
17. Cited in S. Sigal and I. Santi, 'Del Discurso en el Regimen Autoritario: Un Estudio Comparativo', in I. Cheresky and J. Chonchol (eds), *Crisis y Transformación de los Regímenes Autoritarios.* (Eudeba, Buenos Aires, 1985), p. 152.
18. Ibid., p. 80.
19. M. H. Moreira Alves, *State and Opposition*, p. 8.
20. J. J. Brunner, 'La cultura política del autoritarismo', *Revista Mexicana de Sociología*, Vol. XLV, No. 2 (1982), p. 630.
21. Ibid., p. 80.
22. S. Sigal, and I. Santi, 'Del Discurso en el Régimen Autoritario', p. 166.
23. Cited, Ibid., p. 160.
24. L. Gonzalez, 'Transición y restauración democrática', in C. Gillespie, L. Goodman, J. Rial and P. Winn (eds), *Uruguay y la Democracia* Vol. III, (Ediciones de la Banda Oriental, Montevideo, 1985).
25. Cited in C. Perelli, *Someter o Convencer*, p. 40.
26. *Disappeared! Technique of Terror*, A Report for the Independent Commission on International Humanitarian Issues, (Zed Books, London, 1985), p. 20.
27. M. Foucault, *Discipline and Punish. The Birth of the Prison.* (Penguin Books, Harmondsworth, 1977), p. 34–5.
28. C. Perelli and J. Rial, *De Mitos y Memorias Políticas*, (Ediciones de la Banda Oriental, Montevideo, 1986), p. 62.
29. Cited, Ibid., p. 48.
30. G. O'Donnell, 'Democracia en la Argentina: micro y macro', Working Paper No. 2 (1987), The Helen Kellog Institute for International Affairs, p. 4.
31. G. O'Donnell, *Autoritarismo e democratização*, (Vértice, São Paulo, 1986), p. 106.
32. M. H. Moreira Alves, *State and Opposition*, p. 162.
33. J. Dassin, 'Aspectos Culturales de la Transición Brasileña', in S. Sosnowski (ed.) *Represión, Exilio y Democracia: La Cultura Uruguaya*, (Ediciones de la Banda Oriental, Montevideo, 1987).
34. E. Galeano, 'La Dictadura y despues: las heridas secretas', in S. Sosnowski (ed.) *Represión, Exilio y Democracia*, p. 108.
35. M. Foucault, *Discipline and Punish*, p. 201.
36. Ibid., p. 216.
37. G. O'Donnell, 'Democracia en la Argentina: micro y macro', p. 8.
38. C. Perelli, and J. Rial, *De Mitos y Memorias Políticas*, p. 103.
39. J. Brunner, 'La cultura política del autoritarismo', pp. 561–2.
40. Ibid., p. 568.
41. R. Castro de Andrade, 'Brazil: The Economics of Savage Capitalism', p. 165.
42. P. Cammack, 'The political economy of contemporary military regimes in Latin America: from bureaucratic authoritarianism to restructuring', in P. O'Brien and P. Cammack (eds), *Generals in Retreat*, p. 23.
43. See J. Linz, 'The Future of an Authoritarian Situation or the Institutionalization of an Authoritarian Regime: the Case of Brazil', in A. Stepan (ed.), *Authoritarian Brazil*, (Yale University Press, New Haven, 1973).
44. See G. O'Donnell, 'Tensions in the Bureaucratic-Authoritarian State and the Question of Democracy', in D. Collier (ed.), *The New Authoritarianism in Latin America*, (Princeton University Press, Princeton, New Jersey, 1979).
45. P. Cammack, 'The political economy of contemporary military regimes', p. 23.
46. F. Delich, *Metaforas de la Sociedad Argentina*, (Editorial Sudamericana, Buenos Aires, 1986), p. 29.
47. J. Corradi, *The Fitful republic. Economy, Society and Politics in Argentina*, (Westview Press, Boulder, 1985), p. 120.

48. T. Moulián, 'La crisis de la Izquierda', *Revista Mexicana de Sociología*, Vol. XLV, No. 2 (1982), p. 655.

49. P. O'Brien, and J. Roddick, *Chile: The Pinochet Decade*, (Latin American Bureau, London, 1987), p. 30.

50. Ibid., p. 34.

51. N. Lechner, *La Conflictiva y Nunca Acabada Construcción del Order Deseado*, (FLACSO, Santiago, 1984), p. 155.

52. Cited, Ibid., p. 155.

53. Cited C. Perelli and J. Rial, *De Mitos y Memorias Políticas*, p. 56.

54. CINVE, *La Crisis Uruguaya y el Problema Nacional*, (Ediciones de la Banda Oriental, Montevideo, 1984), p. 44.

4. Transitions to Democracy

For different reasons, and following diverse tempos and modalities, the military dictatorships of the southern cone and Brazil began a process of liberalization. Clearly we must distinguish this demilitarization of politics from democratization as such, and certainly not assume some abstract notion of democracy as felicitous end-state. We need to examine why a military regime should seek legitimacy through democratization. We need to evaluate the relative weight of economic, political and other factors in precipitating this dynamic. Just as there was no inexorable logic (e.g. 'dependent development') leading to the installing of the military regimes, there is no univocal logic leading to their downfall. In the 1970s, there were books written on the inextricable link between dependent capitalist development and the authoritarian military state, often seen as the new political party of the bourgeoisie. In the 1980s, there is a temptation to discern a similar overdetermined link between democracy and a new enlightened or 'classical' bourgeoisie in the making. Clearly, as Marx himself recognized, similar socio-economic processes can coexist with quite distinct political forms. One question to ask, of course, is which political form is more favourable to the advancement of the dominated classes. Should the social movements, which invested so much in the overthrow of the dictatorships, now invest similar energies in the maintenance of 'bourgeois' democratic regimes? Would a wide-ranging social pact between the various social and political actors in the southern cone make democracy once again viable? These are some of the questions we need to answer in this chapter, which sets the scene for the national case studies of the 'new democracies' that follow.

The first section below deals with the interrelationship between internal and external factors in the process which leads to the demise of the dictatorships. This distinction between internal and external causation is an aid to analysis rather than a rehearsal of the debate between dependency and internal causation. Furthermore, it refers to the level of the nation-state but also to distinctions between processes within and without the military regime itself. These debates reflect those generated by a research programme on 'transitions from authoritarian rule' under the auspices of the Woodrow Wilson International Center for Scholars in the US.[1] As with the earlier debates on the bureaucratic–authoritarian state (BA), there was an element of formalism and model-building, which we must strive to overcome. This is remedied in part in our second section, which is more concrete, dealing as it does with the relationship between political parties and social classes in the democratization process. One thing we can no longer assume is a one-to-one relationship between a political party and a social class or fraction thereof, which it mysteriously 'represents'. Eschewing determinism (or reductionism), our analysis strives to uncover concrete manifestations of the abstract tendencies we may postulate. A third section takes up the role of social movements in the democratization process, a role acknowledged in theory by the BA theorists but hardly examined in detail. Finally, as in the chapter on the military regimes, we turn to the trends running across the southern cone and Brazil while stressing national particularities, which may help us build up a general picture by determining the factors leading to and those delaying or preventing (as in Chile) democratization.

Internal and external causes

In the dependency debate of the 1970s, considerable energy was expended on the relative weight to be accorded to the internal and external factors affecting Latin American societies. For some the external was 'dominant', while for others the internal had theoretical 'primacy'. Hardly noticed was F. H. Cardoso's straightforward statement that: 'There is no metaphysical distinction (that is, which supposes a static separation) between external factors and internal effects'.[2] The general dynamic of the capitalist order has international effects and operates through particular nation-states. The concept of an 'international division of labour' is, in this respect, misleading, because it implies something at once preordained and mystical, like the 'hidden hand' of the market for others. What this implies for the present debate on democratization is the need to reject simplistic accounts based on a far-seeing imperialism that has now decided, for reasons best known to itself, to encourage democratization in Latin America. While there is no metaphysical distinction between internal and external factors influencing democratization, it can be a useful heuristic device. There is, of course, a complex historical dynamic at play which cannot be reduced to simple formulae. What we can do, in the first instance, is to evaluate the effectivity of the factors leading the democratization at the national and international levels, to pass on to the distinction between factors internal and external to the military regimes themselves.

US policy

There is a general argument in support of the view that democratization, as militarization before it, follows a transnational pattern. So, for example, Herman and Petras distinguish between US policy in Central America, designed to destroy the social movements of the region, and: 'The second track, used in South America, [which] involves support for elections where liberal politicians have gained hegemony over the mass movements and are willing to accept socio-economic policies acceptable to the banks and the armed forces'.[3] Now, this statement is incorrect in its implication that the mass movements of the southern cone and Brazil have fallen under liberal hegemony, but that is not the main problem. The scenario resembles those accounts of the Brazilian military coup of 1964 and that in Chile in 1973 as 'made in the USA', which thus neglected the internal class dynamic. There is here a tendency towards 'intentionalism', with social actors seen as being capable of simply imposing their wishes on a complex reality. For example, the same authors refer to how: 'The military regimes and their US partners, having built up an unmanageable foreign debt and allowed social and economic sores to fester while they "developed" their own bank accounts, have now moved to the wings to wait'.[4] In this manipulative scenario, the new civilian governments are simply the 'fall guys' who carry the can for the economic failures of the military regimes. In this Machiavellian world, democracy becomes a crude ideological smokescreen for imperialism's 'changing of the guard' in its colonial outposts.

Rejecting simplistic visions of foreign manipulation does not mean rejecting an international dimension to democratization. One obvious factor in the democratization process in the southern cone was US President Jimmy Carter's famous human-rights-based foreign policy. Though it was and is common to hear denunciations of the limitations and hypocrisy involved in this policy, it is useful to recall its origins. According to NACLA (North American Congress on Latin America), hardly suspect of an oversympathetic view of the US administration, 'the specific event that galvanized Congress to take action was the shockingly brutal military coup in Chile in 1973 and evidence of US involvement'.[5] By 1976, the US Congress had assumed the power to limit US economic and military aid to 'any country which engages in a consistent pattern of gross violations of internationally recognized human rights'.[6] Subsequently, military and economic aid was reduced in the southern cone countries, which had a considerable effect, even if mainly at the psychological level, on the repressive regimes and their opponents. It is, indeed, very hard to quantify the effect of a newly dominant international democratic discourse, albeit in some cases self-interested and always hesitant. Nevertheless, we can see the regime in Uruguay learning from the international isolation of the Pinochet regime to conduct its repression with a modicum of discretion. The generals in Argentina were also forced by this international climate of opinion to attempt to 'clean up their act' at the time of the football World Cup in 1978.

It is in Chile that we can, perhaps, see most clearly the interaction between international and national factors in the democratization process. Manuel Antonio Garretón has, in this respect, advanced the proposition that: 'in the Chilean case it is evident that the relations with the US and the role that country plays, subordinated always to the internal dynamics, occupies an outstanding role'.[7] For some, the strength and stability of the Pinochet regime leads them to pin all their hopes for democratization on outside pressure. For others, external pressure on the human rights and public liberties front can help create the space for a coherent opposition movement to the regime. Clearly, democracy can only rarely be imposed from the outside, not that this would be the project of the present US administration, which seems more interested in smoothing over 'excesses' in Chile so as more easily to maintain its support for the regime in the international arena. A further, more general, point is that much of the discussion of foreign influence on the democratization process operates with a somewhat unreal picture of independent nation states. Clearly, the nation-states of Latin America have always been subject to foreign intervention, so that the dilemma is not intervention or non-intervention, but how the foreign policy of the big powers can be altered to create the best possible situation for democratic and progressive political forces.

The military dimension

The other dimension of the internal/external duality is that which refers to the military regime itself. One important strand of critical analysis focuses heavily on the internal aspects of the regime and the armed forces in particular, in accounting for the democratization process. Referring to the liberal thesis of a protracted 'struggle for democracy' and the economistic Marxist view of the indispensable character of authoritarian rule for peripheral capitalism, Alain Rouquié maintains that: 'The partisans of both these theses ignore the strictly military dimension of the great majority of Latin American authoritarian regimes'.[8] Liberalism presents the military as an atavistic hangover of a feudal/colonial past: a demon to be exorcised by the virtues of representative government. The economistic view is just as cavalier with the military as institution, in so far as it is viewed simply as the blind executor of generalized 'needs' of capital. The quite distinct forms of military rule in the various southern cone countries and Brazil should alert us to the importance of specific rather than generalized analysis. When it comes to democratization, Rouquié's remarks are also pertinent: 'the return of the military to barracks is above all a military problem, and it would be somewhat paradoxical to study it without considering this decisive angle'.[9] When an institution such as the military assumes functions it was not designed for, such as government, the prolonged exercise of those functions is bound to generate contradictions and ultimately to threaten its internal coherence and ability to fulfil its prime function: warfare.

For Argentina there is a good case for focusing our analysis on the armed forces and their internal crisis as precipitants of the democratization process. Andres Fontana, for example, finds the verdict quite unequivocal: 'The process of transition to democracy in Argentina resulted from the military collapse as a result of its internal conflicts'.[10] He argues, furthermore, that the move to occupy the Malvinas did not result from the tensions between the government and civil society but was determined, rather, by the fear of divisions within the armed forces. At one level we can agree that it was not the mass demonstration of 30 March 1982 that 'caused' the military adventure days later. Yet it was the constant level of working-class resistance since 1976, which was moving from a defensive to an offensive phase by 1982, which alone explains such a bizzare political gamble by the armed forces. The failure of the military campaign in the South Atlantic then, of course, unlocked further contradictions between the regime and its supports, and created more space for a reactivated civil society. It was simply not by choice that the generals in Argentina set about liberalization. As F. H. Cardoso notes in relation to Brazil, we find that 'behind the liberalizing discourse of this or that repressive general of yesterday, lies a resistance focus within society'.[11] Without wishing to underestimate the traumatic effects of the war in the South Atlantic, the military adventure of the generals cannot be explained in purely 'military' terms.

The class struggle

It is now an accepted line of interpretation in the case of Argentina to downplay the significance of popular mobilizations in the democratization process. Thus, for example, Ariel Colombo argues that: 'The decisive factor in the crisis of the regime was not the remobilization of society, but rather the confrontations and contradictions within the liberal–authoritarian alliance'.[12] In this perspective, the military regime simply 'self-destructs' in a suicidal external war, and popular mobilization occurs only in the aftermath of this debacle. Certainly, mobilization increased in the wake of the regime's military defeat by Britain in the South Atlantic. Yet all the journalistic accounts to date show a military institution debating the Malvinas takeover precisely as a means to defuse the growing social conflict within the country. That the military–monetarist policies did not achieve the success expected by the propertied classes is clearly connected with the failure to atomize totally the labour movement. As Nicos Poulantzas wrote in his study of the collapse of the southern European dictatorships: these internal differences 'can only be appreciated if behind this or that measure of policy in favour of this or that fraction of capital, we see clearly the spectre of the struggle of the popular masses'.[13] This, of course, can lead to a mystical appeal to class struggle as *deus ex machina* which explains all, or to concrete analysis which weighs up the role of different struggles in specific situations.

Clearly, there is a complex dynamic at play in the democratization process, between the regime and the opposition. There have been attempts by Guillermo O'Donnell and his colleagues to refine our analysis is this respect by introducing different tendencies within both counterposed camps. Two clearly defined groups are seen as typical of the military regime: the 'hard-liners' (*duros*) and the 'soft-liners' (*blandos*). The first believe that 'the perpetuation of military rule is possible and desirable', whereas the latter are marked by 'increasing awareness that the regime . . . will have to make use, in the foreseeable future, of some degree or some form of electoral legitimation'.[14] The *duros* tend to have greater weight when the regime is implanted, whereas the *blandos* come to the fore when its contradictions demand some form of resolution, usually through liberalization. As to the left opposition, they are characterized by a similar split between a 'maximalist' and a 'minimalist' faction. O'Donnell and Schmitter conclude that: 'One premise of this way of conceptualizing the transition is that it is both possible and desirable that political democracy be attained without mobilized violence and dramatic discontinuity'.[15] The prospects for the consolidation of democracy are more propitious, for these authors, when the incumbents of power can negotiate a transition, without duress, with their 'non-maximalist' opponents. There are both analytical and political lessons to be learned from this perspective.

We must be fully sensitized to nuances within the military regime and the opposition camps. Having said that, there is a certain danger of formalism here, of building just a more complex set of pigeon-holes into which to slot unique phenomena. Already Cardoso has criticized the mode of consumption of dependency theory in the US, and O'Donnell himself has criticized formalistic developments of his own bureaucratic–authoritarian theory in similar terms.[16] History, in these models, takes second place to an intricate game played by disembodied actors. It is not that we should deny differences within the regime, but whether our categories are adequate to a fluid and ongoing political struggle. There is a real danger of our analytical categories taking on a life of their own and of our confusing them with reality. As to the politics of the O'Donnell/Schmitter approach, it is essentially a plea for moderation to allow the regime *blandos* and opposition *minimalists* to put together a deal for democracy. It would be crass simply to counterpose 'revolution' to reform, as was done in the 1960s and 1970s, because there is empirical support for their view that an uncontrolled transition may be aborted. Social and political forces which may look beyond the limits of parliamentary democracy, even while living under a dictatorship, are duty bound to provide a clearer strategy for the transition process than they have hitherto.

The state and civil society
A possible way out of over-schematic accounts of democratization is posed by Alfred Stepan, who concentrates on 'the reciprocal relations between the power of the state and the power of civil society'.[17] Clearly, the modern military dictatorships of the southern cone can be seen as a dramatic affirmation of state power over civil society. Yet it is not always a simple zero-sum situation, where the growing power of one leads to a decline of the other's strength. Stepan posits a range of possibilities: Brazil's occasional situations where state and civil society both acquired additional capacity; Chile's debilitated civil society faced with a powerful state; Uruguay's equally stagnant state and civil society; and, finally, Argentina's decreasing state power accompanied by a greatly strengthened civil society.[18] This pattern of distinct state/civil society relations helps us to understand the particular modes of democratization in each country: democratization through collapse in Argentina; Brazil and Uruguay's pacted or negotiated democratization; and Chile's aborted democratization process. The new military states clearly had a relative autonomy with regard to the dominant classes, but this rested on a fear of the threat from below. When the dominant classes felt they could work within civil society, as it were, they began to feel more constrained by the shackles of an all-powerful state. In all cases (including Uruguay), a reactivated civil society played a major role in the rearticulation of the state and the dominant classes.

The above approach is positive in so far as it recognizes the crucial importance of a popular upsurge (or lack of it) in the democratization process, but it is still somewhat one-dimensional. To refer to the reactivation of civil society is itself an abstraction since it masks the diversity, or indeed contradictory nature, of struggles it may contain. No simple formula can account for democratic transitions in all their complexity and unpredictability. What we can do is follow a hint by O'Donnell and Schmitter and pursue Antonio Gramsci's distinction between the different 'moments' of the transition process.[19] For Gramsci 'a common error in historico-political analysis consists in an inability to find the correct relation between what is organic and what is conjunctural'.[20] We may exaggerate the voluntarist or individual element, or we may, as with economism, overestimate indirect causes. In the relation of forces which lead to a given historical outcome, Gramsci distinguishes the following moments or levels:

1. A relation of social forces — this is the level of production, the development of which ultimately provides the basis for the emergence of the various social classes and the transformation of society;
2. A relation of political forces — this refers to the degree of homogeneity, self-awareness and organization attained by the various social classes, and thus their ability to alter history;
3. A relation of military forces — this includes the military level in the strict or technical military sense, and the levels which may be termed politico-military, and from time to time is directly decisive.[21]

We may wish to add an ideological moment or discourse level; we must also recognize that these moments may overlap and do not unfold mechanically. On that basis they may assist us with our enquiries.

In broad outline, and following O'Donnell and Schmitter's analysis, we can note that each moment of the democratization process has its own set of rules, with its own subset of actors establishing various pacts through negotiation and struggle. The military moment, as in Gramsci's original analysis, must be seen as immediately decisive, In this aspect, the armed forces resolve their own internal conflicts and, if conditions are appropriate, a tendency may emerge which moves towards a liberalized dictatorship (*dictablanda pactada*). However, this first moment opens the door inevitably to the political moment in which the political parties come to the fore and seek a stable negotiated role for themselves in the transition. The military pact which offered the prospect of a transition installs a *dictablanda*, and now the civilian politicians move towards a 'strong democracy' (*democradura*). As the social moment begins to take effect, so the politicians and business leaders seek a social contract with labour to ensure the economic preconditions for a smooth transition. The ideological moment permeates all three processes above, with the democratic discourse being appealed to by all the social and political actors, albeit in their own way. As I will try to demonstrate in subsequent chapers, the level of discourse acquires the dominant role once the transition process is under way.

Political parties and social classes

Moving to the more concrete realm of political parties and diverse social
interests, we need first to make some methodological points. According to
Gramsci's famous formulation, 'every party is only a nomenclature of a
class'.[22] Ever since, Marxism has tended to reduce political parties to the social
classes which they allegedly 'represent' — or 'misrepresent' for the case of most
labour parties. Today we must accept that political parties cannot be reduced
to social classes in this manner, and that they exist in a relatively autonomous
sphere of human society. As Barry Hindess, among others, has pointed out:

> When we examine the forces engaged in particular struggles, we do not find
> *classes* in the literal sense, lined up against each other. Instead we find
> political parties and factions within them, trade unions, employers and
> employers' associations, newspapers and television companies (and factions
> within them), state agencies, and a variety of other organisations and
> individuals.[23]

Class analysis, if it is to have any role beyond a radical gesture, must be able to
explain this multiplicity and diversity in the political arena. If social groups do
indeed develop common interests, we must be able to show how this is
translated into political action without recourse to acts of faith. Too often,
critical analysis operates at an empirical level with another unrelated 'class
analysis' uneasily juxtaposed. The problem, as Hindess argues convincingly, is
that: 'Discussion of politics in terms of class struggle is at best a rather complex
allegory and at worst thoroughly misleading'.[24] We can now only proceed
cautiously and provisionally in our analysis of democratization.

The dominant classes

The dominant classes have an ambiguous relationship with the military
regimes. These regimes usually respond to a challenge to the capitalist system,
private property and the free pursuit of profit and are therefore viewed
sympathetically. Yet the military dictatorship also strips the dominant classes
of many of its economic and political prerogatives. We can theoretically say
that the military state rules on behalf of capital and yet may take measures
detrimental to the interests of individual capitalists. Or that this relatively
autonomous state acts in the long-term, if not the short-term, interests of
capital. Yet this is cold comfort to the actual landowner or businessman who
sees the regime implementing measures which adversely affect him. Clearly
there comes a time when either the military regime has accomplished its
original programme (Brazil), or has failed to do so (Argentina), and the
dominant classes reconsider their original tacit or active support for the regime.
A very long-term view of this issue could argue that the military regimes arise
not so much from a popular order but from a failure by the dominant classes to
establish a stable hegemony over society. The dominant classes may not have a
generic desire for hegemony (any more than the workers do for socialism), but
when their interests are threatened, or conversely the element of threat is

removed, they naturally wish to resume their normal role in politics and perhaps take back some of the state power so rudely and totally assumed by the armed forces.

In the long Brazilian transition to democracy, the entrepreneurs of the industrialized south-east played a key role. In 1977, the *Gazeta Mercantil* (Brazil's equivalent of the *Financial Times*) ran an 'election' for 'the ten most representative spokesmen of the business class', eight of whom signed a highly critical manifesto and, in the words of one of them,

> Once we issued the manifesto, civil society entered right into my office by the window. We received numerous invitations to participate in public forums about Brazil's problems and future with members of the church, trade unions, intellectuals and students, groups we had never worked with before.[25]

In the liberalization process which followed, businessmen played a crucial role, no longer being willing to trust their future to an omniscient military state. The appeal of democratic liberalism was genuine, as was the desire to break the overbearing ties between the state and civil society. According to F. H. Cardoso: 'There is even a degree of similarity between the private sector's view of the kind of society emerging and the views among labour leaders, intellectuals, and the clergy. One can detect a similar tone of general political discourse among these separate groups'.[26] This could be a case of the 'general democratic equivalent' which may fuse disparate struggles and aspirations. Of course, as we shall see below, this rosy period did not survive the wave of strikes that began in 1978, although the entrepreneurs did seek the normal collective bargaining procedures common in the advanced industrialized countries, which in its way is a form of hegemony: coercion plus consent (Gramsci).

We are not trying to revive the idea of a 'national bourgeoisie' inexorably moving towards its destiny of a bourgeois democratic republic in Latin America. Some of the declarations of the Brazilian entrepreneurs during the liberalization process may have had that kind of ring, but essentially they were calls for a limited and state-led liberalization, not a people's democracy. However, the dominant classes must be given a greater role in the transition process than most marxist accounts allow for. For example, we can ask why the Pinochet regime 'won' a referendum (albeit with fraudulent methods), and the generals in Uruguay lost one seeking a similar institutionalization of the regime. Only a small right-wing sector of the political elite supported the military elite's move, and conditions of censorship and so on were similar in both cases. Yet, while in Chile all the major employers' associations published manifestos urging the people to vote for continuity of the regime, this did not occur in Uruguay and, indeed, some key business leaders such as the head of the powerful *Federación Rural*, the landowners' association, made plain their rejection of the regime. In Uruguay, perhaps the threat from below had diminished sufficiently to encourage a highly politicized dominant class to resume business. In Argentina, the rapid deterioration of the military regime after 1982 meant that the dominant classes simply had no option but to join the democratic bandwagon, even if this meant the return of nationalist populism, as seemed likely at the time.

The dominated classes

The dominated classes have, at first sight, a less complicated role in the military dictatorships: that of victim. Yet as we have seen, there are multiple ways in which they may respond to the new regimes, from tacit support, through apathy, to active opposition. The role of the political parties in this period is an ambiguous one. In the first instance, the political parties of the left are the first to be banned, and their leaders exiled, imprisoned or killed. Yet, when liberalization of the military regime begins, political parties begin to play a key mediating role between the state and civil society. The political parties tend to lag behind the social movements. As an editorial in Argentina in January 1983 noted: 'In disorder and inorganically the people (*el pueblo*) were ahead of the parties'.[27] That the military were able to cede power without a major social explosion was due mainly to the reluctance of the political parties to take a lead. This is worth stressing because the political parties were portrayed in the new, post-dictatorial regimes as the saviours of democracy. Thus Marcelo Cavarozzi could argue in Argentina that: 'The citizens can now concretely manifest their position, or displeasure, towards the proposals, orientations, styles and leaders of the temporarily majority party, *within the framework of the institutional system*'.[28] The previous zero-sum conception of politics gives way to compromise and negotiation as the essence of politics, with parliament the privileged arena of that process.

The political party in the Marxist tradition is like the piston of an engine driven by the steam of social movements; without it the latter would be dissipated and unable to drive the train of the revolution forwards. However, in recent decades there has been renewed criticism of the party form. If we listen carefully to what the new democratic left in Argentina is saying, for example, we can understand the problem better. Liliana de Riz argues in this respect that the mediation of the political parties can become 'the principal instrument for the regulation of social conflicts'.[29] Furthermore, the trade unions are urged 'to subordinate the logic of their sectoral interests to that of a party politics which must conciliate the exigencies of the trade unions with the demands of other social sectors . . .'[30] This line of interpretation fits in with the liberal democratic critique of corporatism, with the armed forces and the trade unions being seen as equivalent villains in the plot. Certainly, the trade unions in Argentina, as in Brazil, have a history of subordination to the state, but then political parties have not exactly been characterized by a strong, autonomous, democratic or liberatory practice. The question of democracy cannot be reduced to the party-political and parliamentary arena, if we are adequately to understand the problems facing the new democracies. Of course the trade unions should be subject to a strong campaign for internal democracy, but these organs of working class defence cannot in any meaningful sense be compared to the armed forces so recently driven from power.

Political parties, including those of the left, can greatly affect the smoothness or otherwise of the transition process. In Uruguay, the parties of the left, organized in the *Frente Amplio* (Broad Front), were full participants in the negotiations with the military that paved the way for free elections in 1985. Luís González writes of how 'Throughout the transition process this oiled the necessary formal or tacit understandings. This is perceived by *all* the participants as a "natural" necessity of the system'.[31] Given the closure of the political arena for a long period, parties claiming to represent the interests of the dominated classes act usually on the basis of self-assertion. The left has lost little of its messianic character with each party (or faction) claiming to be *the* party of *the* working class. Where the traditional party form has been questioned, as in Chile, the alternative has been a rank and file-ism (*basismo*) that verges on populism and the educational self-improvement of the masses. However, the model of servant of the masses has been no more successful than the earlier role of missionary. Two possible strategies have followed. Either, political parties of the left enter the political market with all the others and offer up their wares for popular consumption. Or centralism can give way to ultracentralism to avoid future liberal deviations, and the vanguard party once again sets itself up as general headquarters staff of a revolution and everybody else is busy betraying, compromising or selling out.

A social pact

We must turn now to the absolutely essential question of whether a 'social pact' between the fundamental social and political forces is necessary or possible in the transition to democracy. If this were the case, some of the dilemmas identified above for both the dominant and the dominated classes could be resolved. The pact, social contract or *concertación* can take many different forms, but its common currency is compromise. Thus there may be pacts to accompany the different 'movements' outlined above: during the military moment a deal might be made regarding human rights abuses; the political moment usually sees some kind of multi-party (*multipartidaria*) agreement on the rules of the game; and finally, as the social (or socio-economic) moment of the transition unfolds, so employers and trade unionists may attempt some kind of social pact on wages and profits. Certainly, class compromises and political deals are nothing new in Latin America, as elsewhere, but the issue of *concertación* has assumed major proportions during the current round of re-democratization. O'Donnell and Schmitter are far less sanguine than others on the prospects for *concertación* in Latin America, but they argue nevertheless that: 'Pacts are not always likely or possible, but we are convinced that where they are features of the transition they are desirable — that is, they enhance the probability that the process will lead to a viable political democracy'.[32] The chapters on each of the new democracies will return to this theme, but here we outline some of the pacts that were indeed negotiated during the recent transitions to democracy.

If the incumbents withdraw from office by their own choice, then they are less pressurized to agree to any pact with civilians. This was the case in Brazil, but nevertheless a quite elaborate pact does seem to have been agreed.

According to Alfred Stepan, who was able to interview key military figures, in this pact 'the opposition and the government made a tacit agreement that the 1979 amnesty would be a "mutual amnesty". Thus, history allowed the left, in good conscience, to support a moderate candidate, in exchange for the withdrawal of the military'.[33] The situation in Brazil was extremely complex because the opposition had been making steady advances in elections during the regime's long, sometimes reversed, moves towards 'decompression'. By 1984, in control of the key states, the opposition was able to negotiate from a position of strength with the military government. The upshot of these negotiations was agreement on a presidential candidate from within the ranks of the opposition who would be acceptable to the military: Tancredo Neves. These negotiations certainly paved the way for a relatively stable demilitarization process. However, we must note O'Donnell's point that 'the very existence of this pact is not entirely certain and its contents, in any event, are a matter for speculation — including the crucial question as to what extent it may be construed as binding by President Sarney'.[34] Formal pact or not, the negotiations in the Brazilian case seem to have been conducted by two fairly confident parties — regime and opposition — which may explain their comparative success.

In Argentina there was an attempt by the crumbling military regime after 1982 to impose some kind of pact on the rest of society. Unlike Brazil's 'mutual amnesty' between torturers and guerrillas, in Argentina the military granted themselves an amnesty in the vain hope of avoiding retribution. Precisely what was agreed on this issue with the leaders of the main political parties, grouped in the *multipartidaria*, is impossible to know, but subsequent events point towards some limits being set on military accountability to the new democratic regime. It is interesting to note, however, that in 1981, Antonio Trocolli, who was to become Minister of the Interior in the new civilian government, argued in a debate on 'the reconstruction of democracy' that: 'It would be a tremendous error to seek the defeat of the armed forces, because this would recreate in the country a new antinomy, a new split, an abyss between the armed forces and civil society'.[35] Whether this was simply political realism or not, it indicates a willingness to establish some kind of understanding with the dictatorship. As to a social pact, *concertación* between labour and employers, mediated by the state, was to be one of the main priorities of the Alfonsín government. In a country with a powerful trade union movement on the one hand, and a critical economic situation on the other, the future political leaders of Argentina had as a major task some kind of balancing act between wages and profits. This type of social pact was not going to be easy to achieve.

In Uruguay, like Brazil's a relatively smooth transition, but due to a social and political equilibrium rather than any success of the outgoing regime, there was a quite explicit pact, the *Acuerdo del Club Naval*, in mid-1983, between the joint chiefs of staff and representatives of the major parties (excluding the *Blancos* who did not attend and whose presidential candidate, Wilson Ferreira, was banned by the military). A timetable for elections was set and a considerable continuing role for the armed forces was agreed: the National

Security Council would continue in an advisory capacity, and military trials would continue for those arrested under the 'state of Insurrection', the latter being called by parliament if parliament saw fit. Yet the civilian politicians gained considerable ground, including the hitherto taboo legalization of the left-wing political parties. The main point ceded was the head of Wilson Ferreira, leader of the main opposition party, the *Blancos*, and an uncompromising critic of the military dictatorship. In practice, not all the points of the Naval Club Agreement were implemented: this is in the nature of pacts signed under duress. Luís González offers a realistic interpretation of the agreement as neither democratization conceded (from above) or conquered (from below): there was a triangle of negotiating parties comprising the civilian political elite, the military hierarchy and popular pressure, in which no side had a clear-cut dominant position.[36] The nature of the pact that launches the democratization process will have a major impact on the orientation and limits of the new democracy.

Finally, in Chile there is, of course, no pact between Pinochet and the political opposition, but it is interesting to see how much emphasis is placed on the question of *concertación*. The organizer of a 1984 conference in Chile on the issue writes of how: 'Democracy cannot be consolidated and will find it difficult to survive in Chile if confrontation prevails over *concertación*'.[37] Thus employers, trade unionists, politicians and academics were brought together to see how *concertación* could help promote democratization. There appeared to be little substance to *concertación*, which was based on 'the diagnosis that between the diverse social groups and classes there is a basic community of interest concerning the development of the country, which gives meaning to the idea of national community'.[38] There is little here to distinguish this discourse from that of populist nationalism. The limits of this project were demonstrated by an employers' representative at the above conference who praised *concertación* and then proceeded to list those issues 'beyond discussion', which basically amounted to a *pinochetismo* without Pinochet. I am not arguing that the struggle for democracy cannot entail any agreement between social classes, only that these social pacts are usually based on a relationship of forces. Politicians who for long have believed literally their chosen ideology of Christian democracy, democratic socialism, social democracy or developmentalism, seem now to take the rhetoric of *concertación* at face value, rather than an ambiguous discourse of corporatist compromise.

The role of social movements

We have already pointed to a certain neglect, in the democratization debate, of the role played by social movements in that process. This does not mean that we can return to an earlier 'heroic' vision of social movements inexorably rolling back the military state and paving the way for socialism, or at worst, if led astray by reformists and misleaders, for 'bourgeois democracy'. We do need to be specific and examine in turn the various social movements, including labour, community and human rights movements. There are old and new social movements, defensive and offensive social movements, and there are distinct national configurations and histories. We may examine the effectiveness of different movements and postulate a certain role for them in a given democratization movement. We may also show that a given social movement was not as quiescent as some accounts portrayed it. Having said that, there is also a theoretical argument that leads us to believe that social movements are effective actors in the democratization process, even when we cannot detect pertinent effects by them on national politics. It is not unreasonable to suppose that the generals, businessmen and technocrats within the power elite supporting the modern military dictatorships carried out their debates and took policy decisions within a framework deeply marked by the past and possible future actions of what is euphemistically known as the 'popular sector'. The people, even if cowed and lying low, always figure on the horizon of bourgeois political thought.

The labour movement

The labour movements of the southern cone and Brazil were severely affected by their respective military dictatorships, and were to differing extents disarticulated. However, we must beware of blanket statements such as that made by Paul Drake, for example, that 'Up to 1983, labour unions and parties had displayed little capacity to influence or dethrone these authoritarian regimes'.[39] We have already referred to the economic, political, military and social measures deployed by the military regimes, which weakened the labour movements. However, we must distinguish firstly between the Brazilian and Argentine coups, against essentially populist–nationalist labour movements, and those in Chile and Uruguay, directed against labour movements under socialist or communist hegemony. In Brazil, the 1964 military coup confronted a socially weak labour movement, with an exposed statist leadership, largely devoid of workplace roots. In Argentina, in 1966 and again in 1976, there was an organic labour movement, well rooted in the workplace and in society, with a representative, albeit bureaucratic, leadership. In Chile, the labour movement of 1973 was the main social base of a democratic socialist government, but was itself only partly rooted in the class, being more of a political than a labour movement as such. In Uruguay, finally, labour was in a situation in some way between Argentina and Chile, sharing the latter's political traditions but having some of the more organic and workplace-rooted characteristics of its counterpart across the River Plate.

Under the military regimes, there was a quite differentiated level of response in the various countries. In Argentina, a long history of labour militancy and the dense social network uniting the workplace and the working-class community led to a considerable capacity for resistance. By 1979, the first (albeit partial) general strike had been mounted, and on the eve of the Malvinas takeover in 1982 labour was in an openly offensive mode. In Uruguay, the 1973 military takeover was met by an unprecedented general strike, which, though ultimately unsuccessful, helped maintain a certain level of morale while waiting for more favourable conditions for labour. In Chile, the defeat of 1973 was more traumatic and went deeper, given the labour movement's traditional reliance on leftist political parties to articulate its interests, and the lack of solid workplace organizations from which to weather the *pinochetazo*. Nevertheless, by the 1980s, labour had regained the capacity to mount defensive actions as part of a broader popular movement against the dictatorship. Brazil is a case apart, marked at once by the longest period of labour quiescence, in the 1970s, and the most far-reaching and innovative labour movement of the 1980s. This was one case where the relative success of the modernizing military dictatorship helped to forge a dynamic and concentrated working class in some areas, which was to become a major actor in the democratization process. In all four countries the labour movement survived the monetarist–militarist offensive and was able to regroup its forces and move beyond corporatist defensive measures.

As to labour's impact on democratization, Argentina again is the most clear-cut case. After the war in the South Atlantic in mid-1982, a veritable flood of pent-up demands were pressed in persistent and widespread labour protests. There was a normalization of trade union affairs as part of the global move towards military disengagement, but this soon overflowed the official channels. This pressure from below led towards a new general strike in December 1982, which the union leadership called partly to defuse the groundswell of protest. Two more general strikes in 1983 placed the labour movement firmly back on the political map, even though the defeat of the union-backed Peronist Party in the elections towards the end of the year (see Chapter 5) was an undoubted setback. In Brazil, the labour movement did not represent a substantial threat to the military regime for over 20 years, but its impact on the regime's 'decompression' became considerable after the first spate of strikes in 1978 and 1979. A new union movement emerged, centred around the most dynamic industrial regions of the south-east, which through its struggles and its own mode of organization provided an impetus for democratization in the 1980s. In Chile and Uruguay, labour activities were more conditional on phases of regime liberalization, but in Uruguay, at any rate, labour mobilization ensured that the political pact between the regime and the political parties (see Chapter 7) was implemented and deepened. In Chile, a politically divided labour movement mounted sporadic assaults on the dictatorial regime but was ultimately driven back by repression and internal divisions.

Community movements

If the organized trade union movement is the core or backbone of popular resistance to the military project, other forms must be mentioned. To refer to a community movement is not an attempt to unify clearly disparate movements, but to signal their common locale. A late commuter train is burnt by irate travellers; a supermarket is sacked by hungry squatters; an *'olla popular'* (soup-kitchen) is set up in a popular neighbourhood; a rent strike is organized. Outside the workplace people began to organize in myriad different ways —

some quite traditional, others new. They were all in their way popular responses to the military regimes. That is not to say that their claims amount to a global challenge to the state or a call for radical political change, because the state can clearly co-opt, play off one movement against another, and ultimately defuse their more immediate demands. Potentially these social movements can unify with labour and the opposition political parties in pursuit of their common aim of democratization. In practice, as Ruth Cardoso has shown for the case of Brazil,[40] there is no guarantee that the community-centred movements of the oppressed will be able to intervene autonomously in the correlation of forces created by democratization, given their ideological autonomy. In some specific conjunctures joint action is possible, more usually the sometimes contradictory, always heterogeneous, demands of the community social movements cannot be incorporated into a broader project.

In Chile, the urban social movements have displayed greater explosiveness than the organized labour movement. Within the *poblaciones* (urban poor settlements), diverse answers to the exclusionary economic and social policies of the regime have taken shape since 1973. Various producer, consumer, health, education, cultural and other co-operative ventures have flourished. What all these initiatives have in common, according to Cristina Hurtado Beca, is that 'their basis is the initiative and participation of its components . . . [and] . . . their direct relation with the local housing and daily life space'.[41] Self-organization, mutual aid, and self-reliance mark all these responses to authoritarian rule. The trade unions have begun to link up with struggles beyond the workplace, and this multiplicity of struggles around the principle of democratization has had far-reaching effects. Unlike the situation in Brazil, where a self-confident and relatively dynamic military state was able to defuse many urban struggles and co-opt others, the Chilean regime has polarized the situation. The national protests in Chile during 1983 and 1984 represented a veritable 'explosion of the majorities', as one analysis of the events was entitled.[42] The *pobladores* were the main protagonists of these, often violent, protest actions and reaffirmations of popular will. Defensive actions in the struggle for survival in a hostile environment have become transformed, albeit partially and unevenly, into a more direct challenge to the regime, albeit inchoate and prone to unchannelled violence.

In the other southern cone countries and, above all, in Brazil there was a similar flourishing of popular urban movements, which contributed, in varying degree, to the democratization process. Locally based organizations centred around basic needs were able to articulate a more global problematic, which questioned the legitimacy of the dictatorships and posed a popular democratic alternative. In certain situations, such as the wave of strikes in Brazil between 1978 and 1980, the multiplicity of struggles and diverse social movements can fuse explosively. Lucio Kowarick writes of how: 'Along these discontinuous pathways, *bairros* and factories met in mutual opposition to the established order, articulating practices built up, little by little, in scattered and seemingly disconnected day-to-day struggles'.[43] A whole city could become a supportive network for a strike by one particular category of workers. These same workers were of course often members as well of the *Movimento contra o Custo da Vida* (Movement against the cost of living) or one of the Church-sponsored *Comunidades Eclesiais de Base*. The struggle against the military state and for democracy (in all spheres of life) unified once disparate and possibly even opposed social movements. It is perhaps excessive to refer to a rearticulation of the relation between the social and the political, but we can say that the process of democratization involves more than inter-elite negotiations.

Human rights

The 'modern' military regimes also gave rise to a 'new' social movement centred around the former's abuse of human rights. Its main demand was of a startling transparency in the case of Argentina: *'Aparición con vida'* (i.e. the reappearance, alive, of the disappeared). This was a defensive or reactive movement by definition and by conception, yet it took on a major role in challenging the legitimacy of military rule. A discourse of Christian humanism was broadened out to embrace, sometimes, the socialist values espoused by the majority of the *desaparecidos* and persecuted. Private agony fused with a very public challenge to the powers that be. As Elizabeth Jelin writes, what is most noticeable about the human rights movement is how 'a movement may be generated, which though heterogeneous in its social composition and in terms of its demands or slogans, introduces a new ideological dimension in the debate . . . : the ethical consideration, which appeals to a system of fundamental values'.[44] The 'naive' humanist reassertion of the right to live became transformed into a frontal challenge to the very essence of the military state. Or, as Maria Sondereguer puts it: 'Human rights are no longer what we had before and must respect, but that which comes later and must be constructed. They become a horizon, a utopia'.[45] In this way, an old social movement became transformed; appealing to 'old' values, it was introducing a new element into the political discourse of southern cone societies.

With the political arena closed by force, struggles inevitably took a social form. The values advocated were universal ones, centred around individual human rights and shared ethical principles. Yet, as Sondereguer writes, 'this resistance was unexpected. A new social actor is born in this way, establishing a novel practice and opening up space for reflection'.[46] This occurred in a context in which all the major social and political organizations maintained a stony silence on the *desaparecidos*. In Argentina, Radical Party leader Ricardo Balbín could even declare contemptuously in 1980 that 'all the *desaparecidos* are dead', thus attempting to close an unsavoury episode in national history. Nevertheless, human rights activists were able to gather wider support in civil society, as the moves towards democratization began. Ironically, it was Balbín's successor, Raúl Alfonsín, who, of the major political figures in Argentina, most clearly voiced his support for the human rights campaign. Something had changed in Argentina because a once taboo subject could now be openly espoused by a civilian presidential candidate while the military still held the reins of power. Later, under civilian rule, the heterogeneous composition of the human rights movement created great tension when one 'intransigent' wing refused to drop their campaign, now directed at President Alfonsín.

The precise manner in which the human rights issue is dealt with during the democratization process will dictate to a large extent the nature of the new democracies. Alain Rouquié wrote how, 'In Argentina, the specter of Nuremberg haunts the barracks and explains the *fuite en avant* into the Malvinas/Falklands adventure, as well as the uncertainties that have attended the surrender of power to civilians until the last moment on 10 December 1983'.[47] It was the dynamic human rights movement in that country that broke the 'law of silence' imposed by the military, and literally forced the civilian politicians to face the issues. In Brazil, on the contrary, liberalization of the regime was premised on civilians closing the book on the regime's human rights abuses. The armed forces were in a position to impose a veto on any 'revanchist' attempts by civil society to hold them to account, and democratization seemed to be conditional on this compromise. As one opposition weekly headlined: 'The honour of the barracks is above the rights of man'.[48] In Uruguay, likewise, there was a fairly explicit deal on human rights during the democratization process, although this would be a thorny issue for the new democratic regime, as the method of the *caceroleo* (mass beating of saucepans in the street), once used to demonstrate opprobrium to the dictatorships, was later deployed against a civilian regime that vacillated in calling the military to account for their crimes against humanity.

Women played an important role in all the above social movements centred around the workplace, community issues and, above all, human rights. In Argentina, the Mothers of Plaza de Mayo, who agitated persistently on behalf of their 'disappeared' children, in spite of constant repression, were a focal point for the whole human rights movement. It was women, again, who played a central role in the Chilean and Brazilian community movements. These, however, cannot be described as women's, let alone feminist, movements. Certainly in the southern cone countries feminism was a persistent, if minority, current. In the process of democratization it was to flourish, and not only under the influence of women returned from exile, where they had met Western feminism. As one Uruguayan document declares, this was a new stage where,

> with the reopening of traditional channels of participation, there emerges as a concrete preoccupation the specific problematic of women and reflection is increased around the need for a dual feminine militancy, that which accompanies the general revindications for the construction of a project for a new nation (*país nuevo*), and that which specifically relates to the condition of women in that project.[49]

It still remains to be seen if the impetus given to the formation of an autonomous women's movement during the democratization phase can be carried over to the new democracies, given a certain tendency to dissolution as new political loyalties begin to hold sway. Once the unifying focus of the dictatorship has gone, diversity and particularism inevitably seem to prevail. As for the church, this is an 'old' social movement that took on many of the characteristics of the new. The churches (mainly the Catholic, but also others) are no longer simple bastions of the old order, but contain within them deeply contradictory impulses. A song much in use in Brazilian rural ecclesiastical basic communities is indicative of this sentiment:

> We are the people, we are many,
> We are God's people,
> We want land on earth,
> We have it already in heaven.[50]

Faith in the hereafter is replaced by a more mundane claim on earthly goods hitherto monopolized by the rich. In Brazil and Chile, the church has played a very substantial role in the struggle for democracy, whereas in Argentina and Uruguay the hierarchy meekly consented to military rule. Certainly, political differentiation within the body of the church is nothing new, but now the church contains a genuine popular movement for social change, all the more dynamic and explosive because it does not take traditional political forms. As Frei Betto of the Brazilian basic communities has said: 'people who almost always live in a sphere of necessity now for a moment live in a sphere of liberty'.[51] This is not to play down the contradictory connotations of religion in a post-revolutionary situation, or to say that the church-influenced social movements are unambiguous, but only to signal their powerful effect on vast sections of the people.

Trends and differences

Taking up some of the themes developed above, we will outline schematically the main features of the transition in each country, an analysis which will then be expanded in subsequent chapters (except for the case of Chile which is not as yet a new democracy). Brazil must be mentioned first, as it is the paradigmatic case of successful and smooth transition in Latin America.

Brazil

The Brazilian transition to democracy perhaps best epitomizes a successful pacted solution for Latin America. As Luciano Martins indicates, 'the Brazilian "liberalization" was originally triggered by the regime's difficulties of its "internal economy", and did not originate from any substantive change in the correlation of forces between the regime's protagonists and its opponents'.[52] A necessary proviso to this verdict is that the opposition was clearly the main beneficiary of the political space opened up by the regime's 'decompression'. Furthermore, after 1979 and the first major strikes, and the birth of what was effectively a new labour movement, a reactivated civil society was to have a considerable, if not determinant, role in the transition process. We must recognize, however, that when the Geisel regime began to promote an *abertura* (opening) of politics in 1974, it was on the basis of the regime's success — the 'economic miracle' above all — and the complete defeat of all opposition movements, including a brief flourishing of an armed struggle movement, rather than any pressure from below.

The timetable for liberalization was carefully controlled from above. Even so, as Viola and Mainwaring argue: 'The 1974 elections, a surprise to regime and opposition alike, showed more pervasive opposition than expected, especially in the country's most developed regions which had been the primary economic beneficiaries of development'.[53] The regime still had the upper hand, and was able to muzzle the opposition through censorship, and then in April 1977 simply closed Congress and 'reformed' the Constitution and electoral law. The (in)famous *'pacote de abril'* (April package) shifted representation from an electoral to a total population base, thus favouring the government party ARENA, in the more backward north-east. It also set a maximum representation for the more populous states, thus disadvantaging opposition-dominated São Paulo, and a minimum to favour the least populous states. The government was also allowed to appoint one-third of the Senate — the 'bionic senators' — so guaranteeing its control of the upper house. Thus the regime was able to do slightly better in the elections of November 1978, and saw itself firmly on course for a victory in the presidential elections of 1984. What intervened was the popular mobilization already mentioned above. From the industrial heartlands of the south-east to rural labourers in the north-east, from the church-based labour groups to protesting professionals, civil society was on the march and was now effectively setting the parameters of the democratization process. The military had not lost control of the process, but it had become far more uncertain, and required assistance from the political elite to 'manage' the transition effectively.

The Figueiredo administration, which came to power in 1979, was now charged with taking the *abertura* to its logical conclusion, and 'make of this country a democracy', as he pledged in his inaugural speech. Party political life and political competition began in earnest, and by 1980 the new political spectrum seemed to have stabilized. Notwithstanding terrorist activities by dissident (*duro*) elements within the regime, the dismantling of the repressive apparatus began with the scrapping of the notorious Acta Institucional No. 5 and the re-establishment of parliamentary immunities. The November 1982 elections saw the opposition taking control of most of the major states, yet the government party (now, significantly, renamed the *Partido Democrático Social*, Social Democratic Party) retained control of the electoral college, which would name the president in 1985. The campaign for direct elections gathered momentum in 1984, at the cost of the opposition's acquiescence with the government's socio-economic policies. With millions of people on the street, the government political front began to crumble and essentially a whole section passed into the opposition. General Figueiredo himself — who once declared that he preferred the odour of his horses to that of the masses — played a role, in refusing to control the presidential succession process as was customary. As the credibility of the regime eroded, so did the 'responsible' opposition politicians begin to take control, with a potentially threatening mass movement rumbling uneasily in the background.

Argentina

Argentina, of course, represents a transition via collapse of the military regime. The dictatorship had earlier essayed a move towards liberalization with the brief presidency of General Viola in the second half of 1981, but the *duros* reasserted their hegemony with General Galtieri. The now unstable military regime turned towards a military nationalist populism, first threatening war with Chile and then launching the 'recovery' of the Malvinas, which would hopefully create social consensus at home while avoiding a real war. Mrs Thatcher did not permit such a scenario to materialize and the rest is history. For the remainder of 1982, the military was able to maintain a semblance of control over the situation. The loss of legitimacy by the regime was not accompanied by a corresponding gain in legitimacy by the political parties. This was in part due to the failure of the political parties, across the political spectrum, to criticize, or at least distance themselves from, the adventurist episode of the Malvinas war. Allied to this was the ambiguity of the major political parties towards the regime. The Peronists, though it was their government that had been overthrown in 1976, were far from implacable opponents of the regime. The Radicals, for their part, were declaring, through one of their more leftist leaders, as late as 1981 that 'for the rest of this century and for several decades of the next there will not be *populist adventures* in Argentina in the style of Radicalism and Peronism'.[54] Naturally when the military did begin to stumble in the following year, all the parties began jockeying for position in the new *abertura* politics.

The timetable for a redemocratization was at first controlled firmly by the dictatorship, and the fact is that calls for immediate elections were noticeably absent. As Viola and Mainwaring write: 'Parties were allowed to reorganize, but the multiparty front continued to be cautious and did not encourage mobilization'.[55] Towards the end of 1982 the political parties were effectively outflanked by a multifaceted social mobilization. The human rights movement had made the transition to a mass movement capable of mobilizing hundreds of thousands in the streets. Local or municipal protest movements flourished and tax and rates strikes became common. The constant recuperation of the labour movement peaked with a general strike in December which was a notable success. Even the police force kept to barracks in Buenos Aires in a protest over wages. A passing-out ceremony for conscripts who had fought in the Malvinas was marked by unprecedented acts of civil disobedience and open acts of hostility to the hierarchy. All these protests culminated in a major demonstration for democracy on 16 December, which set the seal on the fate of the dictatorship. The caretaker president, General Bignone, announced early in 1983 that elections would be held in October with the winners to take office in January 1984, although they were even forced in the end to backdate this to December 1983. The political parties were now finding their place in the sun, thanks to a popular mobilization they neither encouraged nor controlled.

The non-revolutionary political opposition to a dictatorship has an ambiguous task, because it needs to confront the regime but it also fears 'uncontrolled' mobilizations. Nestor Vicente, a leader of the Christian

Democrats in Argentina, expressed this dilemma in 1981: 'It is impossible to observe passively how social explosions are beginning in the country; we must interpret them and translate into politics the resentment (*la bronca*) of the Argentines'.[56] This, of course, was the worry of the 'moderate' opposition: that the effects of the military dictatorship would exacerbate social conflict to a degree that they would not be able to cope with once constitutional rule was re-established. Now the political party arena became the focus of nearly all opposition activity and it acquired a momentum that no longer allowed the military to set any firm parameters on the transition process. Even the threat of a new coup was an empty one. A leading military figure, when Alfred Stepan questioned him on the military fears of reprisal and whether this would impede extrication, replied simply that: 'There has to be an exit or we will disintegrate'.[57] The power of the state was disintegrating, as instanced by its total failure to control the main economic policies, and a reinvigorated civil society was being mediated by a cautious political elite. *La bronca* had been effectively 'translated' into politics and channelled into the electoral arena.

Uruguay

Uruguay represents another mode of transition, because it was pacted, but the outgoing military regime did not have the solid power base of their counterparts in Brazil. The deterioration of the dictatorship began essentially with its failure to win the 1980 plebiscite, which would have institutionalized the regime, and the significant refusal of the military to resort to fraud, as Pinochet had in similar circumstances. With the military *cronograma* (timetable) in tatters, a process of negotiation with the political parties seemed logical. But, as Charles Gillespie writes, 'the continued weakness of the political parties meant that they were unable to capitalize on their unexpected victory . . .'[58] The armed forces had a bitter debate on whether to continue liberalization or simply close the door on democracy. General Alvarez emerged in 1981 as president, committed to some form of limited democracy or *democradura*. Meanwhile, President Carter, who had actively supported the *cronograma* project, had been succeeded by President Reagan, who exercised less pressure for liberalization. A carefully controlled process of internal political party normalization began, which culminated in the 1982 primaries, which saw the emergence of decidedly anti-regime political leaderships, committed to a full restoration of democracy. Yet there was no demand for an amnesty of the *Tupamaro* and other political hostages held prisoner by the regime, or the legalization of the leftist parties, as a condition for entering a military-sponsored redemocratization process.

In 1983, negotiations began in earnest between the armed forces and the newly elected political leaders, with the signal exception of *Blanco* leader Ferreira, who was still in exile. It appeared that the armed forces were still maintaining their 1980 project of a *democradura*, and their willingness for genuine political negotiation seemed doubtful. Then, in the second half of 1983, according to Luís González, 'a social agitation, unknown since 1973, passed to centre-stage, beginning with a "*caceroleada*" [pots and pans protest] in August and culminating with a massive public act in November'. The latter event, organized mainly by the new union federation, the PIT (*Plenario Intersindical de Trabajadores* — Interunion Workers Plenary), drew in the political leaders and placed them at the head of a social mobilization they had not encouraged. In January 1984, there was a general strike, which was a resounding success, though the two main political parties refused to endorse it. The government promptly declared the PIT illegal, but the mass movement was now clearly back on the scene. Nearly half a million people had congregated in the centre of Montevideo for the November 1983 rally. The student movement had now reorganized, a group opposed to human rights violations prospered (if not on the scale of its counterpart in Argentina), and a flourishing co-operative housing movement articulated the protest and self-activity of the urban poor. It was in this context that a new round of talks began between the traditional political leaders and the armed forces chiefs, in the inauspicious setting of the Club Naval (Naval Club).

The Club Naval negotiations have already been mentioned as an example of a political pact between a weakened dictatorship, a growingly confident political elite and a third, uninvited, guest, the social movements. Following a successful May Day rally in 1984 the opposition planned a civilian strike (*paro cívico*) for June under the slogan of 'democracy, liberty, elections without bannings, amnesty and work for all'. On the eve of this mobilization the *Colorados* accepted the draft proposals from the military for further negotiations. These were to lead eventually to elections in November 1984, which were duly won by the *Colorados*, with the *Blancos*' charismatic leader, Wilson Ferreira, in prison after his return from exile. The transition in Uruguay seems to conform to O'Donnell's model or regime 'soft-liners' (*blandos*) allying with a 'minimalist' opposition faction. But, as Gillespie notes ironically, there was:

> the quite extraordinary twist that no one had predicted a year before, when all parties declared their commitment to free elections at the foot of the Obelisk [in Montevideo]. In their determination to prevent Wilson from becoming president, the military were willing to rehabilitate the Left and keep him in jail.[59]

As with other transitions, the fate of the new democracy is inextricably bound up with the way in which it succeeds the military dictatorship.

Chile
In Chile, there was an aborted transition towards democracy around 1982–84, and there has been a fierce struggle for it to be put back on the agenda in the years since. A failed democratization process is no less illuminating and forms a useful counterpoint to the cases of the new democracies. A decade after coming to power in 1973, the Pinochet regime was beginning to feel the impact of a growing economic crisis, sizeable popular mobilizations and a failure to reconstitute its own social support base. However, the transition to democracy was thwarted by the absence of electoral mediating institutions (Brazil), or

failed plebiscites (Uruguay), or external military defeats (Argentina). According to Garretón: 'The crisis confronting the regime since 1981 did not originate in the actions of the opposition, although these came to play a role in its subsequent development. Rather, the contradictions and problems created by the actions of the regime gave rise to the crisis'.[60] Until 1980, the middle-class supporters of the regime (including the crucial self-employed unions, the *gremios*) were quiescent, given the trauma left by the Popular Unity experience. The left and its social base was equally traumatized by the defeat of 11 September 1973. Pinochet's grandiose scheme for institutionalization, ratified in 1980, helped to 'unblock' the situation because it posed the prospect of a political life 'beyond Pinochet', if very much in the long term. Created largely by its own internal contradictions (above all, the failure of the Chicago economic model) the growing crisis of the 1980s saw unprecedented popular mobilizations.

During the late 1970s, there was a gradual recovery within the popular movement, particularly among the *pobladores*, although some strikes were also beginning to occur. In 1982, there was a hunger march in Santiago which took the forces of repression by surprise. The Catholic Church helped to create the political space for this partial rearticulation of civil society, although the left-wing opposition parties were beginning to become active again. It was the national protest days of May 1983 which gave maximum expression to the accumulated social discontent and posed the first real challenge to the regime in a decade. This was followed by the protest strike of October 1984, based around the slogan 'Without protest there is no change' (*Sin protesta no hay cambio*). This did not produce, however, a situation of 'ungovernability' and the abandonment of Pinochet by the armed forces themselves, as the opposition had hoped. In 1985, the church sponsored a National Agreement (*Acuerdo Nacional*) for the transition to democracy, but this excluded the Communist Party and gradually lost momentum. This difficulty in producing a unified opposition movement for democracy reflects the quite distinct pre-dictatorial situation in Chile, compared to the countries which are now new democracies. A bourgeois opposition to the regime, or *blando* dissent within the regime, is inevitably constrained by the spectre of Allende and the present radicalization of the Communist Party, which has now, apparently, dropped its commitment to a 'peaceful road to socialism'.

The question inevitably arises as to why the situation of regime crisis did not lead to regime liberalization. Pointing to the great personal power held by Pinochet, and his determination to remain in office, is one answer, but an insufficient one. The support of the US is another, but less plausible, because even the Reagan administration would prefer someone less unsavoury than Pinochet in control of Chile. Garretón offers another interpretation, namely that 'the opposition, in all its expressions, did not have a precise proposal to end the regime with which to negotiate and around which to organize and prioritize the social mobilization'.[61] The ultimate aim of all protest movements was clear enough — an end to the dictatorship — but there were little in the way of 'transitional demands' to mediate between present reality and the objective.

Thus the social mobilization of an important minority, and the general discontent with the regime, were not translated into a viable political force capable of accumulating strength, stiffening the organizations of civil society and recovering from the setbacks that would inevitably occur in the struggle against the dictatorship. The regime responded to the wave of social mobilization with the declaration of a State of Siege, and had considerable success in presenting events as a resurgence of the 'chaos and disorder' typical of the Allende years. In a sense each opposition is a product of the regime it faces, and the intransigence of Pinochet has encouraged the revival of 'hardline' opposition stances, prioritizing the armed struggle ('the example of Nicaragua') and an unrealistic 'no negotiations' position, which does not have any impact on the regime.

Notes

1. See G. O'Donnell, P. Schmitter, and L. Whitehead, (eds), *Transitions from Authoritarian Rule. Prospects for Democracy* (Johns Hopkins University Press, Baltimore and London, 1986).

2. F. H. Cardoso, '"Teoria da dependencia" o analises concretas de situações de dependencia', *Estudos 1*, CEBRAP, São Paulo, 1971, p. 30.

3. E. Herman, and J. Petras, '"Resurgent Democracy": Rhetoric and Reality', *New Left Review* No. 155, 1985, p. 97.

4. Ibid., p. 91.

5. *NACLA Report on the Americas*, Vol. III, No. 1, 1979, 'Carter and the Generals: Human Rights — the Southern Cone', p. 6.

6. Ibid.

7. M. A. Garretón, *Transición Hacia La Democracia en Chile y Influencias Externas*, Documentos de Trabajo No. 282, FLACSO, Santiago, 1986, p. 22.

8. A. Rouquié, 'Demilitarization and the Institutionalization of Military-dominated Politics in Latin America', in G. O'Donnell, et al *Transitions From Authoritarian Rule* Part III, p. 108.

9. Ibid., p. 129.

10. A. Fontana, *Fuerzas Armadas, Partidos Politicos y Transición a la Democracia en Argentina* (Estudios CEDES, Buenos Aires, 1984), p. 35.

11. F. H. Cardoso, 'La democracia en América Latina', *Punto de Vista*, Vol. VI, No. 2/3, p. 5.

12. A. Colombo, and V. Palermo, *Participación política y pluralismo en la Argentina contemporanea* (Centro Editor de América Latina, Buenos Aires, 1985), p. 81.

13. N. Poulantzas, *Crisis of Dictatorships* (New Left Books, London, 1974), p. 90.

14. G. O'Donnell, and P. Schmitter, 'Tentative Conclusions about Uncertain Democracies', in G. O'Donnell, et al, *Transitions from Authoritarian Rule*, Part IV, p. 16.

15. Ibid, p. 11.

16. F. H. See Cardoso, 'The consumption of dependency theory in the US', *Latin American Research Review*, Vol. XII No. 3, 1977 and O'Donnell, G., 'Reply to Remmer and Merkx', *Latin American Research Review*, Vol. XVII No. 2, 1982.

17. A. Stepan, 'State Power and the Strength of Civil Society in the Southern Cone of Latin America', in P. Evans, D. Rueschemeyer, and T. Skopcpol, (eds), *Bringing the State Back In* (Cambridge University Press, Cambridge, 1985), p. 318.

18. Ibid, p. 319.

19. G. O'Donnell, and R. Schmitter, 'Tentative Conclusions about Uncertain Democracies', p. 39.

20. A. Gramsci, *Selections from the Prison Notebooks* (Lawrence and Wishart, London, 1971), p. 178.
21. Ibid, pp. 180–3.
22. Ibid, p. 152.
23. B. Hindess, *Politics and Class Analysis*, (Basil Blackwell, London, 1987), p. 101.
24. Ibid, p. 109.
25. Cited in A. Stepan, 'State Power and the Strength of Civil Society in the Southern Cone of Latin America', p. 337.
26. F. H. Cardoso, 'Entrepreneurs and the Transition Process: The Brazilian Case', in O'Donnell, G., et al, *Transitions from Authoritarian Rule*, Part III, p. 148.
27. *Del Colapso Militar al Triunfo de Alfonsín* (Cuadernos del Bimestre, CISEA, Buenos Aires, 1984), p. 31.
28. M. Cavarozzi, 'Peronistas y Radicales: Diez Años Despues', *Debates* No. 1, 1984, p. 52.
29. L. de Riz, 'La hora de los partidos', *Debates* No. 1, 1984, p. 15.
30. Ibid, p. 17.
31. L. González, *Transición y Partidos en Chile y Uruguay* (Documentos de Trabajo No. 93, CIESU, Montevideo, 1985), p. 29.
32. G. O'Donnell, and P. Schmitter, 'Tentative Conclusions about Uncertain Democracies', p. 39.
33. A. Stepan, *Os Militares: Da Abertura a Nôva República* (Paz e Terra, São Paulo, 1986), p. 77.
34. G. O'Donnell, 'Introduction to the Latin American Cases', in G. O'Donnell, et al, *Transitions from Authoritarian Rule*, p. 12.
35. O. Abrieu, et al, *La Reconstrucción de la Democracia* (El Cid Editores, Buenos Aires, 1981), p. 145.
36. L. Gonzalez, 'Transición y restoración democrática', in C. Gillespie, L. Goodman, J. Rial, and P. Winn, (eds), *Uruguay y la Democracia*, Vol III, (Ediciones de la Banda Oriental, Montevideo, 1985), p. 117.
37. E. Boeninger, 'Prologo', in M. dos Santos, et al, *Concertación Social y Democracia* (Centro de Estudios de Desarrollo, Santiago, 1985), p. 5.
38. Ibid.
39. O. Drake, 'Labor Parties under Authoritarian Regimes in the Southern Cone and Brazil, 1964–83' (mimeo, 1984), p. 41.
40. R. Cardoso, 'Movimentos sociais urbanos: balanço critico', in B. Sorj, and M. A. Tavares de Almeida, (eds), *Sociedade e Política no Brasil* (Brasiliense, São Paulo, 1983), pp. 50–64.
41. C. Hurtado Beca, 'Regimen autoritano y sectores populares urbanos en Chile', in I. Cheresky, and J. Chonchol, (eds),*Crisis y Transformación de los Regímenes Autoritarios* (EUDEBA, Buenos Aires, 1985), p. 118.
42. G. De la Maza, and M. Garces, *La Explosión de las Mayorias Protesta Nacional 1983-1984* (Educación y Comunicaciones, Santiago, 1985).
43. L. Kowarick, 'The Pathways to Encounter: Reflections on the Social Struggle in São Paulo', in D. Slater, (ed.), *New social movements and the state in Latin America* (CEDLA, Amsterdam, 1985), p. 84.
44. E. Jelin, 'Los movimientos sociales en la Argentina contemporanea: una introducción a su estudio', in E. Jelin, (ed.), *Los Nuevos movimientos sociales/1* (Centro Editor de América Latina, Buenos Aires, 1985), p. 24.
45. M. Sondereguer, 'Aparición con Vida (El movimiento de derechos humanos en Argentina)', in E. Jelin, (ed.), *Los nuevos movimientos sociales/2* (Centro Editor de América Latina, Buenos Aires, 1985), p. 11.
46. Ibid.
47. A. Rouquié, 'Demilitarization and the Institutionalization . . .', p. 131.
48. Ibid, p. 132.
49. C. Filgueira, 'Movimientos Sociales en la restoración del orden democrático: Uruguay, 1985', in C. Filgueira, (ed.), *Movimientos Sociales en el Uruguay de Hoy* (CIESO, Montevideo, 1985), p. 43.

50. Cited in N. Vink, 'Base Communities and Urban Social Movements', in D. Slater, (ed.), *New social movements and the state in Latin America*, p. 101.

51. Ibid, p. 102.

52. L. Martins, 'The "Liberalization" of Authoritarian Rule in Brazil', in G. O'Donnell, et al, *Transitions From Authoritarian Rule*, Part II, p. 82.

53. E. Viola, and S. Mainwaring, *Transitions to Democracy: Brazil and Argentina in the 1980s* (Kellogg Institute, Notre Dame, Working Paper No. 21, 1984), p. 24.

54. O. Alende, et al, *El Ocaso del 'Proceso'*, (El Cid Editor, Buenos Aires, 1981), p. 401.

5. Argentina Under Alfonsín

Argentina's was the first and the most precipitate of the southern cone transitions to democracy. The new democratic regime also faced the worst economic situation and the most traumatic militarist legacy. Under President Alfonsín, there were to be dramatic political developments, both in comparison to the other southern cone 'new democracies', and in relation to Argentina's prior political development. This chapter examines, first, the collapse of the old regime and the transition to the new in more detail than was the case in Chapter 4. It then considers the new economic policy embodied in the Austral Plan, and economic results and prospects generally. Then the crucial role of labour and the trade unions under the new regime is considered, and in particular the project of a social pact. Finally, we carry out a political balance sheet of the new regime which must, of necessity, be provisional. Given the analytical structure of this chapter, we note a few significant facts in chronological order in this introduction.

The war in the South Atlantic ended in 1982 when Puerto Argentino/Port Stanley fell and the Argentine armed forces were routed. General Galtieri was replaced in June by General Bignone, who was explicitly charged with returning the country to constitutional rule. The politicians grouped in the *multipartidaria* (multi-party) front were not too keen to accelerate the electoral timetable and simply call for an immediate restoration of democratic rule, as they needed time to reorganize. The dynamic of social protest among workers, students, human rights activists, and other sectors, unleashed by the regime's defeat in the South Atlantic, accelerated the transition process. Elections were held in October 1983, after a brief but intensive campaign, and the Radicals, led by Raúl Alfonsín, won a decisive 52 per cent, thus defeating the Peronists for the first time since 1946.

President Alfonsín assumed office in December 1983. In his first 100 days (consciously modelled on Roosevelt's '100 days') he carried out a diplomatic offensive abroad, resolving the border dispute with Chile and reassuming Argentina's role in the Non-Aligned Movement. At home he set in motion the trial of the various military juntas and set up a political dialogue with opposition forces aimed at establishing a social pact. The high inflation rates, inherited from the military process, persisted and, in mid-1985, Alfonsín launched a veritable 'war economy' which froze wages and prices simultaneously. In 1986 an ambitious territorial plan was announced, which would entail moving the capital from Buenos Aires to Viedma in Patagonia, a move reminiscent of the creation of Brasília. That year the trade unions called their seventh general strike since the restoration of democracy, and a general air of '*desencanto*' (disenchantment) had set in. However, in the elections of November 1985, to renew half the chamber of deputies and the provincial legislature, the Radicals obtained only slightly less voter support. At Easter 1987, a brief military revolt by nationalist sectors was decisively put down by Alfonsín, aided by an impressive civilian mobilization including most political parties and the trade unions. Fresh elections in September 1987 saw a setback for the Radicals and a relative recovery of Peronist fortunes.

Two abortive military uprisings in 1988 hinged around the remaining human rights trials and the perceived demotion of the military in Argentine society. Both were put down, but with considerable compromises by the civilian government. In 1989, a military revolt of another character occurred — this time led by an apparently Trotskyist group, but with the hint of intelligence service involvement — and its defeat assisted in the recovery of the armed forces' morale. In May 1989, President Alfonsín completed his mandate, but his Radical party headed for defeat in the polls at the hands of the Peronists.

Collapse and transition

We have already mentioned (Chapter 4) the notion that the military regime in Argentina 'imploded' or simply collapsed from its own internal contradictions. Our own interpretation would lay more stress on the impact of the social movements, old and new. Certainly, towards the end of 1982 it was trade union mobilizations which created the space and set the example for the first political party marches for democracy. It would still be true to say that in 1982 and 1983 the military moment dominated the transition moment. Objectively, the military needed to withdraw from politics and back to the barracks to safeguard their own unity. Intense internal conflict within each branch of the armed forces and between the branches was the natural sequel to the South Atlantic fiasco. There was even talk of a 'Peruvianist' or nationalist faction of officers, about to spring another coup within the coup. At one stage, it seemed that the armed forces would be embroiled in the type of open armed conflict within their own ranks that had occurred in the early 1960s. With the removal of the ban on political activity in July 1982, the political parties could have moved decisively to take control of the transition process. They preferred to play safe and allow the military to resolve their own internal differences by themselves. For the political parties this was a 'safe' transition because the military had already decided to go, and there was not a 'dangerous' level of popular mobilization as had been the case in 1969–72, the background to the previous military withdrawal.

The military moment

During the immediate transition to civilian rule (1983) the armed forces began referring repeatedly to the need for *concertación* or agreement on what they considered the main issues. The *concertación* discourse referred to the economic, political and social aspects or levels of agreement. Essentially, what this meant for the military was an understanding with the political parties: no reprisals for the military's disastrous monetarist economic policy, their conduct of the Malvinas campaign, nor, above all, for the *desaparecidos*. The Radicals accused the opposition Peronists of orchestrating a military/trade union pact, and the Peronists accused Alfonsín of compromising with the military on the extent of their accountability. It is doubtful whether any formal pacts were signed by anybody, because essentially the military were a defeated political force. The military were in fact forced to declare a self-amnesty on the human rights issue with the '*ley de pacificación*' (pacification law) of July 1983. That the political parties did not endorse this attempted whitewash is due in no small measure to the continued activity of the human rights movement, which mounted a demonstration of 50,000 in May, thus maintaining the issue on the political agenda. The military moment of the transition process was crucial from mid-1982 to mid-1983: the reactivation of civil society brought the political party dimension to the fore and set the terms of the electoral campaign that followed.

The moment of discourse

Once the electoral campaign began, the moment of discourse became dominant. It was at this level — and in particular around the idea of democracy — that the campaign was fought. While the Peronists counterposed 'liberation or dependency' (with Peronism being equivalent to liberation), the Radicals counterposed 'democracy or authoritarianism' (with Radicalism portrayed as the only democratic force). Alfonsín's proposals during the election campaign were studiously vague, with a great stress laid on their standing for 'life against death', by which they referred to all the forces of darkness which had taken the country to its current impasse. In a similar way, Alfonsín stressed that the Radicals stood for a '*política antipasado*' (anti-past politics), and one which looked to a future modern Argentina. Democracy was presented as not just a means to elect governors, nor a struggle by civilians to take over the positions vacated by the military. For Alfonsín: 'Radicalism is more than an ideology, it is an ethic. It is the struggle against the corrupt, immorality and decadence'.[1] The choice for Argentina was presented simply as one between democracy and chaos. Alfonsín had only recently assumed the leadership of the Radical Party as head of the *renovación y cambio* (renewal and change) tendency, which he had formed in 1972. In a very brief period his image of honesty and energy, not to mention a smooth, US-style campaign machinery, allowed the Radicals to overtake the Peronists as the most popular party. The *alfonsinista* discourse was of a transparency and lucidity uncommon in Argentina. The populist *bombos* (drums) of the Peronists seemed, indeed, an echo from the past.

Any discourse must construct its other. In this, Alfonsín adopted a quite subtle approach to Peronism, refraining from personal criticism and, above all, honouring the memory of Perón himself as one of the great national leaders. Peronism was able to discredit itself quite unaided, particularly through the figure of Herminio Iglesias, who burned effigies of Alfonsín at rallies and openly promoted gangster-like procedures in the internal Peronist struggles. The figure of Italo Luder, Peronism's presidential candidate, was simply a 'clean' figurehead candidate who did not dispel the distasteful aura of the movement epitomized in its slogan *Volveremos!* (We will return!), which was quite unfortunate, given Peronism's disastrous period in office between 1973 and 1976. Alfonsín sealed the Peronist fate with a persistent denunciation of a military–trade union pact, which, though never proven, was quite plausible and extremely damaging. A union-based party such as Peronism now saw its main support base being portrayed as a reactionary corporation on a par with the military. As Landi notes: 'When Alfonsín denounced the military/trade union pact he displaced the referent of the discourse from empirical facts of the damage caused to the nation by the military government, to the processes of power formation, to political action'. Whereas Peronism appealed to 'reality' — the description of the effects of the military regime and 'We are the largest party in the West' — Alfonsín conducted a discursive operation that changed the terrain of battle, and began to construct his own referent. The element of political will and the widespread aspiration for democracy transformed the very notion of reality.

The 1983 elections

The elections were held on 30 October 1983, and the results soon announced: the Radicals had obtained 52 per cent of the vote, against 40 per cent for the Peronists. The full results can be seen in Table 5.1.

The first obvious conclusion from these results is that the two major parties took between them 92 per cent of the vote, thus squeezing out other parties of the right and left. This polarization reflected a turn, on this occasion, by traditional supporters of both the right and the left to Alfonsín. Peronism 'lost' some 700,000 votes in Buenos Aires (province and capital) in relation to its 1973 vote, which accounted for half of its loss to the Radicals. Peronism did less badly in the provincial elections, winning 12 of the 22 governorships at stake and 21 of the 24 senators' seats. Peronism appears to have lost out particularly badly in the vote of women and youth. Finally, the hope of some political party being able to continue the *proceso* launched by the military in 1976 faded away ignominiously.

The 1983 elections in Argentina witnessed 52 per cent of the electorate voting for the candidate who most clearly expressed the desire for democratization. The Radicals, under Alfonsín, were far more adept than the Peronists at articulating the various democratic demands of the electorate behind their banners. Even the traditional Peronist rallying cry of 'social justice' was successfully appropriated by Alfonsín. The Peronists, for their part, were singularly inept at seizing the new democratic mood, engaging instead in a display of authoritarian images and corrupt internal politics. The 1983

Table 5.1
Argentine elections, 1983

| Political party | Presidential poll | | Congress poll |
	No. of votes	percentage	No. of deputies
Unión Cívica Radical	7,659,630	52	129
Justicialista (Peronist)	5,936,556	40	111
Intransigente (leftist)	344,434	2.40	3
MID (Movement of Integration & Development: ex-President Frondizi)	179,589	1.30	0
Alianza Federal (right)	56,506	<1	
Unión del Centro Democrático (right)	51,986	<1	2
Christian Democrats	46,497	<1	1
Alianza Demócrata Socialista (centre)	42,478	<1	
Movimiento al Socialismo (MAS) (left)	42,359	<1	
Others			9

elections clearly did not dissipate social inequality in Argentina nor did they condemn to oblivion the traditional nationalist/popular project of Peronism. However, the 'new politics' had broken the sterile antinomy between Peronism and anti-Peronism in Argentina. For the first time since 1955 the Peronista-*gorila* (reactionary) mould of politics was broken. Alfonsín simply could not be portrayed as a reactionary anti-Peronist, as though that summed up his ideology. After its disastrous period in office, which led to the military coup of 1976, Peronism had been deserted by the professional classes, many skilled workers and some of its traditional supporters — witness the defeat of Herminio Iglesias in the once impregnable bastion of La Matanza. The vague populist appeal of Peronism no longer seemed viable, when faced by a coherent social democratic project, such as that arguably represented by the Alfonsín wing of Radicalism.

The forces of the left shifted, almost *en masse*, away from Peronism and towards Alfonsín: even loyal Communist Party supporters (and members) disobeyed party directives and voted for the Radicals. As to the Peronist Youth, who had in 1973 taken tens of thousands into the streets and provided a subversive flavour to the Peronist campaign, they were a spent force. The armed struggle of the Montoneros had helped to overthrow the military regime that came to power in 1966; now the armed struggle was perceived as the cause of the 1976 coup. The street slogan '*Somos la rabia*' (We are the fury) reflected the limited appeal of the Peronist Youth and Montoneros in 1983, and clearly did not capture the new democratic mood. As to the far left, they were even further distanced from the situation, believing as they did that the Malvinas campaign ushered in a new revolutionary era in Argentina. The Trotskyist

MAS (*Movimiento al Socialismo*: Movement towards Socialism) argued that with the disembarkation of Argentine troops in the Malvinas 'there begins the most extraordinary revolutionary ascent which has ever occurred in the country . . . the socialist revolution is on the march'.[2] With the failure of their electoral campaign — not inevitable given their considerable organization across the country — the blame was laid squarely on the 'political backwardness' of the working class. The well dubbed *'izquierda malvinera'* (Malvinas left) had little to offer in the new democracy, except denouncing the Radicals as a sold-out, pro-imperialist, anti-working-class, bourgeois government, which would not create socialism in Argentina.

The 1985 elections
Further elections were held in November 1985 to renew the provincial legislatures and half of the Chamber of Deputies. The overall results are given in Table 5.2.

Table 5.2
Argentine elections, 1985

Political Party	Votes (%)		Deputies	
	Nov. 1985	Oct. 1983	Nov. 1985	Oct. 1983
Radicals	43.0	49.0	130	129
Peronists	34.0	40.5	103	111
Intransigente (left)	6.0	1.4	6	3
Unión del Centro Democrático (right)	3.5	0.5	3	2

This was the first time in 20 years that legislative renewal elections had been held in Argentina, and thus Alfonsín could claim, with some right, that it was a 'vote for democracy'. Both major parties lost 6 per cent of their share of the vote compared to the 1983 elections, but whereas the Radicals gained one deputy, the Peronists lost eight. The leftist PI reaffirmed its position as the third largest electoral force, obtaining 6 per cent of the vote, a significant improvement on 1983 but not quite the breakthrough hoped for by some and feared by others. A left front embracing the Communist Party, MAS and some leftist Peronists obtained 350,000 votes, or 2 per cent of the total. The right, in the shape of the UCD, gained votes, but not sufficient to keep them within the democratic game, and they soon began to threaten destabilization.

The discourse of liberal democracy in Argentina is well articulated by Gallo, for whom:

The two great Argentine political movements (Radicalism and Peronism) subordinated, with varied intensity, republican principles to the majority popular will. The counterpart to this is that the people of recognized republican vocation have demonstrated open reticence towards democratic practices and have not vacillated, at times, to use methods openly incompatible with the principles on which a representative regime is based. The *desencuentro* (split) between republican values and democratic practice is, we believe, one of the most painful features of our political life.[3]

Indeed, this has rationalized a system of 'democracy for democrats only' because the people, when allowed to practise it, have elected 'authoritarian' figures. This analysis serves to justify a peculiar republicanism that is not democratic, and reflects the failure of conservatives to achieve a stable and credible political formation in Argentina.

The 1987 elections

Fresh elections were held in September 1987, to renew half of the congress seats and the provincial governorships. The results are outlined in Table 5.3.

Table 5.3
Argentine elections, 1987

Political Party	Votes (%)		Deputies	
	Sept. 1987	Nov. 1985	Sept. 1987	Nov. 1985
Radicals	37	43	116	130
Peronists	41	34	110	102

The Peronists overtook the Radicals in terms of votes cast, and the Radicals' lead in terms of number of deputies was dramatically cut. In the provincial polls, the Peronists did even better, obtaining control of 16 out of 22 provinces, thus constituting an opposition hegemony in the provinces to match the narrow lead of the Radicals in central government.

The governing party's loss of the crucial Buenos Aires district, the largest in the country and by far the most influential, was a serious blow. Peronism had restored its 40 per cent of the vote, still below its historic share, but sufficient to overtake the Radicals. The prospect of 'thirty years of Radical rule', as envisaged by its strategists, no longer seemed viable. Yet the results did not seriously weaken the democratic order in Argentina, nor introduce the political instability which once would have been its inevitable corollary. The rightist UCD gained four seats in relation to the 1985 elections, thus confirming that their votes had helped Alfonsín to get elected in 1983. The leftist PI, on the other hand, maintained a steady, if minority, share of the electorate. Some of the Radical projects — such as constitutional reform, and, possibly, the transfer of the capital to Viedma — received a setback with these results. However, in the cabinet reshuffle that followed, in some panic, it was indicative that the key economy and defence ministries were unchanged. Certainly, the commitment to the Austral Plan remained steady, even though there was, naturally, a renewed emphasis on the need for *concertación* with the unions. As the government itself put it, there was now a need for 'basic agreements' with the opposition. The Peronists, for their part, now seemed willing to play the role of 'loyal opposition', thus aiding stabilization. In the shape of the new

Peronist governor of Buenos Aires province, Antonio Cafiero, a new *renovador* (renewal) current had come to the fore in the movement (see below), which augured well for the moment itself as well as for democracy.

Military revolt

While it appeared that the political moment of the transition process now held sway, renewed interest among the armed forces revived the military moment and brought it to the fore again in April 1987. A group of junior officers, under Lieutenant-Colonel Rico, occupied military installations in Buenos Aires, along with colleagues in Córdoba, in protest against the continued trials of military officers, and demanding the resignation of the Army Chief of Staff, General Ereñu. Popular mobilizations across the country raised the slogan: 'Democracy or dictatorship'. Alfonsín, backed by all the main political parties and social movements, went personally to the Campo de Mayo barracks, where the mutiny was centred, and obtained a climbdown by the military rebels. Beyond the dramatic episodes themselves, several conclusions emerged. The 'military question' had come to the fore again because no one knew what level of discontent this episode represented. Military officers were not actually called upon to fire against their rebellious colleagues, so that uncertainty remained. What was quite clear, however, was the surprising degree of unity manifested by all the democratic social and political forces in defence of the constitutional order. General Ereñu subsequently retired, but Alfonsín denied any deal with the mutinous officers. With some pride, Alfonsín could declare that the house was in order and blood had not been spilt. The democratic pact appeared to be working.

Democratization is a process and not an event that can be reduced to elections. The failure of the Easter 1987 military revolt, and subsequent events, does allow us to say that in the course of four years the democratization process in Argentina has advanced considerably. In its first year in office the Radical government had established an agreement of National Unity with the Peronists and 15 other parties. In the course of the 1987 revolt this was broadened when all the main social forces also subscribed to the defence of democracy. Of course, it is not the signing of documents that consolidates democracy. In 1985, 80 per cent of the electorate had agreed to the Papal terms for resolution of the Beagle Channel dispute with Chile, in an unprecedented referendum. Very few heeded the Peronist call for abstention and their implicit chauvinist message. In 1985, some quarter of a million people demonstrated in Buenos Aires in respose to Alfonsín's call to defend democracy. There were brief flurries of military unrest, but constitutional legality was sustained. There were constant labour criticisms of the economic plans designed to defeat inflation (see next section), but even these measures had widespread popular support, thus confirming the overall legitimacy of the new democratic order. In early 1988, the country as a whole could look forward confidently to the presidential elections of 1989, a considerable achievement considering the marked lack of this constitutional continuity in the past: 60 years ago was the last time a democratically elected president had completed a mandate and handed the office to a legal successor. Colonel Rico's brief military rebellion of January 1988, put down by constitutional troops, did not fundamentally alter this verdict. Colonel Seneldín's revolt in December 1988 was an altogether more serious affair, and it was widely accepted that the Alfonsín government made a deal with the mutineers.

The new economic plan

The success or failure of Argentina's new democracy depended fundamentally on the economic situation, which by 1985 had become critical. As Carlos Abalo notes, the continuing astronomic levels of inflation — in mid-1985, the annual retail price index topped 2,000 per cent — 'express a lack of social consensus over the existing rules of the game'.[4] Aldo Ferrer argues that when the Radicals took office the state no longer controlled the exchange rate, interest rates, the fiscal deficit or prices.[5] When the state is unable to control the key economic variables, and when hyperinflation persists over a period of years, the underlying cohesion of a society must be in question. Democracy and development are usually assumed to advance hand in hand: severe economic recession must inevitably constrain democratization. Fajnzylber notes that 'Democratization and endogenous modernization are possible axes for a new development strategy in Latin America'.[6] Yet endogenous modernization seems a remote possibility in Argentina today, after the de-industrializing strategy implemented by the military dictatorship and the subsequent turning by all sectors of capital to speculative rather than productive investment. The foreign debt, which reached US$48 bn in 1984 (with US$25 bn due within a year), was the major external constraint in pursuing such a policy. The *Plan Austral* (named after the new currency), adopted in 1985, had two main objectives: to encourage a strong agro-industrial development with an export orientation and to reduce the public sector deficit and wages.

The Austral Plan
In mid-June 1985 prices and wages were frozen, a new currency (the *austral*) was created and the state pledged itself not to emit more money and to reduce its expenditure. Employers who had been dismissing workers since the 'war economy' was announced in April, now began to cancel investment projects. Alfonsín declared that the reallocation of resources to carry out the economic plan were necessary 'to save the political system', although the actual mechanisms were still unclear. In adopting this plan, some weight is placed on the recommendations of a German economist from the Konrad Adenauer Stiftung, who warned that foreign investment in Argentina would not increase while inflation ran in three-figure numbers, with its sequel of economic and social imbalances. A similar plan would have been forced on the government anyway by the circumstances, a fact agreed by the more lucid Peronist economists. Its prospects of course depended on the degree of credibility it could attain in the various sectors of the population. The first signs in mid-1985

were that the crash plan had achieved widespread popular acceptance. Strikes planned by La Fraternidad, the railway engineers union and the sanitation workers of Obras Sanitarios, in pursuit of wage claims, were immediately suspended.

The Austral Plan's effects towards the end of 1985 were undoubtedly recessive. Between April and June of that year, industrial output fell by 4.8 per cent, the sharpest decline of the decade — barring 1982, the year of the Malvinas war. Wages continued to fall: one survey carried out in August 1985 detected a 3 per cent decline compared to July, and a 27 per cent drop compared to August 1984. The trade balance for 1985 was approximately US$3.5 bn, well below the US$5 bn forecast. In particular, industrial exports — 17 per cent of the total — were considerably lower than what they had been a decade before. On the main objective of the Austral Plan, namely to combat inflation, the government has, however, had some success. In October 1985 (on the eve of mid-term elections), wholesale prices rose by only 0.8 per cent, and retail prices by 1.9 per cent. This success was at the cost of lower living standards, and — perhaps even more significant in the long run — a growing oligopolization of markets. A report by Economy Minister Juan Sourouille himself shows how in recent years the top 200 companies have achieved a growing control over their areas, especially in consumer durables where national capital prevails, and the Austral Plan has only consolidated that process, and to a certain extent legitimized it.[7]

In Argentina, politics is often primarily about the economy. So, the fate of the Austral Plan two years after its launch in July 1985 is of considerable interest. An objective balance-sheet is difficult, given that opinions are completely polarized between governmental supporters of the plan and opposition detractors. On the positive side, we can note definite signs of economic reactivation, a dramatic reduction of inflation rates, the lowest public deficit in ten years and a favourable renegotiation of the foreign debt. On the negative side, we must note a more severe containment of wages compared to prices, which has done little to alleviate poverty, a continued reluctance to invest, and a failure significantly to restructure the public sector so as to make it more efficient. Clearly, this highly politicized debate on the economy is due to the lack of commonly agreed procedures on political economy: there are few nuances in these 'either/or' counterposed positions. The Austral Plan was seen as a last ditch effort to avert economic catastrophe and even the disaggregation of Argentine society. Two years later, its achievements are considerable — hyperinflation has been dealt with and some economic reactivation has occurred — but it is now entering a crisis, as its failure to meet the deep-seated economic and social grievances of the Argentine people becomes evident. The popular support for the Austral Plan at the outset has faded away, yet no realistic alternative has been presented.

By 1987, some of the effects of the Austral Plan had become clearer. In terms of the consumer price index, the inflation rate had fallen from an annual average of 672 per cent in 1985 to 90 per cent in 1986, the lowest rate for over ten years. But, in 1987, inflation again began to creep up, to reach almost 20 per cent for the month of October alone, thus reflecting how ingrained the inflationary outlook was. Preliminary estimates for the 1987 annual rate of inflation were for over 200 per cent. Nevertheless, the real economy was recovering from its earlier depressed condition, with Gross Domestic Product (GDP) rising by 5.7 per cent in real terms in 1986, the largest increase since 1980. According to the Inter-American Development Bank, 'this rise came about mainly because of the buoyancy of domestic demand resulting from the expansion of private consumption, favored by the relative price stability'.[8] After years when the capitalists showed a marked reluctance to invest in the local economy, in 1986 investment rose by 18.5 per cent, although this still only represented 13.3 per cent of GDP, which is low in terms of the 'capitalization needs' of the economy. The fiscal situation also improved markedly in 1986 with the public sector deficit dropping from 6 per cent to 3.5 per cent. This was due largely to an increase in tax revenues, and to holding down wages in the public sector. The 'reform of the state' proposed by Alfonsín also led to 'de-monopolization', which allowed private firms to take over functions previously restricted to the public sector, with the national airline, Austral, being one of the first companies to be privatized.

The Austral Plan, with its wages and prices freeze and its commitment not to finance the government deficit by printing more money, was initially very successful. Popular support was, arguably, a major factor in this respect. However, as the Economist Intelligence Unit notes:

> some aspects of the financial situation after mid-1985 are similar to what happened under Martínez de Hoz in the late 1970s. The combination of high domestic interest rates and an exchange rate which does not reflect the full extent of domestic inflation has attracted speculative foreign funds.[9]

The so-called *patria financiera*, the financial interests which benefited from a great speculative boom under military aegis, has still not been brought under control. It is estimated that during the years of military rule some US$42 bn was transferred from the productive sector of the economy to the speculative arena. Clearly this process cannot be reversed overnight. Meanwhile, as Carlos Abalo explains, 'speculative coups will not disappear in the immediate future, they will carry on endangering the stability of the productive enterprises, stimulating the rise of costs, and the persistence of inflation'.[10] There has recently been an increase in the practice of 'on-lending', whereby companies with access to the international capital market borrow funds and re-lend them at higher interest rates locally. As the EIU notes laconically, 'As with the Martínez de Hoz period, the central problem is that the funds attracted tend to be short term and volatile, and so do not contribute to growth'.[11]

On the external economic front, a constant issue for the new democratic regime concerned negotiations with the International Monetary Fund over the foreign debt. Under military rule, the foreign debt grew by over 30 per cent each year to reach US$47.8 bn when Alfonsín assumed power. In 1984, agreement was reached with the commercial banks to reschedule (over 12 years) US$13.4

bn of debt which should have been paid by 1985. The International Monetary Fund, for its part, decided in 1985 to suspend payments from a US$2.5 bn standby loan because it was dissatisfied with Argentina's failure to implement an austerity plan. Though originally sceptical of the Austral Plan, when this was implemented in mid-1985, the IMF did then reach a new agreement. As the Economist Intelligence Unit notes, however, 'new difficulties emerged in early 1986, when the IMF held back payments of another tranche of the facility because of a failure to meet targets in the last quarter of the previous year'.[12] A new letter of intent from the government, and a commitment to improve tax collection, led the IMF to disburse the remaining tranche of the standby facility. In 1987, a new agreement was reached with the IMF, as was an agreement for rescheduling US$30.2 bn of the debt owed to foreign private banks, which represented some 60 per cent of the total debt. The Inter-American Development Bank, which was involved in these negotiations, believes that: 'The economic indicators at year's end 1986 show the progress achieved since the launching of the Austral Plan and point to a reasonably optimistic outlook for 1987'.[13] However, this optimistic outlook did not last long. The Austral Plan was eventually succeeded by the Spring Plan of September 1988, designed to counteract the deteriorating economic situation. Inflation was brought down from a monthly rate of 27 per cent, as the Austral Plan crumbled, to a rate of 6 per cent per month.

Argentina's new civilian regime has been in the forefront of regional efforts to resolve the debt question. At the 1987 meeting of Latin American Presidents in Acapulco, Mexico, Alfonsín sought regional approval for his notion that only the 'historic debt' should continue to be honoured. This would entail recalculating the foreign debt on the basis of interest rates prevailing a decade or so ago when it was contracted. Alfonsín has, on occasion, gone further than this, as in a September 1987 speech in which he criticized the 'ridiculous recipes' of the IMF and announced an 'immediate campaign . . . to freeze interest rates at historic levels'.[14] This created some uncertainty among foreign bankers, and at times during 1987 a unilateral moratorium on debt payments seemed possible. Overall, however, Alfonsín and his ministers have maintained the line that any moratorium or unilateral measures on the foreign debt would only isolate the debtor nations. This approach came to fruition in 1988 when the IMF granted Argentina a US$1.2 bn standby loan, followed by an unprecedented US$1.25 bn loan from the World Bank. The foreign debt in Argentina, as elsewhere, remains an overarching impediment to the consolidation of democracy. It gives considerable control over the political economy to international agencies, and severely constrains public finances, thus restricting the prospects of a more expansionist policy. Argentina's economy is in a transitional phase, coming out of military monetarism, but not yet having entered a fully democratic phase of growth with stability and some degree of equity.

A major development on the external front in recent years was the mid-1986 economic treaty signed with Brazil. (This later incorporated Uruguay.) Its main provisions included the exchange of capital goods and the formation of binational enterprises, as well as financial, investment and commercial agreements. The logic of regional economic integration is not new, as witnessed by the Andean Pact of the 1970s, but this particular agreement had as much a political as an economic content. It was not simply rhetoric which brought Argentina, Uruguay and Brazil together as new democracies to strengthen their economies and also their political weight in the region against the remaining dictatorships of Chile and Paraguay. For Argentina to sell wheat and food products to Brazil and receive in turn preferential access to Brazil's advanced electronics industry is a logical move. In the short term, however, they will be more likely to receive coffee and cacao. Industrialists in Argentina, however, fear that they will be overwhelmed by Brazil's superior technology and capacity, while workers in Argentina feel that wages will tend to be reduced to Brazilian levels. However, we should not underestimate the potential effect of integration, now that the political decisions appear to have been taken, and forecasts of a tripling of bilateral trade in five years, from US$1 bn to US$3 bn, seem realistic. Projects in computer technology, military aviation and, inevitably, nuclear power point towards a new regional economic power in the making, centred in a Buenos Aires/São Paulo axis.

To seek an overview of the new regime's economic discourse we can turn, finally, to Alfonsín's famous Parque Norte speech of December 1985. The context of economic policy, for Alfonsín, is set by 'the need to construct a future capable of taking Argentina out of long years of decadence and frustration'.[15] Argentina, with its rich economic and human resources, is called on to play a key role in the new world conjuncture, a transition period as dramatic as the original industrial and democratic revolutions. For Alfonsín: 'In the face of failure and stagnation we come to propose today the path of modernization. But we do not want to go along this path sacrificing the permanent ethical values'.[16] Modernization and an ethical society are seen as inseparable. More specifically: 'With the exhaustion of the agro-import model and with the surpassment of the import-substitution stage, Argentina must propose to itself a project of development which will allow it to escape from marginality as well as complementary subordination [to the world economy]'.[17] As to who will carry out this project, Alfonsín criticizes 'classical liberalism' for its reliance on private power, and 'classical leftism' for its reinforcement of state powers, and proposes instead that his participatory, ethical modernization is based on the 'reinforcement of the, autonomously constituted, powers of society'.[18] The egotism and selfishness of Argentina's ruling elite is fiercely criticized but so also is its counterpart of 'messianic populism' which is seen as a cul de sac that cannot lead to an ethic of solidarity.

The Parque Norte discourse is a rational one, but largely devoid of a concrete social setting. Neither Alfonsín or his economic team around Sourouille can be said to 'represent' the transnational corporations, national industrialists, landowners, organized labour or indeed any other major socio-economic force. If anything, the traditional social base of the Radicals was in small-scale rural and urban enterprises. So the question arises as to how such a 'democratic modernization' project can be implemented. Sourouille may argue that the

Table 5.4

Economic indicators: Argentine growth rates (1982–87)

Production

(%)	1982	1983	1984	1985	1986	1987
Total GDP	−4.6	2.8	2.6	−4.7	5.4	1.6
Agriculture	6.9	1.9	3.6	−1.7	−2.8	1.8
Manufacturing	−4.7	10.8	4.0	−11.2	12.9	−0.6
Construction	−22.9	−13.1	−20.0	−6.7	9.0	14.8

In brief, the recovery of GDP in 1986 was led by manufacturing industry and construction, while agriculture lagged behind, mainly owing to floods.

Money, prices and salaries

(%)	1982	1983	1984	1985	1986	1987
Domestic credit	224.0	400.8	565.7	356.1	86.8	151.7
Money supply (M1)	176.3	362.0	546.7	697.9	70.7	106.6
Consumer prices	164.8	343.8	626.7	672.2	90.1	131.3
Real wages	−10.5	24.1	27.1	−12.2	−5.7	−7.6

In this area we note that credit was squeezed by the Plan Austral, the money supply has been tightened and, while inflation was brought under control by the plan, wages have also begun to decline again.

Foreign Sector

	1982	1983	1984	1985	1986	1987
Current account balance (US$m)	−2,241	−2,440	−2,543	−963	−2,861	−4,702
Terms of trade (1980:100)	89.1	86.4	99.0	87.0	75.0	68.7
Interest on external debt/ export of goods and services (%)	56.8	58.2	57.7	51.0	50.7	52.3

Here we note a decline in the current account deficit for 1985 but which was more than counteracted by a rise in 1986; a steady decline in the country's terms of trade due largely to lower international cereal prices, and, finally, that interests payments on the debt as a proportion of goods and services exported still nearly reaches 50 per cent, although there was some improvement in 1986.

Source: Inter-American Development Bank, *Economic and Social Progress in Latin America 1988 Report* (Washington, Inter-American Development Bank, 1988), p. 328.

current opening of Argentina's economy to the international sphere is different from that implemented by Martínez de Hoz under the military regime. Alfonsín may argue that 'his' participatory modernization is distinct from the 1960s' conservative modernization wave which swept Latin America. Yet essentially the results are the same because no new social force has mobilized behind the Alfonsín economic project, even though a certain breathing space has been granted it by most social forces. From the state Alfonsín argues that society must be strengthened, but this is merely exhortation if it remains at the level of discourse. This critique should not blind us to the true import of this discourse, which is new in Argentina and comes at a crucial conjuncture. There can be no going back to simple economic nationalism and a populist Keynesianism: Alfonsín is correct to say that the future of 'civilized order' in Argentina is now at stake. A new military regime would simply be unthinkable.

Table 5.4 gives us some economic statistics that should allow us some kind of quantitative view of the various economic processes outlined in the pages above.

Labour and the unions

The success or failure of the new democratic regime depends essentially on its handling of the economic crisis and the trade union question. We have already stressed the role of the trade unions in destabilizing the military dictatorship through their systematic and tenacious defence of working-class living standards and organizations (see Chapter 4). They were also to be a major issue for the new civilian regime, which was committed to their democratization. The President argued that 'the worker has a right to his political beliefs; what he has not a right to is to put his union at the service of a political party [i.e. Peronism]'.[19] Thus the quite legitimate aim of introducing an element of internal democracy into the trade unions was allied with a quite distinct project of trade union pluralism which would break the organic tie between the unions and Peronism. The CGT, reunified in January 1984 after a period of division under the military regime, mounted a strong campaign against the proposed trade union laws, which was eventually defeated by the Peronist politicians. There had indeed been a growth of Radical influence within the trade unions, with the party's dynamic trade union tendency *Franja Morada* gaining many recruits in some industries, and the leadership of the university students. However, at a national level, out of 250 trade union organizations, only the leadership of two responded to the Radical Party. The question of trade union democracy was one that could be settled only within the working-class organizations, where there was a long tradition of anti-bureaucracy struggles; they could not be settled from above by the government.

After seven years in which the internal life of the trade unions was virtually frozen, the democratic interlude of 1984 was to open up a process of intense debate and renewal. Internal elections were gradually held across all levels of the trade union movement and the results are an indicator of how the movement will act in the future. By hook or by crook, some of the bastions of the trade union bureaucracy remained secure; such was the case with Lorenzo Miguel's metalworkers union. In other cases, such as the auto worker's union SMATA, the old leadership loyal to Miguel's 62 Organizations (the political leadership of the Peronist trade unions) were replaced by supporters of the Group of 25, who had led many of the struggles against the military regime. Even more radicalized sectors came to the fore in the Buenos Aires printworkers union, where Raimundo Ongaro regained control of the union, and the telephonists union, where Julio Guillán stood for revolutionary Peronism. Most significant was the high turnout of union members to vote in the internal elections, in many cases 75 per cent, and in the power workers' union, *Luz y Fuerza*, 90 per cent of its members voted. There has begun, without doubt, a major process of renewal within the trade union movement, with a significant increase in rank and file participation and a major turn towards more combative and democratic union leadership.

The renewed union leadership did not adopt the radical class struggle attitude of the *clasista* (class struggle) union of the mid-1970s, but it did articulate a clear democratic opposition to the bureaucratic CGT leadership. Victor de Gennaro, new leader of the 100,000-strong state workers' union ATE (*Asociación Trabajadores del Estado*), is representative of the current progressive Peronist trend. The campaign against the old leadership of Juan Horvath was carried out vigorously up and down the country and resulted in a clear-cut victory. As de Gennaro explains, 'power resides with the workers and the apparatus did not represent anybody. We sought legitimacy from below'.[20] One of the first measures of the new union leadership was to sanction a broad amnesty for those who had been disciplined for political opposition in the past. They also strove to decentralize the union by instituting financial autonomy for the provincial sections. Finally, the union statutes were altered to devolve much more power to the *cuerpo de delegados*, the shop steward committees, which had maintained much of the vitality and combativity of the labour movement since the rise of Peronism. De Gennaro is keenly aware of the dangers of bureaucratization — 'we each have a bureaucrat within us' — and has taken measures to ensure rank and file participation, debate and control over the leadership. There is now a broad spectrum of revolutionary Peronist, Communist, Trotskyist and independent socialist union leaders and middle cadre pursuing a more democratic trade union practice.

Though the latter years of the military dictatorship had seen a considerable recovery of working-class living standards, there was inevitably an outburst of pent-up demands in 1984. In the first place there was a series of strikes aimed at regaining lost purchasing power, with claims for 50 per cent and even 100 per cent wage rises. There were also strikes that reflected concern over working conditions, in the context of the military regime's rationalization bid and flouting of health and safety regulations. Finally, there were many disputes over job losses, aimed against further redundancies and for the reinstatement of those dismissed under the old regime. These partial struggles culminated in the general strike of September 1984, called to protest against the effects of the government's economic policies, and heeded massively by the industrial unions, but only patchily in the service sector. In November 1984 the CGT warned the government of a possible 'social explosion' if the economic situation was not rectified. By then, however, the trade union leadership was firmly committed to the *concertación* process, which gave rise to the accusation of a Radical/trade union pact, ironic given the Radicals' previous accusation during the 1983 election campaign of a military/trade union pact. The union leadership is now seriously concerned that it will be outflanked by its social base. An indication of this was the strikes and rioting in Córdoba in January 1985, which served notice on the union leadership that their members would not accept the austerity plan implicit in the *concertación social* treaties, being signed those very same days.

In the course of 1984, there were 717 strikes across the country, in which over 4½ million workers participated, the most seriously affected areas being the metallurgical industry, the construction industry, and the sugar industry.[21] In 1985, this unprecedented rhythm of strikes continued, as all sectors, industrial and white-collar workers alike, sought to make up lost ground. In May 1985, the CGT organized mass demonstrations and strikes in various provinces, followed by a general strike at the end of the month. Then, in July, the 4,000 Ford workers in Buenos Aires occupied their plant in protest against dismissals. After 20 days they returned to work, but not before sparking off a wave of workplace occupations against the growing level of redundancies. This recalled the factory occupations of the mid 1960s, which helped lead to the overthrow of the Radical government of Arturo Illia. Real wages fell by 20 per cent in the first half of 1985 and the union leadership could not afford to be outflanked by its membership. It had to balance its support for the *concertación social* process with its concern for rank and file unrest reflected in advances by the left (which led to the Ford occupation, for example).

The 'trade union question' was temporarily shelved during the military crisis of Easter 1987, when trade union leaders stood beside the President in defence of democracy. Shortly afterwards, however, moves towards social mobilization seemed to prevail over any tendencies towards social *concertación*. Then Alfonsín, in a typically bold move, appointed Carlos Alderete, a Peronist leader of the power workers' union, Minister for Labour. Alderete represented a union grouping known as *Los 15* which united some of the larger industrial and service unions against the more confrontationist tactics of CGT General Secretary Saul Ubaldini. Already in 1986, the union movement had broken ranks, with the larger and more powerful unions settling individually with the government and thus undermining the CGT's role. Now, with the co-option of Alderete into the government, a 'moderate' union tendency was being given a slice of power. In the event, Alderete was able to negotiate a favourable settlement of some outstanding legislative issues, which won him the (temporary) tacit support of the CGT leadership. In exchange for a muting of wages militancy, Alderete (until his replacement in the post-1987 elections cabinet reshuffle) sought a full ratification of the *concertación* agreements, and, in particular, the extension of worker and employee participation schemes. The

Alfonsín government has, over the years, had a flexible labour policy, avoiding full-scale confrontation, co-opting and dividing where possible, but not ceding on the essential economic demands, nor fully rescinding the labour legislation passed by the military dictatorship.

The unions, for their part, have maintained the traditional Peronist policy of simultaneous confrontation and negotiation (*golpear y negociar*). In the four years of civilian rule up to 1987, there were ten general strikes, although the CGT declared on the eve of one in January 1987 that they 'were not aimed at overthrowing the government, but at changing its economic policy'. Nevertheless, labour unrest was intrinsically destabilizing for the Alfonsín government. The unions turned to the Catholic hierarchy in a bid to seek allies against the government, and this exacerbated government–church tension, already there due to the divorce issue. Contrary to what some of its critics argue, the trade union movement in Argentina does have a genuine commitment to the continuation of the constitutional regime. The economic situation of the country has, however, placed the union movement in a position where it must organize general strikes and 'struggle plans' (*plan de lucha*) if it is to retain the loyalty of its members. Unlike the employers' side in the state-sponsored *concertación* negotiations, the unions need constantly to demonstrate their capacity for action if they are to remain credible actors in that process. The problem is that the unions, owing to their political traditions, lack a viable and coherent alternative project of government, so their opposition is mainly negative. It would be ironic if Alfonsín, who created the image of a military–union pact, was able to consolidate a Radical–union pact that would considerably increase the prospects of a stable democracy in Argentina.

An essential element in the democratization strategy of the Radical government was the process of *concertación social* (social contract). The theoretical emphasis of many political scientists on political mediation had its practical counterpart in the government's policy of *concertación social*, designed to bring the trade unions, employers and the state into a united front. After various ups and downs, caused by some reluctance on the part of the trade unions to be absorbed by this corporatist project, an agreement was reached in February 1985. The anti-inflationary package agreed to include a commitment to a wages freeze, which caused serious unrest among trade union members. The government promised a tax reform to 'avoid the worsening of social inequalities', but inevitably it was perceived as an IMF austerity plan. One cannot prejudge the ultimate impact of the government's 1985–1989 economic plan, but 'social pacts' have been tried before in Argentina (as elsewhere) and failed. Basically, they seek to achieve an agreement or compromise, which the class conflict will inevitably tend to disrupt. Grossi and Dos Santos argue that '*concertación social* can be seen as one of those modes of mediation between society and the political systems'.[22] They recognize that this may be just another way to legitimize domination, but argue that the involvement of the social movements may turn this type of pact into a means for the 'progressive transformation of the social order'.[23] All we can say at this stage is that neither the national nor the international experience in this area suggests that a 'social pact' between labour, capital and state can be a means of radical social transformation.

At one level, *concertación social* is simply a form of class collaboration. Luis Maria Blaquieri, vice-president of the employers' association, the *Unión Industrial Argentina*, declared in early 1985 that: 'It is the capitalist project — which we all want to fulfil — that is in question. The priorities of objectives between employers and workers' leaders are different, but less than the areas of agreement (*coincidencias*)'.[24] A month later, a spokesperson for the unions argued that trade unionism in Argentina 'was useful to the mode of operation (*sistema de vida*) of the employers' because 'it sought to humanize capitalism and did not pose a class struggle'.[25] In practical terms, the unions were susceptible to this type of agreement because the employers had agreed to support them in their bid to recover their 'social works' programme, worth US$2 bn annually, from the government. However, the provincial branches of the trade unions were less amenable to the *concertación* strategy. In February 1985, a plenary of all the secretary generals, in Neuquen, resolved to oppose the social pact between the union leadership, the government and the employers, denouncing at the same time the growing lack of communication between the national and regional trade bodies. The economic recession was leading to factory closures and the firing of workers, particularly in the provinces, so that the social pact could at best be only patchy.

From a broader perspective, the *concertación* strategy reflects the different pattern of demilitarization following the 1976 coup, compared to that following the 1966 coup. The *Cordobazo* of 1969 had essentially legitimized the use of violence for left and right alike: violence obtained results. There followed ten years of unprecedented violence in Argentina. The collapse of the Argentine garrison in Puerto Argentino/Port Stanley in 1982 — the culmination of years of internal war — had the opposite effect of delegitimizing violence as a means of conducting politics. The elections of 1983 reflected this new political mood, and *concertación* was essentially a form of non-aggression pact between the major social classes and the state. De Riz, Cavarozzi and Feldman have argued in this respect that *concertación* seeks to 'create a sphere which, through a dialogue between the government and the organized social forces, can establish contacts capable of blocking dispersion and reduce the political isolation of the government'.[26] The government is essentially weak, in terms of its social (as opposed to political) base of support, and the trade unions are a potent organized political force, in spite of their grave social weakening under the preceding military regime. In this context we can expect *concertación social* to continue: it will not establish a mythical social consensus, but it may well attenuate the level of overt political conflict. A powerful incentive in this will be the continuing economic crisis.

As for the politics of the labour movement, it is as yet premature to speak of the 'Twilight of Peronism' as many reports did after the split in the party. The movement is indeed facing a crisis of authority and the form of its resolution is still unclear. However, Peronism still represents for the majority of the popular sectors a form of political identity. In this respect, critics such as Di Tella seem somewhat confused in focusing on the movement's present *clasismo* in contrast to its previous multi-class base of support. Observers such as Di Riz argue that the main task facing Peronism, if it is to become an effective opposition party, is to settle its relations with the trade unions.[27] Yet it is precisely the hegemony of the trade unions within the Peronist movement since 1955 that has guaranteed its durability and given it strength in the political process. The vague populist appeal of Peronism is no longer viable against a coherent social democratic project such as that arguably represented by the Alfonsín wing of Radicalism. In the new democratic era, authoritarian political practices and images (such as Iglesias burning an effigy of Alfonsín in a pre-election rally) are no longer popular. This does not mean that the only option for Peronism is to become a broad multi-class political party firmly embedded in the parliamentary game. The 1945 *Partido Laborista* (Labour Party), rapidly dissolved by Perón, represented an autonomous working-class political project, which could possibly prosper again in the 1990s. A new radical labour party, firmly committed to democratic principles, could present a credible alternative to the Radicals.

The bulk of the left-wing intelligentsia in Argentina has jumped uncritically onto the Radical bandwagon, assuming office in many sensitive positions and generally providing intellectual legitimacy for the new regime. This reawakens memories of the similar infatuation with Peronism in 1973, when the intellectuals (along with much of the middle class) became fervent Peronists. Today, as then, this can only dampen the critical spirit and lead to impoverished social analysis. To be more specific, the new found enthusiasm for democracy requires a deepening of its economic and social components. The much vaunted *concertación social* cannot overcome the class struggle, although it may cushion it. Nor can a rightful condemnation of corporatism lead us to equate the trade unions with the armed forces as equally anti-democratic institutions. We can indeed predict a growing role for the working class and the trade unions in the unfolding process of democratization.

In April 1985, nearly a quarter of a million people marched to Government House 'in support of democracy'. President Alfonsín announced a 'war economy' and warned that living standards could not rise. The crowds under the banners of the Peronist Youth, Communist Party and Partido Intransigente began to file out of the Plaza de Mayo chanting *queremos democracia con justicia social* (we want democracy and social justice). Earlier, the Radical masses and the opposition groups had concentrated their slogans against a threatened military coup. The next day, retired General Onganía (military dictator 1966–1970) condemned this mobilization in defence of democracy 'because it is very dangerous to have the people in the street'.[28] In this episode we find concentrated all the dilemmas, frustrations and hopes of the new democratic government. The present situation is increasingly dominated by democratic antagonisms. Whether these become generalized and unified or not will depend fundamentally on the mode of resolution of the Peronist crisis, and the ability of progressive trade-unionists to forge a democratic labour movement.

Political balance-sheet

In Argentina, history seems to stand still and nothing changes, yet, paradoxically, in periods of crisis events move at a rapid and confusing pace. Many events in 1986–87 pointed to a replay of 1966 when the first 'modern' dictatorship came to power: a vacillating civilian regime, an intransigent and short sighted union leadership, and a rabid, sabre-rattling military. Certainly, the ideologies of the past exercise a powerful set of interpellations over present-day political actors. Yet the Alfonsín regime had in four years survived the general strikes and a potentially dangerous military revolt. The political institutions had become stabilized and their mandates had been renewed without undue concerns. Even the economic situation, a perennial problem in Argentina for military and civilian regimes alike, had been to a considerable degree 'normalized', if not truly stabilized.

A political balance-sheet of the first four years of the new democracy in Argentina must assess, firstly, to what extent the 'military question' has been dealt with; in other words, how far democratization has proceeded. The trial, and subsequent imprisonment for long terms, of five of the first nine junta members is a process without parallel in Latin America. The prospect of a full Nuremburg-type process in Argentina was probably never realistic. However, the political and psychological impact of taking once omnipotent military dictators into the courts, trying them for human rights crimes, and then sentencing them to life imprisonment cannot be overestimated. However, the course of this process did not run smoothly. By the end of 1985, the first batch of military trials had been completed and the general impression was of a civilian government keen not to 'go too far' in its settling of accounts. The prosecution, for example, demanded only a 12-year sentence for General Galtieri, whereas an earlier *military* commission of enquiry had recommended the death penalty. President Alfonsín has expressed considerable sympathy for the principle of 'due obedience' (*obediencia debida*), according to which only those responsible for planning but not those who actually executed the crimes are responsible. The *Punto Final* (Full Stop) legislation of 1987 did not amount to a full amnesty of the military, as some feared, but did represent a concession to constant military harassment. In a way the Easter 1987 aborted military rising showed as much the weakness of civilian control over the armed forces as the determination of political parties to stand together for democracy. Alfonsín has toured military installations — once an attempt was made on his life at one of them — and stressed to the military leaders that the 'war against subversion' that they waged was just, but that its methods were misguided. Towards the end of 1987, one act clearly symbolized the continued haunting of Argentina by the military spectre: against government opposition, Lieutenant Alfredo Astiz (torturer of French nuns and Swedish teenagers) was promoted (retroactively to 1985) to Lieutenant Commander, after the 'due obedience' law and the 'statute of limitations' absolved him of his crimes.

The military trials would probably never have occurred without the activity and constant pressure of the human rights movement, and, in particular, the

Mothers of Plaza de Mayo. It is sad, therefore, that among the critics of the new Radical government were the Mothers of Plaza de Mayo, who suffered an intemperate attack by Alfonsín himself in December 1984. They were accused by the President of promoting political objectives that 'do not coincide with the national interest'.[29] This chilling accusation revived sad memories of how the military regime responded to the human rights campaign by labelling it anti-national (*anti-patria*). Clearly, the 'realistic' indifference to the plight of the *desaparecidos* went beyond the reactionary elements in society. The armed forces, who presumably took some comfort from Alfonsín's position on the Mothers of Plaza de Mayo, continued to play a role in Argentine society. In strikes and labour disputes generally, threatening letters are common and there have even been cases of intimidatory kidnappings. There are daily references in the press to the activities of the 'unemployed workforce', a reference to the formally disbanded parallel repression apparatus. These bodies have also interfered in the judicial process against the military dictators, often with violent means. Clearly, the government cannot be held responsible for the activities of the vast network of terror constructed by the old regime, but many consider that Alfonsín's commitment to demilitarization is at best partial.

We can now draw up a political balance-sheet of 'Alfonsinismo'. The Radicals achieved power not because more than half the electorate — including substantial sectors of the working class — embraced their ideology. Furthermore, the Radicals, or the Alfonsín sector specifically, do not 'represent' any particular social sector. Nor was their political programme of any startling originality, repeating as it did most of the standard nationalist–populist recipes. César Jaroslavsky, leader of the Radical deputies, argues quite simply that his party won: 'Because we expressed the national and popular cause better than the other parties, and because the people believed us and entrusted us with the banners of the national movement, which in this century is Yrigoyen, Perón and Alfonsín'.[30] After five years in power, Alfonsín's personal popularity was as high as ever, but the cracks were beginning to show in the new regime, with a widespread aura of *desencanto* (disenchantment). Predictably, the main problematic area was the economy, which the government had signally failed to bring under state control. The inherited economic crisis has clearly not been reversed by the new civilian government and this would seem to be a precondition for progressive democratization. The Radical Youth (*Juventud Radical*) have explicitly argued in this respect that 'one cannot advance in the deepening of democracy if it is not accompanied by a gradual but sustained uplifting of the more disadvantaged social sectors'.[31] Political participation has, in short, not been matched by increased economic participation. Nor can the Radical inroads into the Peronist vote be expected to continue unless this situation is remedied. As one journal put it somewhat crudely, '*sin puchero no hay movimiento*': without stew there is no movement.

One of the possible options facing Alfonsín is to build a 'Third Historic Movement' to succeed Yrigoyenismo and Peronismo. The advocates argue that the time is now ripe for a new nationalist movement led by a great *caudillo* such as Alfonsín. The President himself may have had some such ideas when he held a referendum in November 1984 to obtain a popular mandate to settle the territorial dispute with Chile. This move was undoubtedly successful with 70 per cent of the electorate voting freely (voting is usually compulsory) and, of these, 80 per cent supporting Alfonsín's decision. However, there are far more tangible expressions of this strategy from among Alfonsín's more left-wing (or populist?) party leaders. Thus former Labour Minister Juan Casella argues that Peronism is moving toward the right, and that the traditionally middle-class Radical Party has broadened its social base, thus creating the social and political conditions for a 'third stage of the national movement'.[32] Marcelo Stubrin, a leading Radical deputy, points to the 'Peronization' of his own party, in the sense that it has now become the legitimate bearer of Péron's original aspirations.[33] This possible new course for the Radical Party is at present simply an interesting hypothesis. Although some Peronists have deserted to the Radicals, the historical conjuncture does not seem to point towards a new social and political movement. Nor do Casella and Stubrin necessarily outweigh the viscerally anti-Peronist elements within the Radicals, and Alfonsín has above all to hold his own party together, especially considering that his internal hegemony is only quite recent.

Alfonsín came to power partly because the Peronist movement lacked a credible image at the 1983 elections. This defeat for a movement that retained majority support since its inception in 1943–46 led to a crisis and eventually a split. The elections of October 1983 witnessed for the first time ever a decisive defeat of the Peronist movement in clean and open elections.[34] Though retaining 40 per cent of the vote, the Peronists lost many of their key bastions in industrial areas, and the overall effect was truly traumatic. The electoral campaign had been largely orchestrated by the old trade union bosses such as Lorenzo Miguel, and their subsequent discredit led to their being labelled the '*mariscales de la derrota*' (marshalls of defeat) by many Peronists. At first the post-mortem following the elections took a confused and recriminating note, but by December 1984 dissent had taken an organic form when the Justicialista (Peronist) Party congress split. On one side was ranged Miguel and the unsavoury leader of the party in Buenos Aires Province, Herminio Iglesias. In spite of their dubious methods (or because of them) the majority of the party went with the dissidents, who became known at the Group of 48. The opposition group gained the support of all the Peronist governors and senators, half of the parliamentary deputies, the combative trade union current known as the Group of 25, and many of the political sectors. The role of Isabel Perón in this process was not clear: although she supported the official leadership, she appears to have withdrawn even further from the movement after the split. A sign of how deep the debate and renewal within the Peronist movement went was that Perón's widow had become practically an irrelevance, in spite of many having accepted that she might continue to play a figurehead role.

In mid-1985, the political parties began internal elections in preparation for the November congressional elections. In Buenos Aires city, the *renovador* (renewal) faction of Carlos Grosso won a clear-cut victory over the old leadership. Grosso now advocates a 'one-member-one-vote' system to elect the national party leadership, instead of the present national council elected by regional representatives. This seems an unlikely prospect, in so far as the present national leadership — Isabel Perón, Jorge Triacca (CGT 'moderate'), Vicente Saadi (regional 'hard' political boss) and Herminio Iglesias (Buenos Aires province political boss) — represents a commitment to the status quo at least until after the November elections. Grosso however has emerged as a reformist leader within Peronism with a clear democratic perspective: 'Today Peronism must become credible again. It will not be through remembering melancholically and nostalgically what we were yesterday. . . . We must construct it, and to achieve it we must start by being, and being seen to be, democratic'.[35] Grosso advocates a modernization of Peronist doctrine to suit it to the new political era opening up. If successful, a 'Peronism without Perón' may yet be achieved.

The rethinking that went on within the Peronist movement after the electoral defeat was far-reaching, with many old articles of faith being overthrown. The new critical Peronists have returned to the sources of their ideology: social justice, economic independence and popular sovereignty. They have squarely rejected the gangster-like methods (*matonismo*) so characteristic of the movement in the past, and accepted that democracy is not a side issue. Peronist economist Guido di Tella goes against historical tradition in arguing that 'Radicalism is not our enemy'.[36] Rather, it is now accepted that in Argentina there are small parties of the right and left (which had a negligible impact on the 1983 elections), and two major parties of the centre: Peronism and Radicalism. They fear quite legitimately that the Radicals are gaining the more progressive image and that there is some truth in accusations concerning the *gorilización* (right-wing turn) of Peronism. In many ways, the critical sectors of the political wing of Peronism represent a social democratic option for the movement. The trade union dissidents reject the *verticalista* (centralist) tendency of Miguel, and preach a looser, practically syndicalist relationship between the trade unions and the Peronist party. The last time the Radicals were in power, the trade unions and the Peronist movement were prime movers in the campaign that led to the 1966 military coup. Then, the Radicals governed because Peronism was proscribed; this time the Radicals do have a democratic mandate, and the Peronist movement is beginning to accept that there are certain 'rules of the game' in a democratic process.

One of the main blind spots of Peronism remains the question of democracy. The orthodox Peronist trade union leadership has been lukewarm towards the human rights campaign on behalf of the *desaparecidos*, even refusing to support their demonstrations in many cases. During the 1985 trial of the ex-military dictators, Peronist witnesses made some startling statements. Thus Raúl Baldassini, leader of the telecommunications union and co-secretary of the CGT, testified to the court that he knew of no trade unionist who had been detained or physically eliminated between 1976 and 1982.[37] When reminded of the disappearance of Oscar Smith, leader of *Luz y Fuerza*, the power workers union, in 1976, he said he had 'forgotten'. Jorge Triacca, also co-secretary of the CGT, testified to the 'exemplary' treatment he had received from naval officers when detained after the coup. In the ensuing furore, CGT leader Saul Ubaldini (one of the more combative leaders throughout the military dictatorship) demanded the 'total clarification of the thousands of disappearances of workers' political and trade union militants, which occurred during the black years of the military dictatorships'.[38] Within the political sectors of Peronism, the Buenos Aires boss, Herminio Iglesias, continued his diatribe against 'communist infiltration', the 'social democrats' in government, and openly justified his gangster-like methods of provincial leadership. A large sector of Peronism has not yet become reconciled to democratic norms of conduct.

Towards the end of 1988 the Peronists selected the La Rioja governor, Carlos Menem, as their presidential candidate. Cafiero, leader of the Peronist *renovadores*, was seen as too much like Alfonsinismo without Alfonsín. With Menem — and his populist image of friend to the poor — Peronism was returning to its classic mould. This included a certain relationship with the military, as witnessed in Menem's ambiguous statements during the military revolts of 1988, supporting democracy but also the military demands for higher pay and better status. An Argentina under President Menem would be an unstable place, to say the least.

There has been considerable debate in Argentina in recent years over the possibility of launching a 'Second Republic', an act of democratic refoundation to match the refoundation projects of the now defunct military regimes (see Chapter 4). Alfonsín's projected constitutional reform is part of this, with its proposal for a new post of prime minister breaking with Argentina's presidential tradition. The proposed transfer of the capital to Patagonia is another aspect of this trend towards renewal and the opening of new frontiers. The government's democratic commitment to a divorce law withstood concerted pressure from the church hierarchy, which included an unprecedented procession through the capital led by the Virgin of Lujan, who is never usually removed from her sanctum. And yet democracy has not percolated through to the socio-economic sphere. The recent unqualified endorsement of democracy by progressive intellectuals in Argentina has been questioned by José Nun among others. Nun argues for an essential distinction between a 'governed democracy' (*democracia gobernada*), which is what exists at present, and a 'governing democracy' (*democracia gobernante*), which we can legitimately aspire to.[39] The present constitutional regime in Argentina cannot be considered a full democracy in this sense. The current revalorization of democracy has been overall a very healthy tendency, but it has tended to fall into a political 'stages theory': first we get democracy established and then we may move on to other things.

Alfonsín has, however, been aware of how much Argentina differs from the 'pacted democracies' of Venezuela and Colombia (see Chapter 8). Even before the elections, he had argued: 'after the elections we should arrive at a government of national unity. I would seek the participation of all sectors, including the independents. Venezuela conducted an interesting experiment in this sense with the Punto Fijo Pact'.[40] As the projected Third Historic

Movement became less and less a viable political project by around mid-1986, Alfonsín began to talk more about a 'democratic convergence' and called for a 'pact of guarantees' (*pacto de garantias*) between the political parties. The Easter 1987 military revolt brought home very forcefully the need for some agreement between the forces of civil society on the 'rules of the game'. To some extent, there are other countervailing tendencies that would hinder this perspective. For example, the constitutional reform advocated by Alfonsín would entail the possibility of re-election of the president for another term, at present barred. In this sense 'Alfonsinismo' has all the potential for creating a paternalist and passive politics, as did early populisms. In many ways the authoritarianism of the political system persists — on the basis of a societal micro-authoritarianism that is reproduced — with President Alfonsín representing what has been called a '*caudillo* democracy'.

Alfonsín's discourse can be seen as a type of ethical Bonapartism: an abstract humanism which sees itself above the day to day political struggles in Argentina. It recalls the liberal evolutionist moralism of Krause, who provided the philosophical backing for *batllismo* in Uruguay. Alfonsín himself declares: 'We should speak no longer of reforms or of revolution, an anachronistic discussion, but rather situate ourselves on the correct path for a rational and effective transformation'.[41] Alfonsín's discourse is centred on the concept of 'possibilism', of democracy as political realism, but it is never clear who defines the limits of the possible. Alfonsín may turn to the 'left' or the 'right', whatever those terms mean in Argentina, in a discourse signed irremediably by its ambiguity. Perón's discourse was demobilizing in its effect, with its constant refrain to workers to go 'from home to work, and from work to home' (*de casa al trabajo, y del trabajo a casa*). Now Alfonsín raises one overarching dichotomy between 'authoritarianism or democracy', with everyone who does not line up behind his liberal, rational and elitist version of the latter being condemned as hangovers of a bad authoritarian past. If formal democracy in Argentina continues to exclude socio-economic advance for the majority of the population, it will inevitably engender subversive movements from both the left and the right, which will terminate the present positive experience of a 'democratic convergence'.

Notes

1. O. Landi, *El discurso sobre lo posible* (Buenos Aires, CEDES, 1985), p. 38.
2. Cited in A. Gilly 'Argentina despues de la dictadura', *Coyoacán* Vol. VIII, No. 16, 1984, p. xiii.
3. E. Gallo, 'Reflexiones sobre la crisis de la democracia argentina', in C. Floria (ed.), *La Argentina Política* (Buenos Aires, Editorial de Belgrano, 1981), p. 21.
4. C. Abalo, 'La economia que vendra', *El Periodista* Vol. 1, No. 17, 1985, p. 9.
5. A. Ferrer, *Vivir con lo nuestro* (Buenos Aires, El Cid Editor, 1984), p. 17.

6. F. Fajnzylber, 'Democratization, endogenous modernization, and integration: strategic choices for Latin America and economic relations with the United States', The Wilson Center, Latin American Program, *Working Papers* No. 1L15, 1984, p. 3.

7. *El Periodista*, Vol. 2, No. 60, 1985, p. 13.

8. Inter-American Development Bank, *Economic and Social Progress in Latin America. 1987 Report* (Washington, Inter-American Development Bank, 1987), p. 215.

9. Economist Intelligence Unit, *Country Profile 1986–87: Argentina* (London, Economist Intelligence Unit, 1986), p. 28.

10. C. Abalo, 'La economia que vendra', p. 9.

11. Economist Intelligence Unit, *Country Profile*, p. 29.

12. Ibid, p. 38.

13. Inter-American Development Bank, *Economic and Social Progress*, p. 217.

14. *Latin America Weekly Report*, 24 September 1987, p. 7.

15. 'Convocó Alfonsín a los sectores sociales y politicos a un "pacto democrático"', *Clarín*, 2 December 1985, p. 2.

16. Ibid, p. 3.

17. Ibid, p. 50.

18. Ibid, p. 51.

19. *Redacción*, January 1984.

20. Reportaje a Victor de Gennaro, Nuevo Lider de los Estatales, *El Periodista de Buenos Aires* Year 1, No. 17, 1985, p. 8.

21. *El Bimestre Político y Económico*, Vol. 4, No. 19, 1985, p. 15.

22. M. Grossi and M. Dos Santos, 'La concertación social: una perspectiva sobre los instrumentos de democratización' in O. Oszlak (ed.) *'Proceso', crisis y transición democratica/1* (Buenos Aires, Centro Editor de América Latina, 1984) p. 138.

23. Ibid, p. 159.

24. Clarín, *Suplemento Económico*, 1 June 1985, p. 5.

25. *El Bimestre Político y Económico* Vol. 4, No. 19, 1985, p. 65.

26. L. de Riz, M. Cavarozzi and J. Feldman (1984), El contexto y los dilemas de la concertación en la Argentina Actual. (Buenos Aires, CEDES.)

27. L. de Riz 'La hora de los partidos', *Debates*, No. 1, 1984, p. 17.

28. *El Bimestre Político y Económico* Vol. 4, No. 20, 1985, p. 98.

29. *El Bimestre Político y Económico* No. 18, 1984, p. 91.

30. *Redacción*, February 1985, p. 30.

31. *El Periodista de Buenos Aires*, Vol. 1, No. 17, 1985, p. 4.

32. *Buenos Aires Herald*, 30 December 1984.

33. *La Prensa*, 7 January 1985.

34. For an assessment of the Peronist defeat see L. Maronese, A. C. de Nazar and V. Waisman, *El Voto Peronista '83. Perfil electoral y causas de la derrota* (Buenos Aires, El Cid Editor, 1985).

35. C. Grosso, 'El desafio de los peronistas', *Redacción* Vol. XIII, No. 146, 1985, p. 44.

36. 'Unamuno, Barbaro, Cafiero y otros', *El peronismo de la derrota* (Buenos Aires, Centro Editor de América Latina 1984), p. 135.

37. *El Bimestre Político y Económico*, Vol. 4, No. 20, 1985, p. 94.

38. Ibid.

39. J. Nun, 'Democracia y socialismo: etapas o niveles?', *Punto de Vista*, Vol. VII, No. 22, 1984, p. 24.

40. *Latin America Political Report*, 11 March 1983, p. 8.

41. *Clarín*, 2 December 1985, p. 53.

6. Brazil Under Sarney

Especially compared to Argentina, the Brazilian transition to democracy appears remarkably successful in its smoothness and capacity to absorb social and political conflict. Fernando Henrique Cardoso, who once coined the term 'dependency' and was the leading radical critic of the military regime, was to be a key political actor in this process as Senator for the opposition PMDB (Partido do Movimento Democrático Brasileiro), and as one of the leading political figures of the new civilian government after. While some so-called left critics accused Cardoso of the cardinal sin of 'reformism' and worse,[1] Robert Packenham was pleased to find a Latin American T. H. Marshall (mentioned in Chapter 1). Packenham, mistakenly to my mind, counterposes Cardoso the intellectual to Cardoso the politician:

> Cardoso's political declarations are significantly different from his academic writings. The latter are full of discussions of capitalism, socialism, class structures, class exploitation, dialectics, modes of production, historical materialism, formalism, dependency, imperialism and so on. These topics are far less prominent in his political works. In these works the focus is on such topics as democracy, elections, parties, participation, economy, economic policy, the people, mass party, and the social question.[2]

Behind these comments of the amused and ironic conservative observer lies a very real point, which is not whether the Marxist leopard can really change his spots, as Packenham is concerned to find out.

According to Packenham, Cardoso's political writings demonstrate a

> dedication to liberal notions of democracy and opposition to radical, Marxist notions of democracy. . . . Thus, Cardoso sounds very much like T. H. Marshall when he states 'the people is the totality of its citizens, and therefore the democratic way can only be found when all citizens participate together'. No class struggle there.[3]

We could say simply that a radical socialist democratic discourse can embrace equally general concepts such as capitalism or imperialism and more specific or 'grounded' interventionist categories relating to elections, political parties or social policies. Nor is Cardoso's current prioritization of the democratic question necessarily a denial of 'Marxist notions of democracy'. Nor is commitment to a 'democratic pact' incompatible with the reduction of social and economic inequalities. We must, however, question whether the Marxist tradition is able to deal creatively and intervene actively in a complex transition to democracy such as that being experienced in Brazil. Some of the old categories of analysis, the simplistic economic and political map and a rather ultimatist political practice seem to have little purchase. Many progressive and socialist intellectuals and economists in Brazil feel that politics is too serious to be left to the old professional politicians, and economic policy too serious to be left to the bankers, and are now engaged directly in the transition process. That our balance sheet of the Nova República (New Republic) will be essentially critical should not detract from this effort to become relevant.

The gradual transition

Brazil's *abertura* (opening), or the more lyrically termed *'distensão'* (lessening of tension), is usually dated from 1975, which makes it a semi-permanent transition process, considering that in 1985 it was not even through direct elections, but through an electoral college, that the first civilian president came to power. We have already mentioned (see Chapter 4) the constant interplay between the military regime's concessions and the opposition's gains, a dialectic of transaction and struggle. The November 1982 congressional elections were a clear pivotal stage in this process, with the massive opposition victory considerably lessening the degree of military control over the *abertura* process. The opposition gained three key governorships: São Paulo (Franco Montoro), Rio de Janeiro (Leonel Brizola) and Minas Gerais (Tancredo Neves). These opposition governors were to play a key part in the negotiations, which now began with the military, on the complete restoration of constitutional rule. As Wayne Selcher writes:

> The inauguration of ten opposition governors proved to be one of President Figueiredo's least pressing problems. These men, well aware of the degree of concentration of state resources in the federal government and the delicacy of the political moment, immediately rejected the idea of an opposition front. They moved cautiously to avoid confrontation and to give the president no grounds for accusing them of aggravating national problems.[4]

They saw the *abertura* as a 'gentleman's agreement' and were firm in the suppression of social unrest in their respective states as the effects of the post-1982 economic crisis began to be felt.

In the course of 1983 the main co-ordinates of the transition process were set. Essentially, the opposition state governors allied with President General Figueiredo to isolate the military hardliners, who wished for a far more restrained institutionalization of the regime, and the intransigent opposition, which sought outright democracy. With record unemployment rates, as the last vestiges of the 'economic miracle' faded away, popular unrest exploded at various stages with the most spectacular actions, including the sacking of supermarkets. The PT (Partido dos Trabalhadores) or Workers' Party saw its popularity increasing considerably during the year. This was in spite of its having gained only eight seats (against an expectation of 25) in the 1982 elections. The International Monetary Fund, for its part, intensified its pressure on the administration to implement austerity measures. Already the foreign debt was becoming a pressing issue, and the opposition's alternative plan of government, drawn up by economist Celso Furtado, included in its proposals the declaration of a moratorium, as well as measures to reactivate the economy and thus increase employment. An anecdotal, yet in retrospect crucial, episode was the 43 days in mid-year when Aureliano Chaves stood in as acting president, while Figueiredo was in the USA for an operation. The military establishment was reassured that civilian politicians could be trusted with the reins of government once again without indulging in populist excesses or economic profligacy. The example of the opposition governors was also a reassuring one.

Whereas Franco Montoro in São Paulo and Tancredo Neves in Minas Gerais were decidedly non-extremist, if steady, oppositionists, Leonel Brizola, who swept to power in Rio, was for the military a more dubious figure. Back in 1964, while governor of Rio Grande do Sul, he had called for workers' militias to thwart the threatened military coup. His populism was far more radical than that of his brother-in-law, President Goûlart. Yet now, as governor of Rio de Janeiro, Brizola was at pains to woo the military, partly of course to clear the way for his presidential ambitions. Brizola was (re)constituting his political identity through a discourse that claimed the old mantle of labourism (*trabalhismo*), but fortified with a dose of European social democracy, which Brizola had absorbed during his long exile. This self-declared socialist was in the forefront of those who supported Figueiredo, so, he argued, 'he could fully democratize the country'.[5] Brizola's political modernism — a discourse that stressed the decentralization of power, and popular participation — came into conflict with a more traditional pattern of Brazilian politics. Brizola defended the effective centralization of state power under his rule in classic terms: 'Blessed centralization is that I have exercised, because it is a democratic centralization, in a democratic atmosphere, carried out by a government of a popular nature and concerned with the public interest'.[6] This 'prefigurative democratization' while the military still controlled the central state paved the way for the accession of a civilian president.

The question obviously arose as to how the civilian president was to be elected or appointed. An electoral college was the established mechanism, but early in 1984 an impressive campaign began for *Direitas já*: direct elections now. This popular movement, eventually endorsed by many opposition politicians, culminated in a rally in São Paulo, which attracted between a quarter and half a million people, according to different estimates. However, the *direitas* amendment was defeated in congress in May, and the electoral college, dominated by the pro-regime PDS (Partido Social Democrático), appeared to provide the necessary safeguards for the military. The leaders of the two main parties, Ulysses Guimaraes for the PMDB and José Sarney for the

PDS, set their seal on the arrangements for redemocratization. When the unsavoury and unpopular Paulo Maluf obtained the PDS nomination for the presidency, the pro-regime party split, with Sarney and others forming the Frente Liberal. Now, with the regime dissidents and the PMDB forming the Alianza Democrática in September, the path was clear for an opposition victory. The candidate chosen was Tancredo Neves, who resigned as governor of Minas Gerais to become a solid opposition candidate, with Sarney as his vice-presidential running mate. Tancredo Neves, in a successful bid to ensure a smooth transition unhindered by fears of *golpismo*, met with the leaders of the armed forces in December to quell any lingering fears they might have of *revanchismo*, a rendering of accounts to the new civilian regime for economic corruptions, if not their abuses of human rights.

The electoral college met in January 1985 and, by a surprisingly large majority of 480 to 180, elected Tancredo Neves as the first civilian president for 21 years, to assume power in mid-March. Neves was a pragmatic, cautious politician who saw the need of fundamental social reform to pay back what became known as the 'social debt' incurred by the Brazilian people in the long years of military-based capitalist expansion. Between 1960 and 1980, income distribution had become even more concentrated, so that 50 per cent of the population earned less than did the top 10 per cent. The UN's children's commission, UNICEF, estimated that 8 million Brazilians, mainly children, were undernourished. So, for Tancredo Neves the *Nova República* (New Republic) would 'begin to promote social, administrative, economic and political changes much needed in Brazilian society. The people are the country; therefore, resolving their problems and attending to their basic needs must be the fundamental commitment of the next government'.[7] However, in keeping with the broad political front that supported him, Neves prepared a basically conservative cabinet. In the event Neves never assumed office, because he was overtaken by a fatal illness, and José Sarney, until recently the leader of the pro-military party, became the interim and eventually full president when Neves died. In the dramatic days of Neves's death agony, a rich symbolic imagery was built up, with suffering and democracy closely intermingled. With Sarney stepping in to avoid further elections, and the military well pleased with the course of events, the first steps of the transition process were assured.

With the televised death of Tancredo Neves there were to be no messiahs or miracles in the new republic, only a lacklustre politician who had been the military's foreman in the political arena. With no social or political base of his own (barring the small *Partido da Frente Liberal*), Sarney had no option but to follow the broad outlines of the PMDB government plan. The *Direitas já* campaign, though defeated, had prevented any backsliding on democratization. Now a wave of strikes in 1985 — including 'unpatriotic' ones while Neves lay on his deathbed — ensured that the labour question would not be postponed. Here a bold reformist strategy was implemented, doing away with the military legislation, and Labour Minister Almir Pazzianotto was one of the few progressive elements in an essentially conservative cabinet. Agrarian reform was another bold reformist measure announced. Yet economic policy appeared to follow in the steps of the military regime's 'economic czars'. An essential element in the regime's political economy was to seek a 'social pact' with the trade unions. Tancredo Neves, before he died had declared that:

> A social pact does not mean that workers ought to be called to make even greater sacrifices. Brazilian workers have hardly any sacrifices left to make. But if they cannot contribute to the economy they could instead make a substantial contribution towards assuring social peace and understanding, which would help create conditions under which the government could achieve more in the interests of the workers.[8]

We examine below the vicissitudes of the social pact and the struggles of workers under the New Republic. Suffice it to say at this point that workers and peasants were not to be passive spectators at the festival of democracy.

In what was considered a major policy speech in mid-1985, President Sarney declared that his government would centre around five main elements: freedom, development, social choice, cultural identity, and sovereignty and independence. There was a blend here of economic liberalism, developmentalism and, as always, nationalism. Yet Sarney seemed unable to present a concrete plan of action. Democratization had intensified the class struggle. Workers and employers, once relatively united in their strategy towards the military government, now fought over the government's proposed strike bill. In the rural areas a more naked power struggle began over the government's proposed agrarian reform. Landowners showed that they too could wage a class struggle, as they mobilized with legal and illegal means to block the government's modest reform proposals. Mobilizations, lobbying and assassinations of peasant leaders and advisers proved effective in making the government backtrack in this key area. In 1985, it was announced that 100,000 families were to receive land in the first year of the reform, yet by the end of 1986 only some 2,500 families had been resettled. The government claimed a lack of financial resources, but a lack of political will was clearly just as important. Democracy was bringing out some of the skeletons of underdevelopment: the lack of a radical agrarian reform was a problem now as much as it was in the 1960s in the run up to Goûlart's overthrow by the military in 1964.

In 1985, President Sarney proposed the formation of a *Pacto Nacional* (National Pact), but this never materialized. The President's lack of a political base of his own and the divisions within the majority PMDB made a solid democratic political pact difficult to achieve. The trade unions, for their part, rejected the government's proposal for a social pact after a wave of strikes in April and then in October. President-elect Tancredo Neves had argued for a social pact that would not make workers carry any more of an economic burden, but which would facilitate 'social peace and understanding'. Towards the end of 1985, a new economic package took shape (see next section) which, with its 'radical' proposal for freezing wages meant that workers would be asked, once again, to carry the social cost of economic stabilization. In the political arena, 1985 closed with the November municipal elections. The

PMDB managed to win most of the major cities except for São Paulo (which we will examine in detail); the President's own Partido da Frente Liberal simply collapsed, thus further weakening Sarney's position; Leonel Brizola's Partido Democrático Trabalhista did reasonably well; and, finally, the Partido dos Trabalhadores made a significant breakthrough in winning the major north-eastern city of Fortaleza. The big question was why Jânio Quadros managed to defeat the PMDB's candidate, Fernando Henrique Cardoso, in São Paulo.

Jânio Quadros had been, briefly, President of Brazil in the early 1960s, in many ways epitomizing the populist politician. His election symbol, now as then, was a broom, to 'clean up' politics, and he appealed above parties, principally on 'law and order' issues. Cardoso, on the other hand, presented a rational radical democratic discourse, and was backed by the powerful PMDB (though not by all sectors) in its heartland. In the event Quadros obtained 38 per cent of the vote, Cardoso 34 per cent, and the PT's Eduardo Suplicy gained 20 per cent. (Clearly, if the Workers' Party had not run, most of these votes would have gone to Cardoso.) The PMDB no longer represented the 'natural' vote of opposition to the military government, which converted each election prior to 1984 into, practically, a plebiscite. Quadros capitalized on the traditional anti-government swing in the electorate, but one cannot deny the effectiveness of the moralism of his campaign, with its slogan of Honesty, Work and Security. Cardoso actually lost many votes owing to a question in a televised interview which asked if he believed in God. To reply that this was not a relevant question was not sufficient in the new, born-again populist era. The more dense intellectual message of the PMDB was put on the defensive by a campaign that hardly mentioned socio-economic matters, and by a candidate who did not have a party machine but who, nevertheless, set the whole discursive terrain of the election. The Workers' Party, for its part, rightly or wrongly, split the progressive democratic vote.

Early in 1986, Sarney appointed a new, more conservative, cabinet to replace that which he had inherited from Neves. Soon afterwards, he announced the new shock treatment for the economy, variously known as the *Plano Tropical* and the *Plano Cruzado*, after the new currency. In its essentials it was similar to Argentina's *Austral Plan*, although we will examine its distinctiveness and its ultimate failure in the following section. The wages freeze initially thwarted labour's capacity to react, and the May Day rallies of 1986 were a poor showing compared to previous years. However, the accumulated grievances eventually broke out, including a series of strikes in August which included bank workers, health and welfare workers and the Santos dockers. On this occasion, a government spokesperson declared that the strikes were attempts to 'destabilize the democratic regime'. As in Argentina, workers' struggles for a living wage began to be portrayed as threats against democracy. In April, the army had occupied the railway stations during a rail workers' strike. Then, in October, on the pretext of a planned day of protest by the unions against the new economic plan, the President ordered the army on to a 'state of alert'. A new round of tax and official price increases towards the end of the year led to riots in Brasília and an unprecedented general strike on 12 December, organized by the two sections of the labour movement (see section below). According to government and trade union estimates, respectively, this action mobilized between 10 million and 25 million people, and marked labour's determination not to pay for the austerity measures.

In November 1986, gubernatorial and congressional elections were held, which were a significant landmark for the New Republic. Not only would it evaluate the progress of democratization, but it would also establish a new constituent assembly (composed of the chamber of deputies and senate), charged with drafting a new constitution. In the event, the PMDB swept the board, winning 20 out of the 23 contested governorships — including, against expectations, the crucial São Paulo state. There the PMDB candidate, Orestes Quercia, appeared to be trailing badly behind the PDS's ex-presidential candidate Paulo Maluf, and the PTB's Antonio de Moraes, who appeared to be heading for a Quadros-style victory. In Rio de Janeiro, Leonel Brizola's candidate, Darcy Ribeiro, who concentrated his attention on the government's economic plan, was badly beaten by the PMDB candidate. The PMDB's success reflected badly on its partner in the Democratic Alliance, the President's own *Partido da Frente Liberal*. The PMDB leader, Ulysses Guimaraes, was particularly concerned that the government should not backtrack on its promised social reforms and that wage earners should not suffer unduly under the new economic plan. However, only weeks after the election, in what was widely seen as a betrayal, the government announced a new more intense austerity plan, known as Plano Cruzado II. In part the government had an eye to the International Monetary Fund, which was due to carry out a report on Brazil, which would, in turn, set the scene for the forthcoming debt talks. This economic adjustment would be resisted by the unions.

In the course of 1987, the future of Sarney's government came seriously into question, although the constitutional system itself had achieved a certain stability. Negotiations at the beginning of the year on a social pact between employers and workers, mediated by the government, came to nought as the state moved towards the militarization of strikes, first in the ports and then in the oil refineries. In May, Dilson Funaro, the minister in charge of the economy, resigned and his successor, Bresser Pereira, had his plans rejected by the unions. Another general strike in July was less successful than the first, mobilizing between 10 and 12 million people. The left was more successful in the political arena, with the revival of the *Direitas já*, campaign, which was to force Sarney, who wanted to prolong his mandate, to call elections. The constituent assembly, though a far less radical body than the left had originally hoped for (and the right feared), did come up with proposals for a parliamentary, as against presidentialist, system, which distressed Sarney. His discomfiture increased in October when his own *Partido da Frente Liberal* withdrew its support from the government, although the majority PMDB, after some debate, and conditionally, continued to back him. Towards the end of the year, with inflation reaching 350 per cent and with continued political instability, the military let it be known that they favoured early elections. Only free and direct elections could fully restore the legitimacy of the democratic system, and in this respect the Sarney period can be regarded as a transition between dictatorial and democratic rule.

In 1988, the crisis of government under Sarney deepened with the government party, the PMDB, going through an unprecedented split over whether to support 'their' President. Political violence increased dramatically, with landowners openly attacking squatters and peasants on the one hand, and the state deploying the full panoply of repression to quell a steelworkers' strike towards the end of the year. The final ratification of a new constitution in October 1988 marked a significant gain by the nationalist left in Brazilian politics. Finally, the breakthrough of the PT (Partido dos Trabalhadores) in the November 1988 elections — in which it gained control over key cities — marked the coming of age of the left in Brazil, and questioned the stability of the conservative transition to democracy.

End of the economic boom

President Sarney always stressed the economic difficulties he inherited from the previous military regime: 'the world's largest foreign debt, the highest inflation in Brazil's history, and a great social crisis'.[9] Certainly, negotiations with the International Monetary Fund had reached an impasse in 1985 with the suspension of a crucial loan, and the balance of payments was deep in the red. Yet in many ways the New Republic found itself in a favourable economic context, especially if compared to the 1982–84 period. The economy was growing after a period of stagnation, even if the high growth rates of the 'economic miracle' of 1968–73 had not yet been recovered. Exports were increasing rapidly and the internal market was recovering steadily. This more favourable internal picture should not be allowed to mask, of course, the high inflation rates that now threatened to get out of control, as had happened in Argentina, and the huge fiscal deficit of the state. On the social front, from which political economy cannot be divorced, unemployment rates remained high and wages had been declining over the three previous years. Yet an organ such as the international *Business Week* could see a very favourable general picture: 'Brazil is booming. Its rebound from a deep recession in the early 1980s is unlike any previous upsurge in the history of this huge country. This time, Brazil is on the verge of becoming an industrial powerhouse'.[10] International capital seemed optimistic about the economic context of Brazil's new democracy.

The first economic team formed by the new civilian government consisted of a mix of progressive (even Marxist) elements and conservatives. Tancredo Neves commissioned the *Comissão do Plano de Ação do Governo* (Government Action Plan Commission) to prepare the economic policy of the new government. It was headed by José Serra, ex-student leader, and composed of Celso Furtado, a veteran radical economist, and Luciano Coutinho, a young Marxist economist on the one hand, and on the other hand two establishment economists who had participated in the military governments. This ambiguity reflected the disparate political support enjoyed by Neves, and the need to reform, while also satisfying the breakaway sectors of the military party, the PDS, who had shifted to the opposition. In policy terms, of course, this led to a tendency towards inconsistency and, ultimately, paralysis. Tancredo Neves had a genuine orientation towards reform — conscious as he was of the explosive social situation in Brazil — but his successor, Sarney, was more unambiguously of an economic liberal persuasion. Thus Sarney could argue:

> I think that private initiative is the engine of economic development. In Brazil we have learned that every time the state's penetration in the economy increases, our liberty decreases. When the state has a 60 per cent share in the economy, we know that only 40 per cent liberty remains to us. I want to diminish the state's presence.[11]

Simplistic political economy this may be, and a poor analysis of Brazilian state capitalism, but it was to inform the post-military economic orientation.

In 1985, Year One of the new democracy, the real minimum wage in Brazil rose by 12 per cent. There was consequently a boom in the sale of consumer durables, and internal demand began to replace exports as the motor of the economy. Idle capacity in industry was taken up and employment increased rapidly as a result. The financial sector was one that did not benefit from this economic recovery, an imbalance which would become more pronounced in 1986 when inflation decreased and thus made financial speculations less attractive. However with the increase in the wage mass, more workers were purchasing consumer durables and this, in turn, was stimulating the capital goods sector. As one report notes: 'Makers of "off-the-shelf" capital goods, such as standard machine tools, have a two-year backlog of orders from manufacturers of consumer products who are scrambling to expand their output'.[12] However, producers began to hold back and stopped deliveries of components, and, most importantly, agricultural producers began to limit the amount of foodstuffs going to the cities. There were calls for Sarney 'to dampen the consumer binge'. In reality, firms were taking advantage of the expansion of consumption to increase their profit margins, and thus inflation by the end of 1985 was reaching 300 per cent. The expansion of the real economy in 1985 was not matched by financial and fiscal reform: the huge fiscal deficit was matched by a rampant inflation, with the foreign debt, of course, looming in the background.

The period of economic uncertainty ended early in 1986 with the announcement of the *Plano Cruzado*. A new currency was created (the cruzado), prices were frozen and the system of 'indexation', which regulated inflation, was abolished. According to President Sarney: 'The government has promoted an extremely important economic change. . . . What we are changing is an inflationary mentality. We have a generation in Brazil that became accustomed to living under inflation. We are destroying that mentality'.[13] The aim was to provide a stable environment for sustained economic growth. Inflation began to decline, but the consumer boom actually intensified with the price freeze, rising real wages and the lower cost of consumer credit. Manufacturing's growth rates reached 11 per cent in 1986, the largest increase in the decade, but the production of capital goods and consumer durables was even more dynamic, with growth rates of over 20 per cent. Of course, by mid-1986, as was to be expected, 'numerous firms were circumventing the price freeze by introducing "new products" with higher prices or by charging black market premiums on top of official prices'.[14] In July 1986, the government acted to dampen consumption by introducing a new surcharge on gasoline, car sales and travel abroad. In November 1986, as the fiscal situation continued to deteriorate, the *Cruzado II* was introduced, which, in addition to further tax increases, authorized substantial price adjustments for the public and private sectors.

The reorientation of the Brazilian economy can be traced to the accession of Dilson Funaro as economy minister in mid-1985. Whereas the first economic team ranged from neo-Keynesianism to monetarism, Funaro appointed a group composed of the 'social development' school from Campinas and unorthodox neo-Keynesians from the Catholic University in Rio. As Paul Singer notes: 'After more than 21 years of authoritarianism, a part of the Brazilian left found itself once again in command of the political economy'.[15] As in Argentina, it seemed that socialists were better at running a capitalist economy than its own most fervent supporters, the monetarists. Their aim was to contain the public deficit without provoking a new recession, and to change the way the foreign debt was negotiated, which involved a rejection of the IMF's monitoring role. The economic stabilization measures implemented by the Funaro team can be divided into short-term measures of readjustment to combat inflation and overcome bottlenecks, and a more long-term project to restructure the Brazilian economy. As to the latter, Campinas school economists Ricardo Carneiro and José Carlos Miranda argue optimistically that: 'the political economy of the Nova República after September 1985 and, in particular after the stabilization Plan (*Plano de Estabilização*) can be considered as a policy of transition to a new pattern of economic development'.[16] In this new economic order, the basis of financial speculation would be eliminated as 'inertial inflation' (inflation caused by its sum inertia) was overcome.

It is sometimes risky to detect the 'underlying' social or political project behind this or that economic plan. Nevertheless, we should note that Funaro is a representative of the big São Paulo national industrial bourgeoisie. According to Paul Singer, a 'progressive' (*progressista*) industrialist, 'the developmentalist orientation became hegemonic in economic policy, thus breaking the paralysis which had hitherto characterized government action'.[17] The break with the International Monetary Fund's monitoring role, though not of immediate impact, was a significant political move. Apart from anything else, this deprived the Brazilian monetarists of crucial foreign backing. The stress on national development policies fitted well with Funaro's social base in the São Paulo bourgeoisie, which prided itself on the fact that their province was the second greatest industrial power in Latin

America, after Brazil. The greatest weakness in the Funaro team's economic policy was the lack of political mobilization behind it. As Singer writes: 'The wage earners and small and medium producers, which supposedly were its main beneficiaries, were not even aware that the government's economic policy had changed'.[18] The technocratic stance of this economic team was its ultimate downfall, because there was no mobilization when Funaro was forced to resign in May 1987. To confront monopoly capital a certain social backing is necessary, and, for example, on the question of price controls, factory committees could have been given a monitoring role, but Funaro's team had little contact with the unions.

It is important to note the significant and growing role of national capital in Brazil to dispel any lingering '*dependentista*' illusions about poor under-developed countries being manipulated by the multinationals and the IMF. In 1985, of the top 50 firms in Brazil, 24 were owned by national private capital (compared to 22 in 1984), 18 were owned by foreign private capital (compared to 20 in 1984), and the remaining eight firms were state-owned companies. If we examine the three types of company in terms of number of employees and profits earned (see Table 6.1), the dominance of the national sector is even more clear cut.

Table 6.1
Brazil: national, state and foreign companies 1985
(%)

	National private	State	Foreign private
Employees	44.7	36.3	19.0
Profits	70.2	loss	29.8
Taxes	40.9	17.1	42.0

Source: Exame No 358 (20 August 1986).

Thus national private firms employ nearly half the number of employees and earn nearly three quarters of the profits. The dynamism of Brazilian capitalists, nearly comparable to that of the 'bourgeoisie conquérante', which Karl Marx wrote about, sets them aside from their counterparts in Argentina where the financial/speculative sector is much stronger. Under the Nova República, companies producing for the internal market have thrived, and there has been a substantial degree of diversification.

Another aspect of Brazil's dynamic outlook is the economic agreement with Argentina in 1986, already mentioned in Chapter 5. Together with Uruguay, these two countries have a combined GNP more or less equivalent to that of the United Kingdom. It is not, however, an economic alliance among equals and Brazil is clearly the dominant partner. The discourse of Brazilian capitalism (as perceived on TV) stresses their civilizing role in the rest of Latin America, and their will to help 'underdeveloped' neighbours, such as Argentina. Whereas, in the 1970s, around 40 per cent of Brazil's exports to Argentina were manufactured goods, by the 1980s, these accounted for over 80 per cent. It is not necessary to revive the theories of Brazilian 'sub-imperialism' — which were rather impressionistic and based on dubious geo-political theories — to recognize that Brazil has become the major economic power in the southern cone. Brazil is now assured preferential access to Argentina's grain products into the 1990s, and will benefit from Argentina's more advanced knowledge in some areas, such as bio-technology. Whereas Argentina in the last decade has suffered a profound de-industrialization, the agreements with Brazil may (if fully implemented, because Argentina's business sectors fear they will become junior partners) lead to the strengthening of a state and private national industrial sector complementary to that of Brazil's south-east. This is undoubtedly a long-term economic development project which will greatly affect the prospects for democracy in the region.

In spite of Brazilian capitalism's undoubted dynamism, the economic prospects of the Nova República in 1987 were far from rosy. Despite the further austerity measures of the Cruzado II in late 1986, 'the economic situation became increasingly unsettled', according to the Inter-American Development Bank.[19] Interest rates had soared to over 400 per cent by the end of 1986, as inflationary expectations were fuelled by partial restoration of the 'indexation' monetary correction mechanisms, and by wage increases gained in struggle by industrial workers in early 1987. Thus, when the price freeze was essentially lifted, in February 1987, prices immediately rose by over one third. To cap it all, inflation was once again running at an annualized rate of about 400 per cent (reaching 1000 per cent in 1988 according to some estimates), which brought it back to pre-*Plano Cruzado* levels. With the promise of zero inflation completely overturned, real wages began to drop sharply, and in the course of 1987 had lost one-fifth of their purchasing power compared to 1986. The public deficit, one of the main concerns of the *Plano Cruzado*, continued to mount, and by the end of 1987 the accumulated internal debt reached a staggering US$70 bn. Whereas President Sarney had set a ceiling for the public deficit of 3.5 per cent of GDP, it nearly doubled that proportion in 1987. The underlying health of the Brazilian economy was overshadowed by the failure to stabilize the economy and inflation while sustaining high growth rates.

Turning now to the external sector, we need to assess firstly Brazil's relations with the International Monetary Fund. The decision by the Funaro economic team to break the clientilistic relationship with the IMF was an important move, but one taken cautiously. This was presented as a technical measure rather than a political confrontation with imperialism. There was no attempt to generalize Brazil's position or to move towards the formation of a debtors' cartel. Nevertheless, when Funaro met with the director-general of the IMF and the president of the US Federal Reserve in 1985, he presented three important non-negotiable parameters, which would set the terms of Brazil's relations with the international credit organizations:

1. the need for a long-term adjustment programme to overcome the Brazilian economy's structural disequilibriums;
2. that economic growth was a *sine qua non* condition for any external agreement; and

3. that domestic adjustment was an internal matter and would be confronted with measures in accordance with the country's socio-historical reality.[20]

Table 6.2
Economic indicators: Brazil growth rates (1982–87)

Production

(%)	1982	1983	1984	1985	1986	1987
Total GDP	0.9	−2.5	5.7	8.0	8.0	2.9
Agriculture	−1.9	1.8	3.2	8.4	−7.9	14.0
Manufacturing	−0.4	−6.1	6.1	8.3	11.3	1.0
Construction	−1.1	−14.1	2.5	11.3	17.7	−3.9

After the slump of 1982–83, Gross Domestic Product in Brazil recovered to practically the level of the economic boom years, apart from one bad year in agriculture due mainly to droughts.

Money, prices and salaries

(%)	1982	1983	1984	1985	1986	1987
Domestic credit	95.8	146.1	203.4	249.0	118.8	282.6
Money supply (M1)	65.0	97.4	201.9	304.3	306.7	133.3
Consumer prices	98.0	142.0	196.7	226.9	143.7	231.7
Real wages	0.5	−11.4	−14.8	12.2	0.1	−27.5

As in Argentina with the Plan Austral, the Plano Cruzado led to a squeezing of domestic credit for the private sector but not so severe; inflation did not reach the peaks of Argentina but nor did it decline so dramatically and the wage sector is seen to be the main loser except for 1985.

Foreign Sector

	1982	1983	1984	1985	1986	1987
Current account balance (US$m)	−15,388	−6,798	55	−335	−4,476	−1,439
Terms of trade (1980:100)	80.3	78.0	86.0	84.0	96.0	92.0
Interest on external debt/ export of goods and services (%)	53.7	43.4	39.5	40.3	41.4	21.7

The current account balance only shows a surplus for 1984; but on the other hand the terms of trade have shown a slight reversion in Brazil's favour by 1986; and the ratio of interest paid in the foreign debt to export of goods and services continues to be high, excepting the low figure for 1987.

Source: Inter-American Development Bank, *Economic and Social Progress in Latin America. 1988 Report* (Washington. Inter-American Development Bank, 1988). p. 360.

As a result of this stance, Brazil suspended interest payments on medium- and long-term debts with commercial foreign banks early in 1987. At around this time, the new constitutional planning body was making radical gestures about the control of transnational corporations, and the government was standing firm against US pressure for Brazil to drop its new informatics law, which would allow the erection of a strong national computer industry, keeping US competition at bay.

However, when Dilson Funaro was replaced by Luiz Carlos Bresser Pereira as Finance Minister in May 1987, a series of retreats began on the Nova República's stance towards the IMF. While Ermirio de Moraes, 'businessman of the year' and ex-candidate for governorship of São Paulo, declared that 'the foreign debt issue is the most important economic issue in Brazil', the opinion among businessmen was that maintaining a moratorium on interest payments was not advisable, 'because this type of radical measure only serves to upset the international financial market', as one leading banker put it.[21] These fears reflected the drying-up of capital flows from abroad and the general difficulty of obtaining credit for imports or exports. Bresser Pereira did produce a radical debt conversion proposal, but was forced into a humiliating climbdown when US Treasury Secretary James Baker called the idea a 'non-starter'.[22] Brazilian business journals now called openly for an end to 'messianic postures' in debt negotiations, and the Nova República authorities seemed inclined to agree. By the end of the year, one international business review could comment that while worsening relations with Brazil's creditors had cost Dilson Funaro his job, his successor Bresser Pereira had 'managed to appease at least Brazil's creditors by starting to mend fences with the IMF'.[23] It would seem that, in terms of international financial relations, Sarney's Nova República had beaten an unseemly retreat.

Table 6.2 shows some basic statistical information that will provide some kind of quantitative picture to complement the largely qualitative analysis carried out above.

Social movements and democracy

Shortly before being promoted to President by the Electoral College, Tancredo Neves declared that:

> If there had not been a softening of the instruments of the '64 regime, we would have reached a social convulsion. The mobilization for *Diretas já* showed that. Those numerous masses did not come on to the streets only for direct elections. . . . It was a great movement for transformations and change.[24]

Indeed, it would be impossible to separate the political mobilizations of the transition period from protest against the rising cost of living, housing, transport, violence and all areas that pertained to the social condition of the people. That the political elite, in the person of Tancredo Neves, was aware of this reinforces our interpretation of the transition by transaction in Brazil as being intimately bound up with the progress of the mass struggle. We can say that the 1978–79 strikes in the São Paulo industrial heartlands speeded up liberalization and also radicalized it. In the ensuing tortuous and complex negotiations between the military and the political elite, sometimes mediated by the church, the definitive parameters of the transition process were set. It is noticeable that the 1980 strikes were far more severely repressed by the military government, suggesting to some observers that a deal had been made with 'civil society' based on re-democratization but with an agreement that labour militancy would not be tolerated during the transition period. In the event, large public strikes did decline in the run-up to the indirect electoral process.

After the big strikes of 1978–80 had imparted a definite social dimension to the debate on democratization, the new radical labour movement turned inwards towards the factory. Between 1980 and 1984 the number of long drawn out sectoral strikes declined dramatically but, as Margaret Keck explains: 'the strengthening of the links between the leadership and the base was reflected in 1984 in the considerable increase in factory strikes (of a total of 626 strikes, 500 were local)'.[25] This temporary lull in mass confrontations between labour and the state (as much as between labour and capital) cannot diminish the important role that the labour movement had achieved in the transition process. The workers in the most advanced posts of the 'economic miracle' — the auto plants — had helped forge a militant independent trade unionism practically for the first time in Brazil, and certainly for the first time on that scale. The active practice of workers' democracy through mass meetings, democratic decision-making and the accountability of leaders was a striking indictment of military despotism, and also showed up the shabby compromises of the politicians. In 1985, with the installation of the civilian government, labour would once again come to the fore with a wave of strikes that sought to make up the ground lost under the dictatorship to capitalist profits and control over the labour process. In the course of 1985 some 500 strikes, embracing most sectors of the working population, drove home labour's new found confidence and ability to have a major impact on the social and economic policies of the Nova República.

The new Minister for Labour, Almir Pazzianotto, a labour lawyer, was undoubtedly the most progressive figure in the first civilian cabinet. Among his early measures was an amnesty for all trade unionists removed from their positions by the military regime; he withdrew the ban on the formation of trade union centrals, proposed that workers should regulate trade union elections themselves, and announced a 100 per cent increase in the minimum wage. It appeared that the promised land, after the long trek through the desert of military rule, had finally appeared. Yet the ambitious plans for a 'social pact', which Pazzianotto proposed, soon foundered. His attempt to liberalize the corporatist labour laws inherited from the military were blocked by the dominant business interests in Congress. In particular, the move to narrow the ban on strikes in 'essential services' was seen as a quasi-syndicalist crime against the national interest. Essentially, in its first year in office, the civilian regime favoured labour more by omission than by deliberate reform. Repression against strikes declined noticeably compared to the last years of military rule, and Minister Pazzianotto refused to exercise his right to intervene in trade unions that were on strike, in spite of considerable pressure for him to do so. The government had deliberately called for a truce with labour in its first year to prevent any authoritarian backsliding. The labour movement took advantage of political decompression to achieve a substantial recomposition of wages and salaries in 1985.

The labour struggles that began in 1985 were not only concerned with recovering lost wages, but took up the essential issue of the working week, with a central unifying demand being its reduction from 48 to 40 hours. In the workplaces, working conditions were taken up, as were industrial safety and hygiene issues and work breaks. The social relations of domination at work were being placed in question by a series of imaginative and persistent worker initiatives. Some 280,000 metalworkers in the interior of São Paulo were out on strike as the media whipped up a popular frenzy, over Tancredo Neves' illness, that was designed to quell labour protest. The national strike by bank employees later in the year was extremely well organized, and received widespread popular support through an effective campaign which contrasted the earnings in this sector with the fabulous profits of the banks. Public transport workers — including rail, air and the urban underground — were joined by hospital workers and other professional sectors in strikes in May. Towards October 1985 there was another round of strikes, in the course of which the trade unions categorically rejected the government's proposed 'social pact', which was by now widely perceived as yet another means to get workers to pay for economic stabilization. With the 'economic shock' administered by the Plano Cruzado in 1986, the conflict between workers and the government was to intensify, as the latter began to weary of the honeymoon atmosphere of 1985.

In 1986, the economic situation deteriorated with inflation rising and a virtual strike of productive investment. In these unfavourable conditions — which included widespread popular support for the Plano Cruzado — labour militancy began to wane, and May Day was marked by an unprecedentedly poor turnout. A rail strike in April led to the government ordering the army to occupy the railway stations in a show of force. The army was again placed on a 'state of alert' by President Sarney in October, when the unions threatened a Day of Protest. When bank workers, health and welfare employees, the Santos dockers, and others went on strike, the government declared that these strikes were aimed at 'destabilizing the democratic government' (as already mentioned above). Following further austerity measures towards the end of the year, the two union centrals called a general strike for December 12, which was remarkably successful, even by the government's own accounts. In 1987, as negotiations for a social pact were once again initiated by the government, the 'iron fist' of strike militarization was also manifest as port workers and workers in the oil refineries were subject to armed forces intervention. A further general strike in August 1987 was not as successful as the first, virtually failing in São

Paulo, but it still mobilized some 12 million workers. In a political culture that shuns open conflict for compromise and dissimulation, Brazilian workers had imposed the generalized practice of collective bargaining and had, if with ups and downs, punctuated the democratization process with their actions. This verdict was confirmed by a 48-hour general strike early in 1989, which, according to the unions, was 'the most successful strike ever', even though the employers claimed that only one-third of the workforce came out. For the first time, the sugar cane cutters of the north-east joined their urban colleagues in the big cities of the south-east in the strike action against government economic policies.

The labour movement was to a considerable extent weakened by its internal divisions. There were two major union centrals: the CUT (Central Unica dos Trabalhadores), formed in 1983, and CONCLAT (Coordenação Nacional da Classe Trabalhadora), which became the CGT (Central Geral dos Trabal-hadores) in 1986. The CUT represented the radical labour strand exemplified by the São Paulo autoworkers, and, although still not in the majority, has been responsible for the major mass mobilizations of this period, including of sectors not under its control. CONCLAT, on the other hand, represents an alliance between the old-style *pelego* (state dominated) unionists and the communist parties (both Moscow- and Peking-oriented). Though on paper the majority organization, CONCLAT, has been characterized by its relative quietism, the formation of the CGT represented a tactical turn towards militancy, as it became concerned that it was being outflanked by the pro-CUT forces. This new militant discourse has led to a certain resurgence of inner union democracy in the old established unions. CONCLAT was at first more inclined to accept the government offer of a 'social pact', but it eventually joined the CUT in rejecting it with the jointly organized 1986 general strike. The new class struggle unionism in Brazil recalls a similar wave of militancy in Argentina a decade earlier, between 1969 and 1974. It has brought workers centre stage for the first time in Brazil under their own leadership rather than that of a populist saviour.

The most significant political development in the labour field in recent years was undoubtedly the formation of the Partido dos Trabalhadores (Workers' Party) in 1980. In a dialectical process, the auto workers' strikes of 1978–79 led their most combative leaders to form a specifically workers' party hitherto lacking in Brazil's populist political spectrum, with the exception of the small and sectarian Communist Party. Subsequently, this party was to help create unions in areas not organized, and launched important strike movements. The PT would organize trade union gatherings (*encontros sindicais*) in weakly organized or bureaucratic trade unions from which would spring internal opposition tendencies and factory level committees. As well, the PT was active in a whole series of social movements beyond the factory, in neighbourhood movements, the Black Movement, the women's movement and others, thus serving as a bridgehead between labour and the so-called new social movements. From the start, the PT defined itself as a class party, against the cross-class 'popular' parties. This has led some of its critics to accuse it of 'workerism', due to which, according to Emir Sader,

> The complex concrete reality of Brazilian capitalist society tends to be conjured away into a rhetorically abstract duel of workers and bourgeois, in which all other strata of phenomena are bundled off-stage into a trunk of useless bric-a-brac with 'petty bourgeois' on the lid.[26]

This may be so, but with a dominant political discourse that privileges the nation, the common good and an abstract *'povo'*, it was something quite new to find a party based firmly on the working class and committed explicitly to socialism through the class struggle.

The achievements of the PT in its relatively brief history are considerable. In the 1982 elections, its showing was disappointing to some, with 3 per cent of the national vote and only eight federal deputies. With the more favourable climate of the Nova República, where the PT gained from being seen clearly as an opposition party, the 1985 mayoral elections in the state capitals proved a breakthrough. The PT achieved a national average of 11 per cent of the poll (1,500,000 votes approximately), electing a woman as its mayor in Fortaleza and gaining 20 per cent of the vote in São Paulo (already mentioned above). The 1986 elections for the Constituent Assembly saw the party make further gains, with 3,300,000 votes in its favour (even if this only averaged out at 5.7 per cent of the vote), thereby doubling its number of deputies in Congress to 16. Party chair, Luis Ignacio da Silva, better known as 'Lula', achieved the distinction of being the highest voted congress representative, with 652,000 votes. Claiming a membership of 200,000 (of which over half are concentrated in São Paulo), the PT reaches an audience over and above its electoral representation through its involvement in a myriad of social movements, including a small but potentially significant breakthrough into the peasant movement. The PT has truly given political expression to the social movements in Brazil. In the November 1988 municipal elections the PT won control over the key industrial centre of São Paulo, three other state capitals and a number of smaller towns. Together with the populist movement of Leonel Brizola, the PT now controlled a sizeable proportion of the urban vote and became a credible challenger for state power.

There are, nevertheless, pertinent criticisms that can be directed at the PT. The party is essentially heterogeneous, with its original nucleus of trade union leaders and activists, being joined by church-linked groups and various Trotskyist and Maoist groupuscules. This leads to a somewhat turbulent inner party life, even though all tendencies claim to fight for the PT. In political terms, the party seems to oscillate between a rather 'maximalist' strategy and occasionally 'opportunist' tactics. Its socialism is ill defined, being seen more in negative terms as not Swedish social democracy and not Soviet state socialism. Party intellectuals have often been influenced by Foucault and other French theorists of power and desire, which leads to a generalized rejection of power. This gave it great vitality under the dictatorship, but it makes difficult a concrete political practice. (The problems of the German Greens may not be irrelevant in this respect.) As to the question of democracy, as Plinio de Arruda

Sanpaio expresses the party position: 'The PT criticizes the formal character of a democracy which contemplates exclusively representative mechanisms and makes them operate in a concrete context of extreme economic inequalities'.[27] Here we find the classic contraposition between 'formal' and 'real' democracy (see Chapter 1), which leads the PT to characterize the Nova República as simply an 'illegitimate government'. Not surprisingly, while the trade union work of the PT has continued to expand apace, its political presence is more muted and it is, indeed, suffering something of a political crisis.

Whereas urban workers had undoubtedly become the central contingent of the Brazilian labour movement, developments in the countryside were no less dramatic. Indeed, one of the most massive mobilizations on the eve of the Nova República was that by the rural workers of the interior of São Paulo and other states. In São Paulo, the movement reached some 100,000 temporary sugar cane workers and had a great political impact. The rural wage workers had been organizing actively in 1984, with prolonged and violent struggles in all the main regions. However, their very mobility, instability of employment, and the sheer misery of their situation made organization difficult. As Ricardo Abramovay writes: 'It was in the struggle for land that the Brazilian agrarian question would show its most dramatic and contradictory facet'.[28] From 1981 onwards, the movement of Workers Without Land (*Trabalhadores Sem Terra*) spread from its base in the state of Pará, largely through the efforts of church militants. Alongside the traditional land occupations, this movement practised the novel tactic of camping (*acampamentos*) on the side of the road after being expelled — usually violently — from occupied land, as a mute and permanent call for agrarian reform. The dictatorship had militarized the agrarian question in the Amazon region and elsewhere, making land struggles into a question of 'national security'. The incoming civilian regime promised a far-reaching and comprehensive agrarian reform to settle the countryside peacefully.

The newly created Ministry of Agrarian Reform declared that the Nova República would implement the 1964 *Estatuto da Terra* (Land Law), which the military regime had never put into practice. This was welcomed by all the rural organizations that spoke for the landless, the smallholders and wage workers. Significantly, the proposal was actually launched by President Sarney at the Fourth National Congress of Rural Workers held in Brasília, before thousands of rural workers. In the event, agrarian reform legislation was watered down in congress, as had occurred with the industrial relations law. The reformist discourse and the populist posturing was coming up against the hard reality of Brazil's powerful, conservative and ruthless landowners. Contrary to widespread opinion on the left, agrarian reform was not indispensable for capitalist development in Brazil — as the years of the 'economic miracle' had adequately demonstrated — and now, once again, it was to be sacrificed in the interests of expediency. The government's claim that resources were lacking, or that agrarian reform could not be accomplished 'overnight', could not mask a grievous retreat by the new democratic authorities on this issue. There was even a quite remarkable conflict between the new government and the Catholic Church, which was virtually accused of fomenting rural discontent, when it refused simply to accept the government's failure to implement the promised and legislated agrarian reform.

The struggle for democracy in Brazil is quite inseparable from a democratic resolution of the agrarian question. Class conflict in the countryside has intensified to such a peak that hundreds of rural workers are killed every year by a militant and armed landowning aristocracy. The possibilities for military intervention multiply, and the failure to carry out agrarian reform threatens the whole democratization process. Tragically, the forces, in favour of agrarian reform have not been able to unite the Movimento dos Sem Terra (Landless Movement) with the rural workers' union, Contag (Confederação Nacional dos Trabalhadores na Agricultura), which is linked to the reformist urban unions. As Abramovay notes, these two sectors 'were not able to overcome their differences to establish unity of action in defence of agrarian reform. The proposal [for agrarian reform], instead of fomenting and provoking an advance in the struggle of rural workers, led to its nearly complete paralysis'.[29] Land occupation virtually ceased with the government's announcement of agrarian reform, and was not replaced by other forms of struggle, precisely when landowners were mounting an astute mobilization against it. The rural movement was not able, either, adequately to sensitize urban public opinion to the issue. The general approval of the government's plan in the countryside — in spite of its limitations and contradictions — was simply not matched by the level of mass pressure that could have forced their implementation and taken the struggle for democracy significantly forward.

The New Republic

The manner of a political regime's emergence will have a major influence on its composition, its policies and, ultimately, its prospects. Brazil's *distensão* or liberalization was initiated by the incumbent military regime, but its outcome was determined by a combination of this initiative and the actions of the social and political opposition to military rule. A useful characterization of this process is 'transition through transaction'. Share and Mainwaring develop this concept through a comparative study of Brazil and Spain:

> The term 'transaction' connotes negotiation (usually implicit) between elites of the authoritarian regime and the democratic opposition. But this negotiation does not take place among equals; the regime takes the initiative in beginning liberalization, and during most of the process it remains in a position to significantly influence the course of political change.[30]

The authors add the caveat, however, that the opposition can win significant victories in this process and thus redefine the political struggle. Certainly this is what occurred in Brazil, because the Figueiredo regime had become worse than a 'lame duck' administration by the end: Ronald Schneider describes it as a 'comatose paraplegic duck'.[31] Nevertheless, we must distinguish transition through transaction from transition through collapse, as occurred in

Argentina. Brazil was launched on a path of conservative modernization within a more democratic framework; this was not a 'democratic revolution', and its limits were apparent in all fields of social and political life.

Transition through transaction, to be successful, has certain requirements. The left must be excluded from the electoral process, although in Brazil the Communist Party and other leftist formations were able to operate within the broad opposition front, the PMDB. A certain level of continuity in economic affairs must be guaranteed by the incoming civilian regime, as indeed has proved to be the case in Brazil. Above all, the military must be provided with guarantees against *revanchism* or any accountability for their human rights crimes. Political continuity itself existed in Brazil in so far as the 'permanent temporary' President Sarney had been leader of the military regime's political wing. As Share and Mainwaring note:

> Continuity is also manifested in the fact that the legitimacy of the authoritarian period is not attacked retrospectively. In transitions through transaction, the democratic leaders are unlikely to assail the policies, symbols and leaders of the authoritarian regime.[32]

Indeed, in 1987 ex-President Figueiredo could offer his services to the nation once again to save the country from chaos, without appearing totally ridiculous. In Argentina, in spite of all the hesitations and retreats on the question of military trials, the leaders of the military juntas remain in prison. In transition through collapse of the military regime, the armed forces do not have the legitimacy they undoubtedly retain in wide sectors of the population in Brazil. Transaction involves continuity, compromise by the opposition, but also an undoubted, if relative, stability.

The major structures of the state remain intact in Brazil, with even the notorious national security doctrine remaining in abeyance but not explicitly repudiated. A text by Senator F. H. Cardoso is illuminating in this respect. The context is set by the shift in the dominant Latin American social science paradigm from the forms of authoritarianism to the institutionalization of democracy. Cardoso finds that in post-authoritarian Brazil,

> Thomas Skidmore who tried to see in the military regime a reformed continuity (*continuismo*) with the old statist tendency (á la Vargas) would be delighted, if he maintained the same perspective, to verify that now, in the Nova República, the old tendencies persist. And Philippe Schmitter, with his state corporatism, would have to reelaborate the concept to allow for this contortionism through which the state continues to have primacy over society, but does not foment corporatism.[33]

The recomposition of the political system in Brazil has, effectively, been carried out under the aegis of a state whose administrative and command structures remain unchanged from the military regime. The problem, as Cardoso argues, is that there is insufficient debate on how democracy can be effectively institutionalized in a society such as Brazil's. Hitherto the main guiding idea has been that 'the people' (*o povo*) is sovereign, and is the guarantee for a democratic political order. This can, as we saw above, result in populism. What is necessary is much more concrete debate on the actual institutional structures and procedures required by democracy, and in this the constituent congress with its deliberations has a role to play. The new Brazilian constitution, promulgated in 1988, in spite of its 'progressive' tone, ratified the continued role of the military in politics, through a re-formed national security council and their ability to restrict the newly acquired right of access to information held by the intelligence apparatus (*habeas data*).

It can of course be argued that all the major political forces, including its more radical representatives such as Senator Cardoso, are simply institutionalizing the subordination of the dominated classes. The PT (Workers' Party), for example, as Rui Falcão explains,

> identifies in the struggles of the popular and the trade union movements the motive force for democratization of the country and to provide workers with social and political rights, while the ideologues of the 'Nova República', above all those of the PMDB, in practice transfer this role to the State.[34]

This is the classic contraposition of reform and revolution, concessions gained or concessions granted. Everyone recognizes the weakness of civil society compared to the state in Brazil. But the state in Brazil today is not occupied by active right-wing ideologues: it is a site of struggle between various competing ideologies, including, let it be said, democratic socialist tendencies. Democratization in Brazil occurred through a mixture of concession from above and struggle from below. The institutionalization of democracy in Brazil is occurring also on many levels and through various means, including of course popular 'social' struggles, but also at the institutional 'political' level. The abstentionist attitude taken by sectors of the left towards the constituent assembly — because the transition through transaction could only mean that a conservative constitution could emerge — is not an adequate answer to the limitations of the Nova República.

Another area relatively neglected both by the advocates of judicious reform by the state, and by the believers in a true 'popular will', is the continued authoritarianism of everyday life. The prohibition by the 'progressive' Ministry of Culture of Jean Luc Godard's film, *Jé vous salue, Marie!*, was but one indicator that cultural liberalism had its limits. For most people, however, it is the repressive action of the police which represents the *continuismo* of the military regime's repressive practices. In São Paulo alone, the police killed 580 people in Year One of the Nova República, compared to 480 in 1984. Furthermore, whereas in 'ordinary' wars the proportion of injured to dead is around 10 to 1, in this particular urban war we find that the number of injured is only half that of those killed, suggesting a deliberate 'shoot to kill' policy. Emir Sader also notes that 'If political torture no longer exists, torture continues to be the rule in police procedures . . . this fact being known and tolerated by the rest of society'.[35] The barbaric conditions in Brazilian jails have achieved international notoriety through various revolts and the desperate practice of inmates killing each other to draw attention to their plight. Some initiatives in prison reform, particularly as it pertains to minors, were taken, but the conservative press and politicians such as Janio Quadros and his appeal to 'law and order' instincts forced a retreat on this front. The popular 'joke' about 'democratic head-breakers' bears witness to the oppressive presence of the police in the daily life of the Nova República.

In the preface to this book I referred to the driving habits of the 'new democracies' as an example of the micro-authoritarianism that still permeates these societies. João Quartim, leader of one of the armed struggle groups of 1968–69, reflects on this issue in a witty article entitled: 'The difficulty of being a democrat — on the road [in English in the original]'.[36] During his exile in Europe, Quartim was not scared to cross the road; now, back in Brazil, he was terrified. Certainly the people (*o povo*) are as uncivil as the bourgeoisie, but as it is the latter which holds power it behoves them to democratize this pretty major area of social life. Quartim argues that:

> Our people, looked down on and assaulted, do not even dispose of the right to cross the street with a minimum of security as they can neither work with a minimum of security: it cannot be coincidence that the world records of work accidents and traffic accidents were won by Brazil under the dictatorship of the generals . . .[37]

For twenty years the dominant classes, in an unbridled process of capitalist expansion, disregarded the rights and sensitivities of the oppressed. The authoritarianism of the elites has percolated to all areas and levels of society, and the Nova República still exudes authoritarianism in its attempts to reform the naked rule of capital, in which the mass media, in particular television, play a significant part in encouraging a passive role for the majority.

At a macro-political level we note a continutiy with the chauvinist discourse of the military, one of whose popular slogans was: '*Brasil: Ame-o ou deije-o!*' (Brazil: love it or leave it!). When the Plano Cruzado was implemented in 1986, the words of politicians and press alike revealed this tendency to confuse the nation with particular groups. Thus São Paulo Governor Franco Montoro declared: 'The package ended with the movement for direct elections (*Diretas já*) in 1987 made workers desist from possible strikes and strengthened the president of the Republic, and, in consequence, the whole nation (*toda a nação*)'.[38] The press reiterated that it was everybody's patriotic duty to support the austerity measures and to believe in their success. The *Jornal do Brasil* was even able to recreate the menace of subversion:

> Nothing would be more illegitimate to counterpose the interest of minorities to the common interest, as insignificant and isolated radical residuals are attempting initiatives to spread chaos . . . act of treason towards democracy. (Sarney) is the supreme commander: everything which injures his authority also hits the nation. The nation will stigmatize as bad Brasilians (*mau brasileiros*) and traitors all those who, because of personal or political

ambition, do not comprehend the greatness of the moment . . . they will not be forgiven.[39]

In this particular transition through transaction, the new authorities had created a particular social pact in which, in the words of Communist Party deputy Alberto Goldman, 'the government made a pact without pacting'.[40]

Legitimacy in the Nova República does not spring from direct elections and thus must be sought elsewhere. The sacrifice of Tancredo Neves, carefully orchestrated, was one means of establishing this legitimacy. For José Sarney it was not simple, as his position was so compromised with the *ancien regime*. Sarney has reiterated the 'big Brazil' theme of the military, and that 'Brazil is the world's eighth economic power', and that as regards foreign policy: 'We must have a policy compatible with the size of Brazil and the defence of our interests. We are not prisoners of any great power . . .'[41] The nationalist strand of Sarney's discourse is matched by his constant appeal to 'the people' (*o povo*). That is how he explains how a 'president by accident' could retain his position and act as though he were the natural incumbent. He tells us how:

The difficulty was that of a man who is advised at 3 o'clock in the morning that he is going to assume the Presidency at 9 o'clock . . . The Brazilian people realized my difficulty and were disposed to help me. The people understood, and this was a great test of maturity: there stands a man who must be helped. That was the great thing.[42]

It was hardly the Brazilian *povo* who decided that Sarney should remain in office; rather, it was the result of delicate negotiations between the political elites and the military. But the point is that Sarney sees it necessary to construct a semi-mythical popular interlocutor to justify his role in politics.

The return of populism to the Nova República went beyond the born-again fervour of the nationalist discourse. Janio Quadros epitomized the pre-1964 pattern of Brazilian populism, and over twenty years later he was recreating that politics. As Mayor of São Paulo, Quadros deployed assiduously his symbol of a brush, and his slogan '*E hora de trabalhar*' (it is time to work) appeared on the walls of the city. An analysis of those who voted for Quadros showed that they were on the whole older and less educated than the PMDB and PT voters.[43] Furthermore, a survey showed that whereas three quarters of those voting for them knew that F. H. Cardoso and E. Suplicy stood for the PMDB and PT respectively, only one third of Quadros's electorate knew that he stood for the PTB. This reinforces the conclusion that Quadros gained a personalist vote reminiscent of the populist era. The 'respectable poor' were attracted to his message of a hard line against urban crime, and his view that work was there for those who sought. His very 'anti-politics' image as an austere family man of unbending honesty also attracted those disenchanted with the reality of opposition government in São Paulo state since 1982. For Bolivar Lamounier, the victory of Quadros raised a question mark over the opposition's faith in the people's ability to vote — a rationalist reversal of the right's view that '*o povo não sabe votar*' (the people do not know how to vote) —

and notes how the decomposition of the political parties has followed on from the enthusiasm of the *Direitas já* campaign in 1984.[44]

Populism in the 1960s had blended nationalism, economic developmentalism, and a vague radicalism under the leadership of a charismatic leader. At one and the same time it represented an upsurge of the dominated classes, who 'participated' in politics for the first time, while also co-opting and imposing a state tutelage over the masses. In the 1980s, populism had acquired a social democratic veneer as in the discourse of Brizola, although even he saved his most vehement attacks for the 'liberals' of the PMDB. Liberalism was, of course, always the main enemy for populism, which redefined democracy in its own authoritarian image. Populism, as we saw in the case of Quadros, tends to disintegrate the political parties. From the start of the Nova República, President Sarney's message was directed to the people above the political parties. This mesage found its medium for the 1980s in television, which did not speak for this or that political party, but for the whole nation. As critic Flavio Koutzii expresses it: 'What better discourse than this, which suppresses the parties, does away with social differences and bases all reality on a homogeneous block which sets up . . . a culture of homogeneity in this country of terrible inequalities?'[45] Populism had always stressed the 'common good' over and above social distinctions, and the whole vocabulary of social class was alien to it. Now, once again, populism was short-circuiting the existence of contradictory realities, and generated a grossly simplified image of society and political practice.

The Nova República came into being without direct presidential elections, and its first president came into the post by accident. It is the social and political isolation of José Sarney which explains many of the particularities of the regime. The government achieved widespread popular appeal at first simply because it was replacing a by now discredited military regime. Sarney even achieved considerable popularity at first with his austerity measures, as people became *'fiscais do Sarney'* (Sarney's officials), checking up on shop prices. But none of this could alter the fact that Sarney had no significant social or political base of his own. This isolation was aggravated by the electoral results of 1985, 1986 and 1988 which saw an advance of the opposition parties, particularly by Brizola and the Workers' Party (PT), followed by the unexpected resurgence of the movement for direct elections (*Diretas já*) for president. Even the successes of the senior government party, the PMDB, were a mixed blessing for Sarney, who was not a member of that party and could only with difficulty bask in its reflected glory. In the heart of government itself was a fatal lack of political and ideological homogeneity, which conspired against the consistent and principled application of policies. The Plano Cruzado owes its arising as much to Sarney's bid to conquer an element of hegemony over his own government by, once again, going over the head of political parties to the people, as it does to economic necessity.

Until the Plano Cruzado, a bold political as well as economic move, the Sarney government was plagued by an image of indecisiveness and general paralysis. This, in turn, led to the deterioration of the president's political prestige and authority within his own government, not to mention the country at large. The way in which he regained popularity, with the economic package that promised 'zero inflation', leads Newtown Rodrigues to question the 'disquieting political lacking, the anxious and resuscitated search for messiahs and miracles'.[46] The emotion surrounding the death of Tancredo Neves was once again revived, if in another cause, but it would prove just as ephemeral. The lack of solid democratic institutions, even prior to 1964, was leading the inevitable post-dictatorial upheavals in unpredictable directions. It is significant that the Plano Cruzado was implemented by the device of the presidential-decree law, inherited from the military regime, and which Sarney had promised not to utilize. It is significant that among the mandarins of Brasília a popular saying is that 'a conservative ministry is necessary to promote reforms in Brazil'.[47] In conclusion, we can say that the Nova República is a form of conservative modernization, distinct from the military regime, obviously, in its neo-populism with a social democratic flavour, but carrying on, in its fundamentals, a lucid bourgeois project of modernization.

Notes

1. See J. Myer 'A crown of thorns: Cardoso and counter-revolution', *Latin American Perspectives*, Vol. 11, No. 1, 1975.

2. R. Packenham, 'The Changing Political Discourse in Brazil, 1964–1985' in W. Selcher (ed.), *Political Liberalization in Brazil* (Boulder, Westview Press, 1986) p. 146.

3. Ibid.

4. W. Selcher, 'Contradictions, Dilemmas, and Factors in Brazil's *Abertura*, 1979–1985', in W. Selcher (ed.), *Political Liberalization in Brazil*, p. 67.

5. Cited in 'Dezoito Meses do' L. C. Guimaraes and M. Carqueira, 'O Governo Brizola a Procura da Identidade', *Novos Estudos*, No. 10, 1984, p. 15.

6. Ibid, p. 17.

7. 'Neves outlines his policies', *Latin America Weekly Report*, 18 January 1985, p. 2.

8. Ibid.

9. 'A talk with President Sarney', *Business Week*, 11 August 1986, p. 33.

10. 'The Boom in Brazil', *Business Week*, 11 August 1986, p. 30.

11. 'A talk with President Sarney', p. 33.

12. 'The boom in Brazil', p. 32.

13. 'A talk with President Sarney', p. 33.

14. Inter-American Development Bank, *Economic and Social Progress in Latin America, 1987 Report* (Washington, Inter-American Development Bank, 1987), p. 249.

15. P. Singer, 'Os impasses economicos da Nova Republica', in F. Koutzii (ed.) *Nova Republica: um balanco* (São Paulo, L & PM Editores, 1986), p. 102.

16. R. Carneiro and J. C. Miranda, 'Os Marcos Gerais da Politica Economica', in R. Carneiro (ed.), *Political Economica da Nova Republica* (São Paulo, Paz e Terra, 1986), p. 25.

17. P. Singer, 'Os impasses economicos da Nova Republica', p. 89.

18. Ibid, p. 101.

19. Inter-American Development Bank, *Economic and Social Progress in Latin America*, p. 249.

20. P. de Arruda Sampaio Junior e R. Alfonso, 'A transição inconclusa', in F. Koutzii (ed.), *Nova Republica*, p. 73.

21. Cited in 'Business, military back Pereira', *Latin America Weekly Report*, 15 October 1987, p. 10.
22. Cited in 'Bresser Pereira might have to go', *Latin America Weekly Report*, 24 September 1987, p. 7.
23. 'Sarney founders as economy worsens', *Latin America Weekly Report*, 24 December 1987, p. 5.
24.'A versão Tancredo', *Lua Nova*, Vol. 1, No. 2, 1984, p. 11.
25. M. Keck, 'El nuevo sindicalismo en la transicion de Brazil', *Estudios Sociologicos* Vol. 5, No. 13, 1987, p. 60.
26. E. Sader, 'The Workers' Party in Brazil', *New Left Review* No. 165, 1987, p. 97.
27. P. de Arruda Sampaio, 'O PT na encruzienada', E. Sader (ed.), *E Agura PT?* (São Paulo, Editora Brasiliense, 1986), p. 123.
28. R. Abramovay, 'O velho poder dos parves da terra', in F. Koutzii (ed.), *Nova República*, p. 212.
29. Ibid, p. 221.
30. D. Share and S. Mainwaring, 'Transitions through Transaction: Democratization in Brazil and Spain', in W. Selcher (ed.), *Political Liberalization in Brazil*, p. 175.
31. R. Schneider, 'Brazil's Political Future', in W. Selcher (ed.), *Political Liberalization in Brazil*, p. 244.
32. D. Share and S. Mainwaring, 'Transitions Through Transaction', p. 183.
33. Senator F. H. Cardoso, 'Transição para a Democracia: O Modelo Politico'. Institucional, no date, p. 6.
34. R. Falcão, 'A Republica que fez plastica', in F. Koutzii (ed.), *Nova República*, p. 37.
35. E. Sader, 'Povo, policia e direitos do cidadao', in F. Koutzii (ed.), *Nova República*, p. 200.
36. J. Quartim de Moraes, 'A dificultade de ser democrata — on the road', *Presença*, No. 6, 1985.
37. Ibid, pp. 60–1.
38. Cited in R. Morais, 'Cardapio trabalhista de Nova República', in F. Koutzii (ed.), *Nova República*, p. 245.
39. Ibid, p. 345.
40. Ibid, p. 246.
41. 'A talk with President Sarney', p. 33.
42. Ibid.
43. B. Lamounier and J. Muszynski, *A eleição de Janio Quadros*, Textos IDESP, No. 16, 1986.
44. Ibid.
45. F. Koutzii, 'Por tras das antenas platenadas', in F. Koutzii (ed.), *Nova República*, p. 109.
46. N. Rodrigues, 'Uma nova estagnação institucional', in F. Koutzii (ed.), *Nova República*, p. 15.
47. Ibid, p. 43.

7. Uruguay Under Sanguinetti

The transition to democracy in Uruguay stands, analytically, between the cases of Argentina and Brazil described in the chapters above. It was a transition through transaction as in Brazil, but the military regime of Uruguay lacked the solid record of its Brazilian counterparts and rapidly sought only a dignified retreat from power. In this respect there was a similarity to, and, indeed, a significant influence from Argentina even though, of course, the Uruguayan military were not defeated in a foreign war. The liberalization of the military dictatorship in Uruguay came about largely from an exhaustion of the military project rather than any marked reactivation of civil society, although this did occur once the regime began to liberalize. A significant landmark was the 1980 plebiscite organized by the military to sanction a new constitution, following the initiative of their colleague Pinochet in Chile. Unfortunately for them, the electorate rejected this move to institutionalize the regime and thus the transition dynamic was unleashed. This dynamic, however, had no predestined conclusion, and the nature of democratization was to depend essentially on the role of Uruguay's old and solidly implanted political parties, as well as the social movements which, in part independently, began struggling for democracy. The new democracy that was to emerge in Uruguay in 1985 has exhibited a considerable degree of political continuity with the pre-dictatorial regime (unlike the case of Argentina), but the military appear to have decisively bowed out of the political and economic arenas (unlike the case of Brazil).

Pacts and transition

Following the democratic response of the electorate to the military's constitutional referendum of 1980, a series of negotiations began with the leaders of the traditional parties. This meant fundamentally the *Blancos* and *Colorados*, the two multi-class formations that between them usually attracted over three-quarters of the electorate. The first move in the military state's liberalization dynamic was to normalize the political party structures and personnel to produce valid interlocutors, who could mediate between the dictatorship and the people. Though the parties themselves appeared weak, and unable to take advantage of the 57 per cent vote against the 1980 military constitution, a vigorous opposition press emerged, committed to hastening the transition to democracy. In the forefront was *La Democracia*, aligned with the charismatic and now leftist leaning *Blanco* leader, Wilson Ferreira. When polls were held in December 1982 to elect party conventions (in Uruguay the whole electorate can vote in primary elections), the internal candidates most firmly opposed to the dictatorship came to the fore. For the *Blancos*, Wilson Ferreira became the undisputed leader, and in the *Colorados*, ex-president Pacheco Areco suffered an ignominious defeat, with figures such as Julio Sanguinetti and Enrique Tarigo, who had spearheaded the 1980 'no' campaign, receiving most support. As in 1980, the elections of 1982 served as a plebiscite for or against the dictatorship, with an overwhelming majority (at least 80 per cent) against any form of '*democradura*' (strong democracy) or any other form of disguised military continuity.

In 1983, with the party conventions in place and party executives in turn having been elected, negotiations could begin in earnest with the military rulers, who now sought only to extricate themselves with some degree of security. The future of the 1,500 political prisoners held in the jails of the dictatorship had not been an issue in the primary elections, and thus the traditional political leaders appeared to be adopting an accommodationist stand. Interior Minister General Trinidad reinforced this caution when he warned in April that the transition to democracy could be endangered if the parties 'failed to act and speak with reason and moderation' or insisted on dwelling on the past.[1] If the political leaders were willing to avoid 'maximalism', to engage in O'Donnell's 'safe transition' model with the regime '*blandos*' (soft liners), the popular movement was not so accommodating. For May Day 1983, a new labour co-ordinating body, the PIT (*Pelenario Intersindical de Trabajadores* — Workers' Inter-union Plenary), organized a rally in Montevideo, which brought 100,000 people out in the streets. To the chant of the Chilean slogan '*El pueblo unido jamás sera vencido*' (The people united shall never be defeated), trade unionists, political leaders, and, significantly for the first time from a public platform, relatives of the political prisoners, called in unison for an immediate return to democracy. Shortly afterwards, formal talks between COMASPO, the Armed Forces Political Affairs Commission, and the political leaders began at the Parque Hotel in Montevideo.

The Parque Hotel negotiations did not come to fruition, however. The military insisted that Cosena, the National Security Council, should be inscribed in the new constitution, and that this condition was non-negotiable. The military also wanted to retain the sole right to declare a 'state of emergency', and insisted that military courts should try 'subversion' cases. In June 1983, the talks were suspended owing to the death of Interior Minister General Trinidad, their main instigator on the military side (which was far from united in its approach). When talks were renewed, the political parties decided to walk out, as negotiation seemed paralysed. A student demonstration had been violently repressed and over one hundred arrests were made. In August, an opposition rally was banned and press censorship reintroduced. The military threatened to rewrite the constitution without the co-operation of the political parties, in their bid to create a 'protected democracy' in keeping with their aspirations. In response, the parties of the left began to organize Chilean-style 'days of protest' to shake the dictatorship from its complacent position. These began modestly with people staying indoors for half an hour at a set time with all lights off. The union central, PIT, for its part, organized a series of ten-minute stoppages in September. This social and political opposition culminated in an 80,000 strong march in Montevideo on 26 September, organized by the main political parties and the trade unions, followed by a *caceroleo* (banging of pots and pans) in the evening.

Popular pressure for democratization mounted with a third day of protest in October 1983, in which thousands of workers in Montevideo converged on strategic points, calling for a return to democracy. Informal talks between the military and the political leaders began shortly afterwards, and Vegh Villegas, the main civilian economist under military rule (see Chapter 3), was returned to office with the role of bridging the gap between the military state and civil society. The victory of Raúl Alfonsín in the elections across the River Plate led to spontaneous celebratory demonstrations in Montevideo. Then, on 27 November, some 400,000 people rallied in Montevideo on what was the 12th anniversary of the last time elections were held. If the provincial demonstrations are included it is estimated that nearly half the electorate of Uruguay was out in the streets on that occasion. A sign of the times was that, towards the end of the year, the landowners of the *Federación Rural* (Rural Federation) declared that it was time for democracy to be reinstated, if only because they were clearly concerned at the growth of social and political tensions. As 1984 began, the military regime was clearly in disarray, and General Alvarez had few options, even though he had called for the formation of a new political party which could carry on the work of the military regime in the new democratic era. Pressure from below and negotiations by an astute and representative political elite were between them pushing the military regime into a corner.

1984 began with a general strike on 18 January, organized by the PIT, in the face of which Labour Minister Colonel Bolentini declared: 'I don't need to be told [about its success]. I can see the empty streets for myself. The strike has completely paralysed the city'.[2] President Alvarez threatened retribution for this act of popular defiance: a subsequent anti-government demonstration was violently dispersed, and when Wilson Ferreira returned from exile in Buenos Aires in April, he was immediately imprisoned. Nevertheless, after another 'civic strike' in June, talks were resumed, this time at the Club Naval, giving rise to the agreement of the same name (see Chapter 4). By August, there was agreement on an electoral timetable: elections in November 1984 with handover of office in March 1985. This agreement reflected the changed balance of forces compared to the earlier round, with Cosena being retained in a purely advisory capacity and military tribunals being reserved for military personnel. Though the *Blancos* had withdrawn from the negotiations, the leftist *Frente Amplio* had been brought in from the cold and became an active agent of the transition process. President Alvarez warned that 'whether we are in or out of power we will continue to keep a close watch on events'. This last minute stand could not diminish the impact of the November elections, which duly elected Julio Sanguinetti as the next civilian president. As a footnote to history we can mention the 302 votes gained by the regime's own *Unión Patriotica* (Patriotic Union), whose candidate, Labour Minister Colonel Bolentini, symbolically died on the eve of the elections.

The results of the 1984 elections are detailed in Table 7.1.

Table 7.1
Elections in Uruguay, 1984

Political party	No. of Votes	% of votes
Partido Colorado	777,701	41.2
Sanguinetti	(588,143)	(76)
Pacheco Areco	(183,588)	(24)
Partido Nacional (Blancos)	660,767	35.0
Zumaran	(553,193)	(84)
Others	(97,917)	(16)
Partido Demócrata Cristiano (Frente Amplio)	401,104	21.3
Others	47,184	2.5

We note a clear, if not overwhelming, victory by the 'moderate' *Colorados*, within which Sanguinetti's list obtained three quarters of the votes cast for them. The *Blancos* saw only a small decline in their historic vote, not surprising given the imprisonment of their natural leader, Wilson Ferreira, whose candidate, Zumaran, obtained a clear majority of the party's votes. The leftist *Frente Amplio*, under their legal name of the Christian Democratic Party, saw a slight increase in their vote to achieve one-fifth of the total. The elections for the new chamber of deputies saw a less clear-cut *Colorado* hegemony, as they achieved only 41 seats, compared to 35 for the *Blancos* and 22 for the *Frente Amplio*. In the Senate they took 13 seats, compared to 17 for the combined opposition. Clearly, President Sanguinetti would have to rely on the continuation of inter-party agreements, as demonstrated in the run-up to the elections.

The elections of 1984 represent, in general terms, a move towards the centre. Sanguinetti's discourse repeatedly turned to the themes of the 'safe transition': a vote for him meant 'a President for all', and he would achieve 'a change in peace'. There was a general 'social democratization' of all political discourse during the run up to the elections. The *Colorados* tried to shed their image of the party who had called in the military in 1973, the *Blancos* moved away from their conservative rural image, and even the *Frente Amplio* was a model of moderation and caution. The electorate supported this tendency, voting, for example, within the *Frente Amplio* tickets, for the currents who most clearly repudiated their earlier image of people who were politically sympathetic to the *Tupamaros*. The other major characteristic of these elections is that people voted for what César Aguiar has called 'political goods' (freedoms, rights and guarantees), rather than for radical socio-economic transformations.[3] The election was a mechanism whereby the legitimacy of constitutional rule was reconsecrated, which would lead to a renewal of the social integration so characteristic of the earlier *Uruguay feliz* (happy Uruguay). The younger, more educated voters for the *Frente Amplio* were particularly against a prioritization of 'economic goods' (wages and employment), and declared themselves, in a pre-electoral survey, overwhelmingly for a joint prioritization of wages and freedom (*Libertades y Salarios*), by 75 per cent, against only 50 per cent of the *Colorado* electorate, 42 per cent of which thought wages was the main priority.[4]

Sanguinetti assumed office in March 1985 committed to the formation of a 'government of national unity'. Already, before the elections, the inter-party body *Conapro* (*Concertación Nacional Programática* — Programmatic National Concertation) had worked to produce a common approach to economic policy (for example for foreign debt), and to basic political procedures. However, the *Frente Amplio* was keener to engage in 'co-participation' than were the *Blancos*, still smarting from the banning of their presidential candidate and its acceptance by the other parties. Significantly, one of Sanguinetti's very first moves was to lift all restrictions on the Communist Party, legalize their paper *El Popular*, legalize the CNT (*Convención Nacional de Trabajadores* — Workers' National Convention), dominated by the CP, as well as the university student's union FEUU. A pacification bill was also negotiated between the political parties, which eventually led to the freeing of the remaining 200 or so *Tupamaros* still in jail. By mid-1985, there had been some 160 strikes, but liberal Labour Minister Hugo Fernández Faingold, who had good relations with the unions, declared that they were not the result of subversive destabilization plans but were rather the natural result of twelve years' suppression of all trade union activity. After a general strike in September, however, Fernández was declaring that the trade unions were deliberately attacking democracy, and the government withdrew from the 'social pact' talks it was sponsoring with employers and trade unions, accusing the latter of intransigence. However, substantial wage increases in the first year of the new democracy in Uruguay assured a relative social stability.

In 1986, a new round of 'national dialogue' talks was initiated by president Sanguinetti, especially to deal with the pressing problem of economic development, but also to create the political space for what was, after all, a minority government. Following another successful general strike in March, the opposition *Blancos* were given government posts. The new National Accord government effectively brought the two traditional parties into uneasy coalition and froze out the leftist *Frente Amplio*, whose usefulness in the transition process had been outlived. Wilson Ferreira, once an uncompromising oppositionist, was now calling on the opposition to 'allow the government to govern'. Wilson also took the lead in urging the government to deal with continuing military unrest over criticism in parliament through a 'political solution', which was the accepted code word for an amnesty. For the rest of 1986, there was an ongoing debate in parliament, and popular protest outside, over the government's proposed amnesty bill for the military criminals. Towards the end of the year, negotiations with the military produced a Club Naval Agreement Mark 2, which set the terms of the bill, which was then finally approved. The 'labour question' was also to the forefront in the second half of 1986, with three consecutive escalated general strikes in July protesting over pay conditions, but also the government's growing restrictions on the right to strike and against their economic plan, which involved considerable privatization. In December, a strike in the state oil company, Ancap, was banned by the government, the armed forces were called out, and the PIT/CNT called a general strike, which was eminently successful.

In 1987, political debate was largely dominated by the reaction against the government's amnesty bill. Human rights organizations, the *Frente Amplio*, and a faction of the *Blancos* began to raise the 600,000 signatures necessary to call for a referendum on the issue, an enterprise in which they were successful, contrary to the government's expectations. Wilson Ferreira made the campaign for a plebiscite on the amnesty issue into a dividing line between those who were for or against democracy: those who called for a referendum were against! The trade unions played an active role in this campaign not to allow the military impunity for their crimes, mobilizing some 100,000 people for a May Day Rally. By November 1987, the unions had also mounted their fifth general strike since the return of constitutional rule and showed themselves as active participants in the democratization process, in spite of internal divisions. Wages had risen in 1985 and 1986, but by 1987 they had become more or less stationary, and workers had not been able to recompose their historic level of wages and salaries. The government's economic policy was characterized by a lack of dramatic measures comparable to the Plan Austral or Plano Cruzado in Argentina and Brazil (see below). In political terms, the overall characteristic of the transition process (also dealt with in a separate section below) was the marked level of continuity from pre-military political patterns: this was truly a 'safe transition', although the question of a military amnesty was still potentially explosive.

Economic prospects

The Uruguayan economy, as we have noted above, was characterized by an underlying stagnation from around the mid-1950s. In 1982, a deeper conjunctural economic crisis overtook the economy, which led to a sharp rise in the fiscal deficit and in unemployment. It was this economic crisis that set the scene for the transition to democracy and, presumably, led to the withdrawal of whatever dominant class support remained for the military regime. This represented the failure of yet another dominant class economic project of modernization and economic recovery, various of which had been essayed since the 1950s. Economic stagnation had sharpened inter-bourgeois conflicts as much as it had accentuated the daily struggle between workers and employers over wages and profits. In 1959, the *Blancos* had come to power, after a long period of *Colorado* rule, at the head of a ruralist coalition determined to halt the traditional transfer of resources from the rural to the urban/industrial sphere. This attempt at readjustment did not prosper, and by 1968 a more solid coalition of industrial, banking, and large cattle owners had taken control of the economy. The sharpening of the class struggle under this regime led to the 1973 military coup and the predominance of financial interests in the new economic leadership, in keeping with trends in the other southern cone dictatorships. Its eventual failure paved the way for redemocratization.

The Sanguinetti government did not appear to represent directly any particular faction of the dominant classes, and its discourse centred around modernization as the key to renewed social and political stability. As in the political arena, there was a marked continuity in the economic policy it was to pursue. Even the opposition seemed reluctant to advocate radical policies, and there was a general consensus on economic policy between *Colorados* and *Blancos*, in keeping with their similar social base and political orientation. At a conference on re-democratization, organized by the Wilson Center in 1984, the opposition economists laid out their position. Ramón Diaz argued:

> The military regime which took power in 1973 has been responsible for many grave errors, in the field of the economy as in most others, but the removal of exchange controls, and the timid reduction of import duties, do not deserve to be counted among them.[5]

Indeed, for Diaz the military can be credited with the economic expansion of 1974–80, which was unique in recent economic history. The very title of Diaz's presentation was indicative of an old strategy: 'Small country must be an open country' (*País pequeño debe ser país abierto*). As with conservative romantics in Argentina, this discourse harks back to the 'golden era' of the agro-export economy prior to 1930, when the Plate's economies were integrated into a dynamic international circuit of capital accumulation, albeit on a subordinate basis.

Uruguay is, of course, a small country, with less than 3 million inhabitants, and there is a greater control over economic policy than there can be in gigantic Brazil or Argentina with its naked sectoral power struggles. This time, economic modernization would be carried out by a strong democratic state on the basis of consensus, and not tied to the interests of any particular dominant class fraction. The key element, according to an opposition economic team, was the development of an agro-industrial complex which, with the current consumption industry (and its associated capital goods industry) would be the leading sector (*sector de punta*), which could drag behind it the other economic activities.[6] The modernization of agriculture — where there is an important technological frontier to be occupied — is potentially a viable economic strategy. Yet the dominant tendency has been to perpetuate the economic liberalism of the military regime. Thus, according to the Inter-American Development Bank: 'Basically, the policy applied [by the new government] has been characterized by freedom with respect to prices, exchange rates, and flows of capital with the rest of the world'.[7] Associated with this opening of Uruguay to the world economy are monetarist-influenced policies to reduce public spending, control internal credit, and to put state-owned enterprises on 'a sound financial footing'.

Uruguay's economic authorities are conscious of the role of financial intermediation it could play between Argentina and Brazil in a regional division of labour. With its unique financial and exchange freedoms, it could become the Switzerland of the São Paulo–Buenos Aires industrial axis. Separate economic and trade deals signed with Argentina and Brazil in 1985 may lead to more ambitious economic integration in the area. In 1986, the presidents of the three new democracies met in Buenos Aires and set out an ambitious regional economic agenda. The choice for Uruguay, according to J. M. Quijano, in this alliance between unequals, would be 'to enter this integration or sink into nothingness'.[8] Uruguay has, however, preferential advantages for its products, so much so that Argentina's business leaders have complained of 'unfair competition'. Whatever the case, as the Inter-American Development Bank notes, these agreements 'could provide a powerful stimulus to the expansion of Uruguayan exports and to investments conducive to structural change and to the modernization of its economy'.[9] What we are seeing is a new assertive role for the industrial bourgeoisie in the area, in alliance (by no means subordinate) with the transnational corporations. Though still only a tendency, with Brazil by far the most advanced case, a new, lucid bourgeois leadership may be emerging, which recognizes the importance of the internal market and thus of a democratic regime.

Since 1985, the expansion of economic activity in Brazil has had a considerable economic impact in Uruguay. Brazilian demand for meat and other products, as domestic consumption increased, created a boom for the export sector in Uruguay. As the Inter-American Development Bank noted: 'External demand, stimulated by Brazil's vigorous economic expansion . . . rose impressively [in 1985–86]'.[10] This in turn stimulated the manufacturing sector, with its considerable idle capacity since the recession of 1982, which responded to increased demand. The contraction of all sectors since 1982 ceased with the recovery of agriculture in 1985 and of the construction industry in 1986, which in turn regenerated employment. The only deleterious side effect was the increase in meat prices as a result of the heavy exporting to Brazil, which was reflected in a failure to meet inflation-reduction targets. However, the rise of exports to Brazil was a one-off phenomenon, not repeated in 1987. Likewise, tourism, which expanded in 1985–86, is a notoriously fickle industry, and results in 1987 were not encouraging. The inflow of foreign private financial capital in 1986, which was a decisive factor in the favourable balance of payments, was not repeated in 1987. Overall, thus, we can note a favourable economic context for the new democracy, but not one built on particularly durable foundations, and, given that the dollar is the transaction currency of most Uruguayan exports, subject to external fluctuations.

As to the foreign debt and relations with the International Monetary Fund, the situation in Uruguay is possibly less dramatic than in the other new democracies. In 1986, Uruguay's interest payments on the foreign debt amounted to 24.5 per cent of the amount of exports of goods and services, compared to 43.3 per cent for Brazil, and 46.4 per cent for Argentina. Of course, the net amount of Uruguay's foreign debt does not raise it to an international issue, as is the case with Brazil, for example. The financial package agreed with the International Monetary Fund in 1985 set a target of reducing inflation from over 70 per cent to 50 per cent, an objective that will probably be met in 1988. In addition, as the Inter-American Development Bank notes, 'the lowering of the interest rate applicable to the renegotiated Uruguayan debt had an appreciable impact on payments abroad and on the balance of services'.[11] After new terms were set for servicing the foreign debt, government policy was restricted to monitoring movements of international reserves and changes in the exchange rate, to prevent fluctuations in the money market. This reasonably optimistic scenario has been undermined by the after-effects of the October 1987 global stock market collapse. Likewise, it neglects the considerable weight of the foreign debt, which has reached unprecedented levels for Uruguay, and represents a considerable drain on national resources, and thus the funds available for redistribution and improvement of the 'social wage' to promote consensus.

The question obviously arises as to how Uruguay's workers have fared under the new democracy, because that would be an essential element in facilitating or frustrating social consensus. Taking 1957=100 as an index for real wages, we find that by 1973 the annual average had declined to 70, and by 1983 wages had plummeted to 39 per cent of their 1957 levels. So, although wages rose by 14 per cent in 1985 and 6.7 per cent in 1986, there was still a lot of catching up for workers to regain their historic wage levels. As for unemployment, it had risen dramatically under the dictatorship, in a historical context of nearly full employment. Under the new civilian regime, unemployment fell from 13 per cent in 1985, to 11 per cent in 1986, to 8 per cent in 1987. However, unions argue that these figures mask the considerable level of underemployment. Furthermore, it is estimated that some 50 workers emigrate from Uruguay every day. We may recall that under the dictatorship a considerable proportion of Uruguay's working population left the country. During the 1970s, tens of thousands of workers emigrated annually, but in the 1980s this level dropped to a few hundred. However, a survey carried out in Montevideo in 1984 concluded that 20 per cent of the population wish to emigrate, a proportion that rises to 44 per cent in the 25–29 age group.[12] This does not reflect a stable social formation, and shows the limits of social integration, which has only partly recovered its historic levels under the new democracy.

Uruguay has not experienced the shock treatment of the economic plans of Argentina and Brazil under their new democracies. The relatively benign economic context of Uruguay's redemocratization obviously favours its consolidation. As John Sheahan writes, the political economies of the new democracies must meet two requirements that pull in contrary directions:

Table 7.2

Economic indicators: Uruguay growth rates (1982–87)

Production

(%)	1982	1983	1984	1985	1986	1987
Total GDP	−9.5	−5.9	−1.5	0.3	6.6	4.9
Agriculture	−7.3	2.1	−6.8	4.5	6.7	0.8
Manufacturing	−16.9	−7.0	2.8	−1.6	12.1	11.0
Construction	−3.0	−33.6	−11.0	−30.1	−1.7	10.4

The deep depression that commenced in 1982 was halted in 1985, and in 1986, the first year of civilian rule, there was a remarkable recovery of growth rates led by the manufacturing sector.

Money, prices and salaries

(%)	1982	1983	1984	1985	1986	1987
Domestic credit	116.8	2.6	65.7	83.4	37.1	64.4
Money supply (M1)	18.7	11.4	57.0	101.3	77.6	67.3
Consumer prices	19.0	49.2	55.3	72.2	76.4	63.6
Real wages	−0.3	−20.7	−9.1	14.1	6.7	4.7

Inflation continued to rise under the new civilian regime, even though domestic credit was adjusted to the targets set by the financial programme agreed with the International Monetary Fund. Wages, as we have seen above, rose considerably in 1985 with the commencement of economic recovery, even though they had still not regained their pre-1973 levels.

Foreign Sector

	1982	1983	1984	1985	1986	1987
Current account balance (US$m)	−221.1	−60.0	−129.0	−107.9	91.0	−124.4
Terms of trade (1980:100)	96.2	94.0	98.0	89.0	103.0	105.8
Interest on external debt/ export of goods and services (%)	23.8	24.8	34.8	34.3	24.7	23.2

The external sector reflected the economic recovery after 1985 with the first positive balance of the current account being registered in 1986 (although not repeated in 1987). Likewise, the terms of trade showed a return to 1980 levels, and even the interest on the foreign debt declined as a proportion of exports.

Source: Inter-American Development Bank, *Economic and Social Progress in Latin America. 1988 Report* (Washington, Inter-American Development Bank, 1988), p. 512.

> One is that they have the consistency necessary for a viable economy able to function without constant crises and to achieve some economic growth. . . . The other is the ability to answer enough of the expectations of the politically aware groups in society to gain and hold their acceptance.[13]

The first requirement clearly implies restraints, and it is no coincidence that economic reports identify 'excessive' wage adjustments as the main danger in creating 'economic distortions'. President Sanguinetti's own discourse has centred on the notion of 'efficiency', faith in the 'market economy', the necessarily subsidiary economic role of the state, and modernization guided by 'the spirit of competition'.[14] In a context of still low popular consumption power, a dramatic housing shortage and poor schooling, particularly in the rural areas, it is not surprising that one opposition newspaper declared: 'We, the socialists also want modernization. But not this one'.[15] The fact remains that no coherent and viable economic alternative has been advanced, and the government's *continuismo* has worked to its advantage.

We examine some statistical trends in Table 7.2, which allows us an overview of basic economic tendencies during the transition period.

The left and democracy

The left played a crucial role in the transition to democracy in Uruguay. The freeing from prison in March 1984 of General Seregni, leader of the *Frente Amplio* left coalition, was a key episode of the transition, representing the *de facto* recognition of the left by the military regime. Seregni immediately adopted a cautious and compromising stance, with his discourse centred on the term *concertación*, which he is credited with introducing into Uruguay's political vocabulary. With the *Blancos* adopting an uncompromising stance towards negotiations with the dictatorship, the left had to be involved: as one general put it, a table can stand on three legs but not on two (i.e. negotiations between the military and only the *Colorados*). With the left moderating an already moderate political discourse, it became clear that their role (as far as the military were concerned) was to contain the labour and other social movements that they hegemonized. As Oscar Bruschera, a writer sympathetic to the *Frente Amplio*, remarks bitterly:

> From the Frente's perspective it was a case of mobilization, negotiation, concertation. Mobilization — at least in the form expressed through the contestatory presence of the people on the streets existed, and what a scale this was! It was, however, annihilated to enter the difficult terrain of the Club Naval Pact. Thus we passed from mobilization to negotiation, with the country demobilized.[16]

The result was to grant the military a trouble free retreat, and the new government — assumed to be one of the two traditional parties — a dominant hand in the *concertación social* process.

The left in Uruguay, and in particular the Communist Party, had built up a dominant role within the trade union leadership. Workers in Uruguay voted predominantly for either of the two traditional parties — the *Blancos* and *Colorados* — but within their trade unions they recognized a different leadership: the left. Its role in the labour movement gave the left considerable political leverage. There was, however, a kind of dualism within the unions, with the politicized leadership having a long-term political strategy, while the rank and file sought largely short-term economic benefits from their trade union membership. Alfredo Errandonea has argued that in the present post-dictatorial period, the traditional dual political/trade union membership of the leadership is not balanced, with political affiliation largely dictating and subordinating trade union strategy.[17] Many observers comment that strikes in the new democracy have occurred in spite of the leftist leadership of most unions, and not as part of a strategy of demobilization. This 'real self-demobilization with the appearance of mobilization' — as Errandonea calls it[18] — has been carried out in the name of *concertación*, and to ensure 'governability' under the new regime. Workers are resorting increasingly to wildcat strikes, or mobilizing through some of the social movements outside the workplace, but the overall result is one of confusion, and ultimately demoralization, as workers once again feel themselves victims.

The popular movement as a whole had, as we have mentioned, a major impact on the transition process, preventing an authoritarian backsliding and setting an urgent 'social agenda' for the incoming civilian regime. The Plenario Intersindical de Trabajadores, or PIT, grouped together some 120 unions, and mounted an unexpected general strike in January 1984. This confirmed the trade unions' role on the political scene, already established on May Day 1983, with a 100,000-strong rally calling for the immediate return of democratic rule. Romeo Perez, a Christian Democrat writer, has referred to how Uruguay's national security regime 'retreated under the pressure of a formidable democratizing effort by the popular masses'.[19] This is an important point, not only in terms of the debate on the causation of the transition process, but in drawing the link between democracy and the popular movements. The left is often accused of posing a threat to democracy, of authoritarianism and neglect of formal political liberties. The left did, of course, maintain a certain uneasy responsibility for the dictatorship of 1973, in so far as it tacitly supported the guerrilla campaign of the *Tupamaros*, in spite of the latter's lack of social support (as against diffuse sympathy). Now, ten years later, the left was in the forefront of the struggle for redemocratization, and the various social movements — some under its control, some more independent — were the main social motor underlying the political engineering of pacts and compromises.

When President Sanguinetti assumed office in 1985, the labour movement did not cease its largely unplanned and uncoordinated pursuit of better wages and conditions. The left leadership of the unions had to be seen to deliver on these issues if they were to maintain their political base in the labour movement. In March 1985 the government telephone company (*Antel*) employees went on strike, as did those in *Pluna*, the government's airline, the latter complaining that military personnel remained in key positions within the company. Uruguay's state sector employees represent about one-third of the total working population, so that their actions have considerable repercussions, particularly in the capital, Montevideo. The left leadership of the unions was, however, mindful of the impact of strikes in what was considered essential services, and these were curtailed, partly due to their impact on public opinion, but also so as not to give the government a pretext to attack the unions. By mid-1985, the recently reactivated national wages councils had granted wage increases of between 25 per cent and 33 per cent which went some way to compensating for the 28 per cent deterioration of wages between 1981 and 1985. Nevertheless, what was considered relative peace on the labour front consisted of 160 strikes by mid-1985, and President Sanguinetti was forced to offer talks to the now unified PIT–CNT union leadership. Year One of the new democracy closed with strikes in the transport sector, by metalworkers, health workers, bakers, in the chemical sector, and among civil servants.

Negotiations for a social pact between politicians, employers and trade unionists had begun even before the elections. A constant stumbling block was that the employers sought one overriding non-negotiable commitment by the trade unions to a 'wage truce', to allow a recovery of production. In practice, employers were seeking to bind the trade unions to a no-strike clause — a strange kind of *concertación* indeed. Once the honeymoon period of the new regime was over, the class struggle seemed to resume in all its previous glory. In 1986, the government issued plans to institute secret compulsory trade union ballots, and to ban strikes in essential services. Under the latter clause, a strike in *Ancap* (the state oil company) was banned and the army called out. Workplace occupations were forcefully dislodged and a campaign accusing the unions of endangering democracy was launched. The trade unions, for their part, mounted a series of successful general strikes in 1986 over wages and also the government's threat to the right to strike. These general mobilizations, apparently forced on the union leadership by a restless rank and file, served to unify the various wages struggles occurring across the country. The year ended with a general strike called by the PIT–CNT in support of the *Ancap* workers, and in protest at the government's militarization of industrial conflict. It achieved almost 80 per cent support from the working population.

In 1987, the unions kept up the pressure against the effects of the new government's economic policies (outlined above). May Day 1987 was celebrated with a 100,000-strong rally in Montevideo followed by a demonstration outside Congress House in protest against the government's economic policies. The PIT–CNT had also now become active in the campaign to force the government to call a referendum on its planned amnesty bill for the military, and for repudiation of the foreign debt. In June 1987, the PIT–CNT staged a successful 12-hour general strike in protest against the government's increase of petrol prices by 25 per cent. In November, there was a 24-hour general strike demanding 25 per cent wage increases, against the government's recommendation to employers of a 14 per cent maximum rise. As one report noted: 'The protest marked the fifth during the administration of President Julio Maria Sanguinetti'.[20] Whereas the organized labour movement had made its presence felt during the first two years of civilian rule, the 'new' social movements that had developed during the military period, such as the housing co-operatives, tended to be marginalized. These movements lacked the potential veto represented by labour's capacity to paralyse the economy, and the *concertación* negotiations did not consider them as valid interlocutors. As Rial notes: 'for the new social movements which were attempting to establish their new identity, this type of political game was not appropriate. And they are the net losers'.[21] The real loser is, of course, democratization itself, which is thus losing the powerful autonomous impulse of these movements.

The newly unified PIT–CNT was severely wracked by internal dissent, which may have curtailed its capacity to mount effective action. The basic tension was between the old-guard CNT leaders returned from exile, and mainly Communist Party supporters, and the newer, younger, often independent labour leaders who formed the PIT under the dictatorship. As one commentator put it: 'Today no one is scared of dissenting, though the scandalized orthodoxy may tear its clothes'.[22] Thus the PIT–CNT was split at its 1985 Congress, as all the old bureaucratic methods were deployed to prevent criticism or even debate of the Communist Party role and positions. The government took advantage of this internal dissent, declaring its support for those (Communist Party) leaders acting with 'seriousness and maturity', against the 'impetuous, radical and destabilizing youths'.[23] The ruling *Colorados* could find a tactical ally in the Communist Party, with its rigid discipline and control over its union supporters, and an ability to force acceptance of the *concertación* line designed by General Seregni back in 1984. The loser from this dispute — only cosmetically overcome in 1987 — was the labour movement, which found itself fighting isolated wages battles (with gains being rapidly eroded by inflation) while lacking a general plan of struggle to unify discrete groups of workers behind a common social and economic programme.

Turning now to the political formations of the left, we must note certain evolutions within the *Frente Amplio* coalition. The Communist Party retains its dominant ideological role, but this has been contested by the Socialist Party and various other smaller tendencies, which have also acquired a certain base in the unions. The Communist Party has striven to regain influence lost during the years of exile both within the *Frente* and, particularly, within the unions. The Party's orientation is to 'advance in democracy', with a moderate programme of social and economic reforms. It deploys its influence within the social movements to seek negotiations with the government, but is keen that the *Frente* should not become an alternative for government; the spectre of the Chilean Popular Unity collapse of 1973 is still fresh in Uruguay. One of the most interesting tendencies within the *Frente* is the so-called *Comites de Base* (Rank and File Committees), which Gerónimo de Sierra refers to as 'undoubtedly representing one of the most original innovations in Uruguay's modern political history'.[24] Thousands of these mainly young *Frente* activists

— most of whom were children at the last elections in 1971 — have displayed a great degree of internal democracy and participation, which contrasts markedly with the authoritarian *dirigisme* of Communist Party political practice. General Seregni remains a moderating, if unifying, presence within the *Frente Amplio*, but there are signs, particularly the experience of the *Comites de Base*, that this leftist coalition could set the tone of political debate once the inevitable *desencanto* (disenchantment) with the new regime sets in.

A significant development, towards the end of 1988, was the break-up of the *Frente Amplio*, as the moderate Christian Democrats and the *Partido por el Gobierno del Pueblo* (Party for the Government of the People), led by senator Hugo Batalla, decided to support the latter's candidacy to the Presidency against General Seregni. It remains to be seen whether this tendency will create 'a new left-of-centre political space' as proposed, but it should certainly accelerate the renewal and democratization of the left.

As for the *Tupamaros*, they came out of jail and into the new regime declaring that democracy was a 'blinding reality'. There was little explicit evaluation of the armed struggle of the 1970s — seen still as a defeat rather than a disaster — but an empirical adaptation to the new situation. The 'historic' MLN (*Movimiento de Liberación Nacional*: National Liberation Movement) around Raúl Sendic, the movement's founder and most prominent of the military regime's political hostages, put forward an emergency plan entitled 'For land and against poverty' which they handed to President Sanguinetti. They also engaged in populist *mateadas* (*mate*-tea-drinking rap sessions) with other political tendencies, and with whoever cared to 'meet a *Tupamaro*'. Another sector of the movement, which was imprisoned at the ill-named *Libertad* (Liberty) penal institution, now considers that the MLN project has been exhausted, and that membership of the *Frente Amplio* (which was refused) was the only option. A third tendency, mainly organized in exile, has become essentially pro-Soviet, considering the USSR as the 'international revolutionary vanguard', with its regional representative being Cuba. It revindicates the 'revolutionary method of the armed struggle', and seeks an alliance with Uruguay's Communist Party. Whether a new left can emerge from within the *Frente Amplio* in alliance with some sector of the ex-*Tupamaros* remains open to question. At the moment there is certainly much debate, within and between tendencies, and a certain prospect of renewal.

In conclusion we should note the considerable political influence of the left in Uruguay's new democracy, compared to Argentina and Brazil. The left claims the allegiance of one-fifth of the electorate and dominates an influential labour movement. Yet its capacity to articulate an alternative programme of government to that of the *Colorados*, or even to generate a new political alliance, seems to have been thwarted. In purely mathematical terms, the left holds the balance of power in Uruguay's chamber of deputies, but the opposition *Blancos* have thrown in their weight with the governing *Colorados*, with whom they have more in common, in spite of their radical discourse during the phase of the dictatorship. The particular position of the left in Uruguay has been explained by Juan Rial in terms of 'negative integration' that is: 'supporting the existing regime while questioning its fundamental bases on the discursive plane'.[25] A 'responsible' left has become essentially social democratic in terms of its overall orientation in practice, while retaining the Marxist–Leninist vocabulary as its own internal referent. To a certain extent the left in Uruguay has accepted that the political system consists of 'two-and-a-half parties', as the saying goes, with themselves representing the poor half that can never aspire to office. Whether or not this is advantageous to the consolidation of democracy in Uruguay, it is tending towards a certain flattening of political discourse, with all political parties claiming the centre ground and none seeming able to articulate hegemonic projects of the fundamental classes.

Political continuity

Compared to Argentina and Brazil, the transition to democracy in Uruguay was marked by a considerable degree of continuity with pre-dictatorial political processes and discourses. The traditional political parties — and we saw above how much of the left falls into this mould — served an essential role in facilitating a smooth transition. Certainly there was struggle as well as negotiation — the role of the social movement was probably crucial in 1984 in forcing the military back to the negotiating table — but the element of compromise was probably dominant on all sides. Whereas in Brazil the long years of military rule had created new political formations, and in Argentina a new democratic discourse emerged, in Uruguay there was a quite remarkable restoration of the pre-dictatorship politics. There was a certain amount of renewal within the political parties — which are really coalitions — but the dominant trend was one of restoration. Sanguinetti was no Alfonsín out to 'break the mould' of Uruguayan politics; the *Frente Amplio* was no new and dynamic *Partido dos Trabalhadores*. As Juan Rial notes:

> The participation of the traditional political parties [in the transition process] produced an element of integration which reopened channels of communication with civil society recreating political society, in a way of assuring the autonomy of the armed forces within it.[26]

Indeed, the military question was to become surprisingly controversial as the democratization process unfolded.

There is no absolutely reliable account of what agreements were made at the Club Naval between the representatives of the armed forces and those of the political parties, which paved the way for redemocratization. Wilson Ferreira, leader of the *Blancos* who pulled out of the talks, has claimed that there was a hidden agenda, which included a deal on no human rights trials. When challenged on this, he replied: 'I do not say that an actual deal was made, but that *that* was the basis for the agreements'.[27] This seems probably to be the case, in view of subsequent government reluctance to press the cases of military trials even where the evidence was uncontroversial. Such was the case, for example, with the prominent politicians, Zelmar Michelini and Héctor Gutierrez Ruiz, who were murdered in Buenos Aires by a joint Argentine–Uruguayan armed 'task force'. There was a congressional investigation into human rights abuses, which reported towards the end of 1985, showing that there had been 164 'disappearances' (most of them in Argentina) and 156 dead under torture. However, as criticism of the military impunity for its crimes mounted, government representatives began to make complacent comparisons. For example, it was noted that the *desaparecidos* were not a product of a deliberate strategy as in Argentina, but largely 'accidental'. It was claimed that the 'subversives' had in fact caused more armed forces deaths than vice versa. In short, a litany of repressive measures and the most systematic use of torture in the southern cone was largely swept aside.

The military themselves clearly believed they had a deal, and were taken aback by criticism in parliament and in the streets. Private prosecutions were allowed and some of these went ahead. The military personnel accused simply refused to appear before civilian courts, and the Sanguinetti government seemed unable or unwilling to force them to do so. The *Tupamaros* expressed widespread revulsion at this apparent military impunity for their crimes when they declared in mid-1986 that:

> It is criminal to speak of amnesty when torturers, kidnappers and assassins carry on holding arms. It is criminal to speak of amnesty when there are still kidnapped children. It is spitting in the people's face to speak of amnesty while the intelligence services carry on spying on us all.[28]

The military high command had decided, by no means unanimously, to begin an orderly retreat after their failure in the 1980 plebiscite. They were politically defeated by a combination of political manoeuvres and the reactivation of civil society, but their collapse and demoralization was in no way comparable to that suffered by their counterparts in Argentina. A moralistic move by the military as they left power promised prosecution of those accused of 'economic crimes', but this could not mask their determination to prevent military accountability to the new civilian regime. As popular protest mounted, the military leadership tried to convince the new political leadership that the very unity and integrity of the armed forces were at stake, which led to the Club Naval II agreements of December 1986.

The essentially conservative Sanguinetti government found itself on good terms with the military once the amnesty question was apparently resolved. The military, for their part, admitted to certain 'excesses in the fight against subversion' and pledged themselves 'to defend democracy'. There was, of course, a genuinely constitutional streak in the military of Uruguay, and now the armed forces did seem to want to return to a more 'non-political' role, acting as a last resort should the constitutional regime lose control of the situation. Political positions in the country polarized around the amnesty question, with the *Colorados* receiving the whole-hearted support of the once fervently anti-compromise *Blancos* against the *Frente Amplio* coalition, the

Tupamaros (or, more properly, the *Movimento de Liberación Nacional* — National Liberation Movement) and the now revived human rights organizations. As the popular movement revived, the *caceroleo* (pots and pans) protests from the military era, to campaign against the planned amnesty in 1986, provoked the military to react fiercely, warning of the possible 'extremely grave consequences' of these 'irresponsible' actions, while the government dubbed the protest 'anachronistic'.[29] The left, for its part, saw the amnesty issue as symptomatic of the conservative restoration carried out by Sanguinetti, and a benchmark for the whole democratization process. The *Blancos*' leader, Wilson Ferreira, one time political hostage of the military, turned things on their head and declared that all democrats had to support the amnesty and allow the government to govern as it had been elected to do.

By early 1989, a date had finally been set for a referendum on the proposal to repeal the amnesty for the military personnel accused of human rights violations. A broad campaign had gathered over half a million signatures (one-quarter of the electorate) to meet the requirements for a referendum that neither of the two main political parties wanted. Thus, the question of the military amnesty, eventually ratified by the referendum, became an essential ingredient in the run-up to national elections towards the end of 1989, which were this time to occur without military interference, as had been the case in 1984.

Uruguay's political system has demonstrated considerable capacity to absorb or defuse opposition. When Wilson Ferreira returned from exile, he did so in a grand dramatic style on a chartered steamer, accompanied by the press, aiming to emulate Perón's 17 October 1945, when a mass uprising took him out of jail and set him on the road to power. The regime was apparently crumbling and 'Wilson' was a popular figure. However, in the event, the promised popular rising or *pueblada* was stifled by the military presence, and Ferreira went to jail. From his prison cell, Ferreira declared:

> The solidarity which has been forged at a popular level during eleven years of struggle against the dictatorship does not coincide with the political alliances today in force . . . the Partido Nacional [*Blancos*] is the only one which can reach government without extraconstitutional compromises with the military apparatus.[30]

During his exile Ferreira had even forged an alliance with the Communist Party, to form *Convergencia Democrática* (Democratic Convergence), an alliance which, however, had little reflection within the country. Nevertheless, Wilson Ferreira had, in little over a year, passed from a radical populist anti-imperialist discourse, to become the main proponent of a 'political solution' to the military question (i.e. an amnesty), and equated all opponents of this move as enemies of democracy. This cannot be put down simply to individual adaptation or opportunism but must be seen in the context of Uruguay's integratory and compromise-based political system.

Clearly, there was no 'democratic revolution' initiated in Uruguay in 1985. The tendency towards continuity applied equally in the economic, political and social arenas. The predominance of restoration over renewal was clear cut. There is no obvious hegemonic project emerging from either the dominant or the dominated classes. A major problem is that there is no room for an expansion of political citizenship which could, potentially, lead to a qualitative leap in democracy, as, for example, in Brazil. As Juan Rial notes: 'Political citizenship [in Uruguay] ceased to be a problem early on at the turn of the century. . . . There are no new sectors to incorporate as may be the case in most other countries of Latin America'.[31] Social citizenship, or participation, is, however, more problematic. Uruguay enjoyed a precocious development of a welfare state, spurred on by the discourse of Batllismo and the consensual development policies of the post-war era. A considerable degree of social and political consensus ensured the stability of democracy. However, the conditions that made this felicitous state possible were eroded by changes in the international and national economic conditions in the 1960s, and definitively shattered by the post-1973 military dictatorship. The question now arises as to whether Uruguay's new democracy can restore T. H. Marshall's social citizenship, achieve a renewed level of income distribution and thus recreate the social conditions for political legitimacy. There is, of course, a tendency in this type of discussion simply to look back to a mythical past as a way into the future: to seek a better yesterday for tomorrow.

Uruguay has a highly organized civil society, with a plethora of corporatist institutions and means of representation. On the face of it, *concertación social* (social concertation) could work better here than in the highly polarized, disorganized capitalism of Argentina. However, the *concertación* perspective is still limited, being aimed at the incorporation of the 'live forces' (*fuerzas vivas*) of society, at functional groups, to the detriment of the unorganized. Sectoral revindication, for example by the trade unions, have tended to neglect the basic social needs of those at the bottom of the social pyramid, much as the trade unions may wish to speak for all the oppressed. Thus we find that the human rights movement has now faded in importance:

> Human rights do not today effect the upper and middle class sectors in terms of their corporal liberty. This does occur basically with members of the lower classes but this only provokes occasionally an isolated commentary in the press and does not mobilize vast social sectors.[32]

Individual human rights, once the political referent of the dictatorship had disappeared, are now posed in terms of social inequality, and represent a challenge to the whole of political democracy. When police forces carry out mass arrests and house searches in the poor sectors of Montevideo, on the pretext of crimes against property, this is also an attack on democracy. However, at present, few social or political sectors have incorporated this type of issue into their new democratic discourse, which seems to centre on the problem of 'governability'.

Clearly, the traditional parties did not have to reimpose their hegemony over a hostile or recalcitrant civil society; there was a remarkable degree of 'fit' between the politicians and the society they represented. As Juan Rial has written: 'Behind the resurgence of the traditional parties lies the link with a society which continues to think its future within frameworks and formats of the past'.[33] Political discourse on social justice assumes a return to a political style 'based on paternalist state action [which] has strong roots in the thinking of civil society, in the collective memory which has transmitted it to the present'.[34] Political parties thus express a generalized desire for social reform that might return Uruguay to a mythical harmonious past. Of course social inequality always existed in this *Uruguay feliz* (happy Uruguay), but it was ameliorated by state welfarism and denied by a widely shared ideology of a general, if mediocre, level of equality. The left bears witness (people on the left are known as *testimoniales*) to a better society, but in practice acts as a semi-loyal opposition to the new democracy. The two main political parties do not represent any fundamentally opposed social or economic forces or doctrines, and thus can operate lazily together. With the Club Naval Pact of 1984, civil society was effectively demobilized by the political forces that had encouraged its reactivation. Under the new democracy, mobilization has occurred spontaneously and over the question of the military amnesty, but on the whole it has imposed a reluctant acquiescence to a new order.

The political legitimacy of the democratic order in Uruguay must, however, be in question while it cannot satisfy the basic social needs of its population. We cannot simply divorce the social and the political aspects, or moments, of democratization. If the political moment appears to be dominant in the first phases of the transition, as this progresses, the social moment inevitably comes to the fore. The social movements provided a powerful impetus to the transition process, but now they appear as 'threats to democracy' according to government rhetoric. Political realism, in the cold light of the post-dictatorial day, seems to preclude any fundamental expansion, let alone rethinking, of social citizenship in Uruguay. The military regime was unable to impose a new political common sense, but it did fundamentally alter the social structure. In the name of efficiency, urban poverty in particular has increased dramatically, as many studies have shown. As Mazzei and Veiga demonstrate, however, 'The conjuncture of transition leads the political strategy, or rather the "tactic" of concertation to reproduce, once more, the postponement of the treatment of the expanding urban poverty in Uruguay'.[35] Poverty leads usually to a lack of political resources, and certainly of political leverage, such as that possessed by the union movement. For this sector of the population the new democracy has brought few changes, a characteristic common to the post-dictatorial regimes in Argentina and Brazil as well, of course.

As we have said, Uruguay's new democracy has not been as innovative, dynamic or controversial as those in Argentina and Brazil. This does not mean, of course, that it is any less likely to be a stable restoration of democracy. Uruguay, with Chile (as we saw in Chapter 2), represented historically a more stable competitive political system than the predominantly populist pattern of politics in Argentina and Brazil. Whether this historical stability can now be recovered and 'modernized' is, of course, open to question, but the first three years of the new democracy indicate that it is possible. There is a certain stability in stagnation, and nothing like the pressing and growing problem of social integration of a rapidly modernizing social formation such as Brazil. Nor is it to deny the crimes of the military in Uruguay to recognize a constitutional vocation quite lacking in Argentina. Uruguay's military have simply not been involved in politics directly, as they have been continuously in Argentina since 1930. Furthermore, as Charles Gillespie notes: 'the incorporation of the Left into the transition has the added bonus for the future of Uruguayan democracy that it committed the leftists to a peaceful and democratic (i.e. electoral) road to socialism. The contrast with the Chilean Left is stark'.[36] Of course, democracy cannot be reduced to elections, but the point is clear: Uruguay's new democracy has been able to produce the elements of a new democratic consensus with the left having, in practice, lowered its sights from socialism to some more humane version of capitalism.

Notes

1. *Latin America Weekly Report*, 22 April 1983, p. 12.
2. *Latin America Weekly Report*, 27 January 1984, p. 6.
3. C. Aguiar, 'Perspectivas de democratización en el Uruguay actual', in C. Aguiar et al, *Apertura y Concertación* (Montevideo, Ediciones de la Banda Oriental, 1985).
4. J. Rial, *Uruguay: Elecciones de 1984* (Montevideo, Ediciones de la Banda Oriental, 1985), p. 49.
5. R. Diaz, 'Pais pequeño debe ser pais abierto: analisis de la estrategia de desarrollo optimo para el Uruguay', in C. Gillespie et al, *Uruguay y la Democracia/*Vol. 11 (Montevideo, Ediciones de la Banda Oriental, 1985), p. 51.
6. L. Macadar, C. Barbato de Silva (CINVE) 'Fracasos y expectativas de la economía uruguaya', in C. Gillespie et al, *Uruguay y la Democracia*, Vol. 11, p. 21.
7. Inter-American Development Bank, *Economic and social progress in Latin America — 1987 Report* (Washington, Inter-American Development Bank, 1987), p. 402.
8. J. M. Quijano, 'Alianza entre desiguales', *Cuadernos de Marcha* Vol. 11, No. 10, 1986, p. 67.
9. Inter-American Development Bank, *Economic and Social Progress in Latin America*, p. 80.
10. Ibid, p. 401.
11. Ibid, p. 402.
12. C. Aguiar, 'Perspectivas de democratización en el Uruguay actual', p. 46.
13. J. Sheahan, 'Economic Policies and the Prospects for Successful Transitions from Authoritarian Rule in Latin America', in G. O'Donnell et al, *Transitions from Authoritarian Rule* Part III (Baltimore, Johns Hopkins University Press, 1986), p. 154.
14. Cited in *Alternativa Socialista*, Vol. 1, No. 36, 1986, p. 5.
15. Ibid.
16. O. Bruschera, *Las Decadas Infames — Analisis Político 1967–1985* (Montevideo, Linardiy Risso, 1986), p. 181.
17. A. Errandonea, 'Sindicatos y democracia tutelada', *Cuadernos de Marcha*, Vol. 11, No. 9, 1986.
18. Ibid, p. 21.
19. R. Perez, 'La izquierda en la fase post-autoritaria', in C. Gillespie et al, *Uruguay y la Democracia* Vol. 11, p. 128.

20. *Latin America Weekly Report*, 19 November 1987, p. 12.

21. J. Rial, *Concertación y Gobernabilidad*, (CIESU Documentos de Trabajo No. 124, 1985), p. 32.

22. I. Seré, 'Una crónica del III congreso del PIT–CNT', *Cuadernos de Marcha*, Vol. 11, No. 9, 1986, p. 31.

23. Ibid, p. 33.

24. G. de Sierra, 'La izquierda en la transición', in C. Gillespie et al, *Uruguay y la Democracia*, Vol. 11, p. 153.

25. J. Rial, *La Izquierda Partidaria Frente a la Redemocratización*, (CIESU, Documentos de Trabajo, No. 109, 1985) p. 11.

26. J. Rial, *Partidos políticos, democracia y autoritarismo*, Vol. 11 (Montevideo, Ediciones de la Banda Oriental, 1984), p. 61.

27. *Latin America Weekly Report*, 21 June 1985, p. 3.

28. *Mate Amargo*, Vol. 1, No. 2, 1986, p. 4.

29. *Busqueda*, 14 August 1986, p. 8.

30. Cited, S. Blinder, *Uruguay: Las Visperas de la Democracia* (Montevideo, ALA, 1985), p. 52.

31. J. Rial, *Partidos políticos, democracia y autoritarismo*, p. 87.

32. C. Perelli and J. Rial, 'La estrategia de las apariencias: transición a la democracia y derechos humanos', in C. Perelli and J. Rial, *De Mitos y Memorias Politicas* (Montevideo, Ediciones de la Banda Oriental, 1986), p. 86.

33. J. Rial, *Partidos politicos, democracia y autoritarismo*, p. 79.

34. Ibid.

35. E.Mazzei and D. Veiga, 'A propósito de la concertación social y la expansión de la pobreza urbana', in CIESU, *7 Enfoques sobre la Concertación* (Montevideo, Ediciones de la Banda Oriental, 1984), p. 104.

36. C. Gillespie, 'Uruguay's Transition from Collegial Military–Technocratic Rule', in G. O'Donnell et al, *Transitions from Authoritarian Rule*, Part 11, p. 19.

8. The New Politics

More than most, this is a conclusion without conclusions. That is because the story of the new democracies in Latin America is barely beginning, although it could also have finished by the time this book appears. It is inconclusive in another sense, though, because it eschews theoretical certainties and, above all, political prescriptions. The new politics of Latin America are all about realism and 'possibilism', against messianic and 'principlist' (*principalista*) politics. We have, in the course of this text, deconstructed many things, from the marxist notion of democracy to the discourse of the new democracies. In our post-modern era we are supposed to be post-politics, post-marxist and post-vanguardist. Yet, given the contradictory nature and incompleteness of modernization in Latin America since 1930, this may be premature. We thus turn in this final chapter to consider in more detail the new democratic ideology, which many see as ushering in a new era in the region. For many, the dominant position of the 'question of democracy' leads them to bid farewell to socialism as we know it. We consider these debates as carefully and dispassionately as possible, because there is nothing to be gained from repeating old orthodoxies. But before we can take up these issues we have to examine the prospects for democracy in the region, on which all the debates are premised. By recapitulating briefly the constraints, ambiguities and limits of 'actually existing democracy' in the region, we hope to ensure that our subsequent speculations at least start off grounded in the reality of the post-dictatorial situation.

Prospects for democracy

In 1973, when the military dictatorship in Argentina was crumbling and a radicalized Peronist movement was assuming power, a popular chant on demonstrations was: 'Se van, se van, y nunca volveran' (They're going, they're going, and they'll never be back), referring, of course, to the departing armed forces. Though this sentiment has been echoed since then in the southern cone, we cannot be quite so sanguine about the prospects for democracy in the region. Democracy has 'worked' in Latin America in particular periods and for quite specific and identifiable reasons; it is by no means a 'natural' form of government, national constitutions notwithstanding. In general, we can say that the stability of democratic forms of government depends on some level of integration of the dominated classes, and a modicum of class compromise. The peaceful coexistence of capitalism and democracy rests heavily on the issue of compromise: the welfare state, Keynesianism, state education, collective bargaining and many other aspects of contemporary capitalist society represent forms of class compromise. Clearly, in periods of austerity, compromise is also possible — the 'war economy' model — but economic prosperity certainly oils the wheels of democratic compromise. To implement a democratic pact — in this broad sense — a certain stability of political institutions is also necessary, to mediate the various social interests that must be negotiated. Finally, a 'democratic culture' is necessary, to legitimize these arrangements, and, indeed, to provide the motivation to enter into them, otherwise simple force would prevail.

Pacted democracies

In Colombia and Venezuela, 'pacted democracies' (*democracias pactadas*) were established in conditions of a relatively weak civil society. In Venezuela, there was an explicit political agreement, the Pact of Punto Fijo of 1958, which set the norms whereby the elites have been able to regulate interest disputes since. In Colombia, until recently, the Liberals and Conservatives have operated a complex system of power sharing, which ended the *violencia* of the 1950s, and has survived a longstanding guerrilla threat in recent decades. It was the oil wealth of Venezuela that provided the economic room for manoeuvre that allowed both elite prosperity and limited structural reform to coexist. As to the political parties, according to Terry Karl,

> they provide a degree of stability and predictability which is reassuring to threatened traditional elites. The rules they establish limit the degree of uncertainty facing all economic and political actors in a moment of transition and therefore are an essential element of successful democratization.[1]

This negotiated compromise, which establishes the 'rules of the game', sets the parameters of socio-economic development, guaranteeing the position (albeit negotiated) of the dominant classes and an element of reform (albeit restricted) to benefit the dominated classes. The pacted democracies are limited; political stability is not reflected in social or economic democratization. This conservative democratization is not a simple sham, however, as some of its critics allege, and it is a path which can be usefully compared with the current transitions towards democracy in Brazil and the southern cone.

Fragile democracies

Other more recent, and more troubled, transitions to democracy in Latin America occurred in Peru and Bolivia, the latter country, in particular, suffering an on-off democratization process since 1977. Democracy exists in a very unstable political environment, with great social polarization, and is essentially accepted as the 'least bad' option. Julio Cotler writes of Peru — but it is applicable also to Bolivia and Ecuador — of how:

> In this context of crisis, both civil society and the state manifested their fragile constitution, unable to organize and mobilize the resources to create a relatively coherent and consistent new order. In such conditions a democratic conception of social relations could only take on . . . an abstract and vacuous form.[2]

The very notion that the dominant classes might achieve social and political hegemony over the popular classes, when they could not even unify their own ranks, is thus discounted. For the dominated classes, democracy cannot, in this context, appear as an objective in its own right, given its formal and instrumentalist nature. A democratizing pact, given such overriding structural and historical constraints, seems inconceivable, as does any long-term perspective. In Bolivia, the attempted transition to democracy from 1977 to 1980 ended with another, even more criminal, military regime. Its own failure in 1982 did not prevent its setting the tone of the new democracy, as Laurence Whitehead notes: 'Given the shortsighted, indiscriminately repressive, and parasitic nature of the outgoing military regime, the redemocratization of mid-1982 was a fairly unplanned and disorderly affair'.[3] A highly repressed, demoralized and socially disarticulated country does not offer a good setting for democracy.

   If we turn now towards the southern cone cases we can examine the prospects for democracy there in a more comparative context. In general terms, we can say that the situation there (in spite of variations) lies somewhere between the 'pacted democracies' and the fragile, demoralized democracies just discussed. Democratic theorists need to confront the question of 'governability' in this context. The left has studiously avoided an issue which smacks of an imperialist or elitist concern. Whitehead writes that: 'The economic and social conditions of the country make Bolivia an extremely difficult country to govern well . . .'[4] This verdict is seen to apply equally to authoritarian and democratic government, and goes beyond a technocrat's ambition for stability and order. The so-called 'crisis of governability' lay behind the ultimate failure of the modern military dictatorships in the southern cone, the case of Chile notwithstanding. Now, the new democracies face a similar crisis, if for different reasons, caught as they are between the pressure of the foreign debt and the pressure from below. Interestingly enough, Trotsky, referring to Mexico, wrote of the particular conditions of state power in which: 'The government veers between foreign and domestic capital, between the weak national bourgeoisie and the relatively powerful proletariat. This gives the government a Bonapartist character of a distinctive character (*sui-generis*). It raises itself, so to speak, above classes'.[5] For the present southern cone democracies, particularly Argentina, this is a suggestive analogy, and one which helps explain the apparently endemic crisis of governability.

Theoretical perspectives

The image of a Bonapartism *sui-generis* to characterize the new democracies does suggest an element of continuity, if that is how Trotsky saw Mexico in the 1930s. We must not, however, minimize the impact of the modernizing military dictatorships on the political system. One line of interpretation of the post-dictatorial regimes is that they simply take up where the old democratic regimes left off. Another line of interpretation, developed by Karen Remmer, argues, on the contrary, that 'Latin America's experience with redemocratization demonstrates that authoritarian rule tends to promote political change rather than freeze preexisting political patterns'.[6] A key variable, of course, is the duration of military rule, and here the case of Brazil is clear confirmation of this dictum given the radical change of post-1984 politics compared to pre-1964 politics. In Argentina, too, the intensity of military rule has led to some considerable change in the valorization of democratic procedures and politics. Uruguay, and possibly Chile in the future, show rather more continuity with regard to the pre-military period. Even so, we cannot imagine a post-Pinochet political system in Chile simply continuing with the pattern set prior to 1973. The new democracies begin life in a social and political world whose parameters were set by the military dictatorships: the social structure was radically modified; political cleavages were restructured; new social movements emerged. The fact that the democratic political process has been put into cold storage for a considerable period of time, in some cases, does not mean that politics had somehow become 'frozen' under military rule.

A related problem in analysing the new democracies is the assumption of continuity in terms of the social and political actors involved, as though pre-existing identities could be simply reactivated. In this class-reductionist perspective, classes are preconstituted subjects whose role is determined by the capitalist production process: the class subject (with predetermined political and ideological position) exists in abstraction from social practice. Empirical analysis of democratization would be unnecessary because we already know how the classes in struggle will line up. There is no class struggle in this vision, because bourgeoisie and proletariat simply act out their pre-allotted roles. Our own account of democratization shows a much more fluid, complex and uncertain set of social processes at work. As Oscar Landi argues for the case of Argentina, 'the access to political citizenship by the population takes the form of a process of formation of political actors with capacity to generate and stabilize a virtual regime'.[7] It is not a case of subjects who are invariable and exist *ex ante* — capitalists, workers, women, peasants, students, etc. — simply being wound up and set in to a pre-existing regime of political representation. Our emphasis must be on the construction, or reconstruction, of social and political identities, and the open-ended analysis of political processes, which cannot be reduced to a mathematical conception of a balance of forces. What we are saying is that neither is the political arena simply reconstituted as it was before the 'military interlude', nor are social and political subjects objectively given, but constructed in an inter-subjective signifying practice (which we will return to).

Constraints on democratization

Having examined some analytical issues in relation to the new democracies, we must now assess the constraints that severely temper their prospects. The main external constraint is, of course, the foreign debt, which amounted to US$388 billion in 1986 for the whole of Latin America, with interest alone amounting to a staggering US$33.5 billion. The region has experienced an economic deterioration since the crisis of 1982, which marked the beginning of the process of democratization. The situation today, according to the Inter-American Development Bank (IDB), is that 'as long as there is no solution to the external debt problem and the region does not have a sound financial foundation for sustained economic growth, direct investment will not grow'.[8] The reasons for the region's difficult financial situation, particularly since 1982, are located in the increasingly unfavourable terms of trade for Latin America's traditional exports in the world market: high interest rates; slow economic growth in the developed countries, since aggravated by the 1987 stock market collapse; excessive speculative borrowing. Recognizing the importance of what in Argentina is called the *patria financiera* (financial nation), the Bank recommends that the countries of the region learn from recent experience (under the military regimes) and 'prevent speculative capital inflows and outflows by better controlling short-term capital movements'.[9] Current moves towards a regional strategy on the foreign debt, and efforts to stabilize the financial sector, may just provide a more favourable context for democratization in the 1990s.

The main internal constraint on democratization in Latin America remains the unequal distribution of wealth and power. During the 1970s the Latin American economies grew at an average of 6 per cent per year, with aggregate GDP (Gross Domestic Product) expanding by more than 80 per cent in the course of the decade. According to the IDB, 'this made possible a rapid rise in average incomes', with GDP per capita rising from US$1.615 in 1970 to US$2,288 in 1980.[10] This pattern of growth in output and employment has not, however, been maintained in the 1980s. A marked recession from 1981 to 1983 was only slightly eased in the years after 1984, with GDP increases barely keeping pace with population increase, and unemployment rates rising steadily. The problem, of course, goes deeper than this, because even the relatively successful Brazilian economic performance masks, as we saw in Chapter 6, growing social inequality. Even the IDB Report for 1987 admits that: 'there is a case to be made that health conditions are worse today than at the beginning of the decade. It is known, for example, that illnesses transmitted by vectors have become more common: malaria, Chagas disease and yellow fever are some examples'.[11] Government spending on health, and other aspects of the 'social wage', had been declining in real terms, while falling personal incomes and rising unemployment are, in the restrained language of the Report, 'probably raising general morbidity and increasing the demand for public health services'.[12] The general picture is thus of a slackening in the rate of capital accumulation and an increase in the general oppression of the people, of which health is just one, albeit significant, 'indicator'.

Moments of democratization

One way of drawing up a balance sheet of the new democracies could be in terms of the 'moments' of democratization (Chapter 4). Firstly, we may consider the military moment, or how far the demilitarization of social and political life has proceeded. The case of Argentina shows clearly that the military do not simply fade into the background but remain a profoundly destabilizing force. In Uruguay too, the attempt to block the new regime from settling any accounts of military crimes has been symptomatic. In Brazil, Luciano Martins asks, 'what new role can be assigned to the military, after two decades of authoritarian rule, in order to justify the existence of professional soldiers in a geopolitical context without real external enemies at whom to point their guns?'[13] It is indeed strange that the military question in this sense has not been confronted squarely through an explicit reformulation of the 'national security' doctrine. As to the socio-economic moment of democratization, the balance-sheet is also quite bleak. Political democratization has simply not been matched by social and economic democratization. Just as obvious is the conclusion that democratization cannot be consolidated on the basis of a highly unequal distribution of wealth. Poverty, in brief, is just as much a latent obstacle to democratization as the military who have moved to the wings but not off the scene. Whether a democratic social pact can deliver the level of socio-economic reform to at least attenuate this factor must remain in question, on the basis of our analysis in the chapters above.

Considering the political moment of democratization, we note the most significant changes and advances. There is no new 'way of doing politics' yet established, but certain transformations can be detected: the church, in some cases, playing a major role for democratization; the birth of the first genuine independent workers' party; a decline of political ultimatism and a growth of genuine political intercourse. Cardoso writes, furthermore, that: 'The new democratization includes a reequilibrium of powers between the State, civil society movements, and parties'.[14] The autonomy of the social has, practically for the first time, achieved acceptance in the Latin American political horizon. Political parties look more towards the social movements now than the state. Progressive politics is no longer directed solely towards the state, which has been devalued by the military experience as democracy has become revalorized. Yet if we shift our attention from the macro-political to the micro-political sphere or 'moment', we find that democratization has not had such a great effect. Certainly the cultural sphere has been opened up and education has been democratized. Yet the violence of daily life for the vast majority of the population has in no way decreased. Authoritarian practices are still the rule in most interpersonal relations, and the heavy hand of the state, in the shape of the police, still marks heavily the day-to-day existence of the people. Democratization of every sphere of social life is still on the distant horizon in Latin America.

The uneven advance of the various 'moments' of democratization leads us inevitably to consider the various paths of advance that are possible. Fernando Faynzylber, among others, has advocated squarely a strategy in which 'democratization and endogenous modernization become the basis for achieving Latin American development goals'.[15] The two aspirations of democracy and a self-reliant modernization which can meet the accumulated social needs of the region cannot be separated. An integrated policy of economic modernization needs to take an eclectic rather than a dogmatic view of the transnational corporations, export promotion, protectionism and so on, and not simply repeat mechanically the policies of the import substitution era. As to the popular camp, the general advice by social scientists seems to be to not 'rock the boat' while enlightened technocrats ('progressive', this time round) get on with their task. F. H. Cardoso confronts this call for demobilization and argues persuasively that: 'It is not a case of advancing slowly, negotiating every step, to avoid a retreat [of democratization], but of having the resources to, once the liberalizing dynamic has been unleashed, force political situations which transform the regime'.[16] There is a need to broaden the horizon of possible alternatives and not simply accept the present order as it exists. Self-reliance also applies to the popular camp, as does the need for creativity, which the new democracies have created the space for.

Constructing democracy

In conclusion, we must consider the serious gap between the new democracies in theory and in practice. The first flush of post-dictatorial democratic enthusiasm is over and now *desencanto* (disenchantment) has set in. Perhaps the 'theoretical inflation' previously applied to socialism had, for a while, been applied to democracy. In principle, democracy was to be many wonderful things; in reality it was shabby compromises, backdoor deals and backsliding. Of course, democratization cannot be conceived as a one-off act; rather, it is an ongoing process, always seeking but never achieved. What has probably not been stressed enough in our own analysis is the subjective and symbolic aspects of democratization. As Norbert Lechner puts it: 'To construct democracy it has to be imagined. And imagination is one of the scarce resources, above all under authoritarian regimes. To construct democracy it is not sufficient to have a plan, as drawn up by an architect'.[17] To draw up a programme of radical reforms for the new democracies is a necessary but not sufficient condition for progress. That is because the type of measures implicit in such a programme — nationalization, participation, workers' control, military reform, debt repudiation, etc. — take on meaning only within a broader horizon of meanings, which leads to an affective identification either for or against these reforms. Thus the project of a radical democratic pact can only make sense ultimately if it is articulated at an ethical level, so that it may become the new 'common sense' of the era.

Democracy is defined in many different ways. For Adam Przeworski: 'The process of establishing a democracy is a process of institutionalizing uncertainty, of subjecting all interests to uncertainty'.[18] The essence of democracy is that no one's interests can be guaranteed. Democracy is about compromise, about consensus, about consent. It is certainly about all these things but it is also something more. Lechner again points in the direction when he notes that: 'All social practice (even the economic) is a signifying practice. Every social relation is a process of production and reproduction of signifiers'.[19] Social reality is not simply 'given' but is constructed and classified by a continuous elaboration and articulation of signifiers. This is an integral and fundamental part of the production of material life. Politics is inseparable from this ongoing production of meaning, which has obvious implications for any study of democracy. The symbolic dimension of social life has only recently been receiving attention in the social sciences. A radical democratic socialist practice requires far more sustained attention to this dimension. Its objective would be to construct a new democratic socialist imaginary which could have a genuine impact on the moral structuring of social practice. There is no socialist subject out there, waiting for the scales of 'false consciousness' to fall from their eyes; these subjects need to be constructed and articulated in a liberation project appropriate to the new democracies and aware of their constraints.

A new democratic ideology

The prospects for democracy in Latin America are bound up with the development of a new democratic ideology. There are signs, albeit incipient, that in the southern cone in particular, the experience of the dictatorships has led to a democratic convergence and renewal. According to Angel Flisfisch, this new ideology is seeking a political practice based on the following principles:

1. the diffusion and consolidation of effective practices of *self-government*;
2. a process of expansion of the spheres of life subject to *personal control*;
3. the need for a process of fragmentation or *socialization of power*;
4. the restitution of the collectivity of *personal capabilities and potential.*[20]

This new democratic ideology is clearly anti-statist; it rejects the concentration of power in the hands of the state, which it would see dissolved into civil society. It is hostile towards all forms of bureaucracy, and the spurious legitimacy of the expert. It seeks to deprofessionalize politics and move towards its definitve socialization. If these terms renew the message of a libertarian Marxism, there are others which are more akin to the neo-liberalism of Friedman and others. Thus there is a great stress on personal freedoms and potentials, which are seen as being hitherto subsumed under the weight of social structures. To assess the prospects and contradictions of this new democratic ideology is an urgent task.

The post-dictatorial political debate has undoubtedly placed the question of democracy centre-stage, for the first time in many decades. The modernizing military regimes of the 1970s, as we saw in Chapter 3, orchestrated a wholesale revision of economic, political, social, and cultural norms. Somehow, after this experience, it was easier to argue that a simple reversion to the pre-dictatorial, populist, nationalist variant of democracy was insufficient. After all, the military regimes responded to a very real crisis, particularly in the economic domain, of the previous state systems. The struggle against repression was couched largely in the discourse of human rights: not surprisingly this element permeated the new socialist liberalism. Faced with the sheer intensity of the military onslaught and the strength of its monetarist economic project, the autonomy of the political became easier to perceive. A much more difficult issue is the undoubted level of popular support that some of the southern cone regimes obtained at certain times. The call for order did not come merely from a hysterical pro-fascist petty bourgeoisie. The siren calls of the 'property-owning democracy' did not affect just landowners and big business. The dictators' tirades against politicians of all stripes found considerable popular echo. It is in the context of all these factors that certain sectors of the left sought a new way of doing politics. Once again, politics, in the classical sense, would be in command: the economic projects of the post-dictatorship would be evaluated on the basis of whether or not they were conducive to a deepening of democracy.

Human rights

We might start with the question of human rights, because its impact was so profound on the new democratic ideology. For the Marxist tradition, human rights were largely a mystification, in that they contrast individual formal rights with social inequality. Against the reality of power, class antagonism and poverty, the very idea of citizenship appears illusory. Yet under the military regimes of Latin America in the 1970s, human rights and citizenship became crucial issues for the opposition. In part, this was a politics of defence, once the offensive politics of the earlier period had received such a rude defeat at the hands of the military state. Human rights was a political space with considerable legitimacy both at home and abroad. This was a classically bourgeois democratic discourse, taken up assiduously by the left when other avenues of advance were closed. There were some of the usual pragmatic instrumentalist attitudes at work in 'taking up' the human rights issue: a good stick to beat the bourgeoisie with when it did not even respect its own canons of political practice. However, while the politics of human rights began as a defensive and conjunctural response to military rule, they became, as Waldo Ansaldi notes, 'a strategic component, a structural part of the project for reinforcing civil society and the new democratic ideology'.[21] Human rights were to become the ethical principle of the new democracies in Latin America, as never before in their history. Human rights became an absolute principle, against their relativization by right or left. In particular, the left was not so quick to subordinate individual human rights to some inherently superior collective social rights to the daily necessities of life.

The revalorization of human rights has reintroduced an ethical and moral component into Latin American politics. In many ways, the classical discourse of human rights has been transformed and radicalized by the human rights movements under the military dictatorships. The new politics of human rights sought nothing less than 'a strategy which would put in place and preserve the conditions for the existence of an order of which it could be said that effectively all enjoy certain basic rights'.[22] At first it was an extremely small minority, usually only relatives and a few small support groups, who were interested in the plight of the *desaparecidos*. Yet they gradually broke through the official silence and popular apathy. By the time democratization was imposed on the military regimes the issue was to the forefront of political debate. By the late 1980s, there was a report on the disappeared by an eminent international commission composed of bishops, ex-presidents and prime ministers, the Red Cross and Robert McNamara, former US Secretary of Defense and President of the World Bank.[23] Human rights had become established as an absolute principle, which could not be relativized for reasons of state. This had clear implications for the politics of armed struggle, which much of the left abandoned in favour of peaceful means. It also prompted the left to 'take democracy seriously' and not advance the slogans of the 1970s, such as: '*Ni golpe, ni elección: revolución!*': 'Neither coup, nor election: revolution!'

The rule of law

Apart from human rights, the other major component of the new democratic ideology concerned the so-called 'rule of law'. In societies where for so long the rule of law had been flouted by the forces of law, this appeal had considerable resonance. The theorists of the new '*estado de derecho*' (state based on the rule of law) stress the formal, institutional mechanisms of parliamentary democracy. For Juan Carlos Portantiero 'democracy is necessarily "formal" and it could not be any other way, because it concerns the construction of a political order'.[24] Democracy, as participation of all in all decision-making, necessarily involves parliamentary-type institutions based on universal suffrage, rather than corporative-type bodies. Liliana de Riz takes this argument further in criticizing the role of corporative bodies, such as the armed forces and the trade unions, in Argentine politics: 'the weight of the corporative phenomenon had as its counterpart the lack of consciousness of belonging to a project of "all" and the lack of solidarity with the remaining "parts" of the social body'.[25] Under the military regimes, this corporatization of society reached its paroxysm, to such an extent that politics itself faded into the background. Under the new democratic order, it is up to political parties to mediate and articulate the various social demands of the population. In relation to the labour movement, of course, this strategy implies a subordination of the trade union aspect to the political party domain, which looks to parliament as the arena for its struggles.

There is a parallel between the Latin American advocates of the '*estado de derecho*' and E. P. Thompson's commitment to the rule of law as an 'unqualified human good'.[26] For Thompson, it is the 'rule of law', in the classical liberal sense, that distinguishes liberty from despotism; for the southern cone theorists, it stands between democracy and authoritarianism. Yet, as Bob Fine has argued, 'the rule of law does not have to be an unqualified human good for its superiority over authoritarianism to be recognized and acted upon'.[27] To recognize the values of the liberal state it is not necessary to deny its bourgeois form and its basis in class exploitation. Against a crude

Marxism, which reduces the law to class dictatorship, we are presented with an equally reductionist view of law as trusty restraint against state power. From the idea of law as instrument of this or that social class, we pass to the idea of law as unsullied champion of good against evil. Bob Fine correctly points out that: 'A critical understanding of the rule of law requires that we comprehend the many functions of law and the conflicts between them; not that we give privilege to one function of law as law's essence'.[28] Likewise, in considering the new *'estado de derecho'* in Latin America, we should bear in mind the contradictions of the new democratic order for the subordinate classes, while clearly pointing out its unqualified advance over the military regimes, against all who would see it as a mere 'sham' or clever imperialist ploy to change the guard over their dependent states.

A democratic pact

The institutional form that the new democratic ideology took in practice was the socio-economic pacts proposed by the new democratic governments. The various social pacts proposed and practised during the transition to democracy in the southern cone were designed to regulate wages and profits under the aegis of the state. Yet they were (or wanted to be) much more than mere wage agreements. Mario Dos Santos writes that: *'Concertación* implies somehow making compatible different interests, but perhaps much more important is the inter-subjective dimension of collective creation and legitimacy created by this process for a given social order'.[29] Social reality is somehow transformed by this foundational getting together of once-opposed actors as social partners. Social participation in the construction of democracy has as its prioritized realm the social pact. This pact clearly must recognize the existing socio-economic framework in which it operates, while seeking, to varying degrees, its progressive reform. Non-cooperation with the social pact runs the risk of jeopardizing the very existence of the national community itself. Against the previous zero-sum conception of politics, the proponents of the social pact envisage a situation where all can benefit or, at least, all suffer equally. Social actors have the strategic choices of using social pressure to advance their claims or abstaining from using that resource. The alternative for Flisfisch is that: 'If all the actors employ social pressure, they will generate the conditions for a new cycle of militarization'.[30]

Against the advocates of the social pact for democratization, we could argue that they are trying to make compatible the incompatible. Capital and labour do usually operate in a zero-sum situation, where a loss for one is a gain for the other. Political equality is incompatible with social inequality. We may question, as Lucio Colletti does in relation to Bernstein, 'the capacity of the parliamentary government or modern representative state progressively to iron out the tensions and conflicts arising from class differences. . . .'[31] We can point to the massive social inequality in Latin America as a barrier to the progressive reform of capitalism. Nevertheless, the social and economic pacts have arisen from a deeply traumatic process and cannot be so simply brushed aside as 'mere' reformism or 'class treachery' by labour leaders. We should not underestimate the purchase of the new democratic ideology on wide layers of society. What is necessary, however, is a preliminary task of disaggregation of the various meanings of the term 'pact'. There are pacts and pacts, as Guillermo O'Donnell reminds us: 'It depends who is pacting, on the basis of what resources, on what questions, with what purposes, with what probable consequences and the degree of exigibility of the respective compromises'.[32] There is a growing orthodoxy under the new democracies of Latin America that 'the pact' is virtuous in and of itself, and anyone who opposes it is an enemy of democracy. The pitfalls of populism and the subsequent horrors of military rule do not automatically make the social pact 'a good thing'.

The socio-economic pact is always set in a particular historical context: its significance will depend on the conjuncture at which it is introduced, and the relationship of social forces that prevails. In some cases the discourse of conciliation and compromise actually masks a desire by one party to have another (usually the workers) accept the *status quo ante*. The pact thus becomes a displaced discourse of domination. As we saw in preceding chapters, the mechanisms for restraining wages were invariably more efficient than those restricting profits or interest rates. There is often the implicit price of demobilization, which popular parties must pay, to enter the pact negotiations. Safely diverted to the parliamentary arena, popular protest then has less effect on the transition process. But there is also what O'Donnell has called the 'democratizing' political pact (*pacto político democratizante*), in which the various parties agree to the procedural norms that will prevail in the new democracies, and commit themselves to an overriding allegiance to the framework of the new order.[33] This does not preclude conflict, nor does it preach an impossible consensus; it simply sets the 'rules of the game'. Clearly, the socio-economic pact is riven by contradictions, but it cannot be reduced to a simple reformist (or even counter-revolutionary) ploy. In the variant of the democratic political pact, there is a manifestation of the new democratic ideology that includes a genuine commitment across social sectors to maintain democratic norms. In this way, the political space for democratic and socialist struggles may be maintained, and threats from the old military authoritarian order rebuffed through a united front of the democratic forces in civil society.

Class compromise

The underlying issue behind the debate on the socio-economic pact is whether class compromise is possible under capitalism. As Adam Przeworski argues, 'Any compromise must have the following form: workers consent to the perpetuation of profit as an institution in exchange for the prospects of improving their material well-being in the future'.[34] Capitalism is not a zero-sum game, because profits are necessary to maintain the accumulation cycle. This does not necessarily mean that the relationship between worker and capitalist is a co-operative one, however, or that workers have no material interests in socialism. A logic of co-operation must relate future wages of workers to current capitalists' profits. This in turn implies that investment cannot be left in the sole hands of capitalists, and that profits will become wage increases in the future. Given these conditions, class compromise is possible but not necessarily in the best interest of workers. That is because, as Przeworski explains:

> The decision to compromise depends, in the end, on a comparison of the best compromise that can be obtained with the consequences of no compromise. The question of the balance of political power becomes paramount; the outcome highly uncertain.[35]

Here we meet the limits of an economistic approach to the socio-economic pact: it is simply insufficient to balance up expected benefits, on the basis of rational calculations, in moments of crisis such as those following demilitarization. When the degree of uncertainty is high (as in Argentina), workers may seek short-term gains, and capitalists will disinvest rather than seek a viable pact or compromise.

The structural heterogeneity of the dominated capitalist nation poses insuperable barriers to a durable class compromise. Workers in the advanced capitalist sector could participate in a socio-economic pact through their trade unions, but this leaves out of account the vast majority of peasants and unorganized rural and urban workers. Wages could be evened out within the competitive national sector, but wages in the internationalized sector controlled by monopoly capital would not be subject to this control. There is an essential contradiction, which Przeworski notes, between the transnational level, at which the reproduction of capital is organized today, and the national level, at which political consent is sought.[36] This implies the need for a coherent *international* democratic strategy, which goes beyond the ritual denunciation of 'imperialism and the multinationals'. All this is not to say that the contradictions of 'dependent capitalism' are so explosive that only immediate revolution can be the order of the day. The depth of social and economic problems makes a strategy of reforms eminently viable. The nature of the political systems makes political reform urgent. The revolutionary upsurge of the late 1960s and early 1970s, and the subsequent counter-revolutionary backlash, create a certain space for a reforming political practice. Above all, the creation, or recreation, of democratic institutions and practices is a necessary precondition for any advance by the labouring classes. The democratizing political pact may not create the conditions for class compromise, but it is the foundation for effective class struggle in the present conditions.

Revolutionary reforms
In discussing the Marxist tradition on democracy, we mentioned Edward Bernstein's position that democracy was not just a means to an end but an objective in its own right. Could it be that the father of the dreaded 'revisionism' was, in spite of Lenin's withering critique, actually right? For Bernstein, the Social Democrats were effectively 'a party that strives after the

socialist transformation of society by the means of democratic and economic reform', so that it would be more honest and fruitful to 'make up its mind what it is in reality today: a democratic, socialistic party of reform'.[37] Bernstein criticized the verbal clinging to 'outworn' revolutionary phraseology. Kautsky, while criticizing Bernstein's sometimes crude 'revisionism' of Marx, also argued for a revolutionary advocacy of reforms in the context of a gradualist class struggle, while retaining the ultimate objective of socialism. The Austro-Marxists, from the First World War to the Second, also developed a new conception of socialist politics, of 'revolution through reform' or 'slow revolution', by which Otto Bauer referred to the conquest of power by the working class through a gradual construction of socialist institutions. The Austro-Marxists examined the new role of the state under capitalism and urged the extension of social policies regarding housing, health, education, welfare and cultural facilities to the working class. While rejecting the Soviet model of socialism, the Austrian socialists did not discount the use of extra-parliamentary methods and the use of violence. They in fact maintained their own armed organization — the *Schutzbund* — and the possibility of an armed insurrection was always taken into account when considering political strategy.

To refer to Austro-Marxism in relation to Latin America is quite apposite, in so far as some political thinkers have explicitly turned to the 'Austrian model'. Chilean socialist Ernesto Tironi argues that: 'The case of Austria is of singular importance for Chile, and diverse elements of the socio-economic system which were developed in that country seem, in effect, applicable to Chile'.[38] The Austrian system of *Sozial Partnerschaft*, in which the state, employers and trade unions negotiate together, is seen as the means whereby that country overcame the great social divisions of the inter-war period. Chile, like the other southern cone countries beforehand, is emerging from a long period of political authoritarianism and economic neo-liberalism, which have been profoundly divisive. A degree of social peace seems essential, as it did in post-war Austria. For Tironi, and many other Latin American 'neo-revisionist' socialists, Austria was a case in which 'there was a consciousness that it was urgent to find forms of government to build a country for all [*una patria para todos*]'.[39] That Austria and the Scandinavian countries are not Chile or Paraguay is obvious. Yet when all metropolitan socialists (practically without exception) are engaged in reformist political work, there is no overwhelming case for apocalyptic revolutionary practice in the Third World. The type of revolutionary reformism advocated by the Austro-Marxists finds a viable path to advance precisely because of the failure of statist, militarist, instrumentalist and other variants of Marxism in practice. It is well to remember, however, that the Austrian socialists did have the *Schutzbund*.

Farewell to Socialism?

The revalorization of democracy by the left has led many to bid farewell to socialism, at least in its present forms. The antagonism between authoritarianism (of all forms) and democracy has largely superseded that posited between capitalism and socialism. Or, rather, it is widely argued that this is the case. This section does not attempt to set out a socialist project for Latin America, but simply seeks to demonstrate the continued relevance of socialism to the continent, in spite of all the reservations expressed, including those expressed in this book.

Politics regained

Norbert Lechner has expressed a general feeling among Latin American intellectuals in stating that: 'If revolution was the articulating axis of the Latin American debate in the 1960s, in the 1980s the central theme is *democracy*'.[40] In the 1960s, a rather apocalyptic vision of the 'development of underdevelopment' (things could only get worse) led to a rather stark political choice between 'socialism or fascism'. The victorious Cuban Revolution meant that socialism was possible: the condition of 'dependency' meant that it was necessary. The forthcoming socialist revolution was seen as an inexorable product of the explosive social contradictions, and the perceived failure of capitalist modernization in the 1950s. When the military coups occurred in the 1970s and produced something akin to fascism, this momentarily strengthened the illusion that socialism and fascism were the only alternatives open to Latin American societies. In defeat, much of the Latin American left accentuated its previous dogmatism. Indeed, it is not exaggerated to refer to a quasi-religious conception of politics: hence the current call of the 1980s to 'desacralize' politics.

Under the military regimes of the 1970s, intellectual endeavour turned from the social and economic aspects of 'dependency' to the origins and nature of the new 'bureaucratic authoritarian' states. Around 1982, with the growing international economic crisis shaking the stability of the military regimes, the theme of democratization became the major focus of intellectual debate. The struggle against military rule had centred largely around the issue of human rights, a defensive politics which took over from the vision of a socialist alternative. The overwhelming presence of the state under the military encouraged a self-criticism of the left's own statism. The megalomaniac visions of a new order, articulated by the Pinochets, made the left sceptical of its own previously confident vision of a future as a guide to political practice in the present. Above all, the logic of war, as practised by the military regimes, led the armed left to question its own past militarism. The concept of difference had not been accepted, and political adversaries had been enemies to be liquidated. The horrors of military rule — and the undoubted, if rarely expressed, feelings of culpability — led to a serious revision of how politics should be conducted. If the messianic concept of revolutionary politics had to be overcome, so too would politics have to be demilitarized.

As the logic of war gave way to a political logic, there was a revalorization of civil society against the now omnipotent state. The study of social movements — both old and new — was an expression of this new-found interest in what lay beyond the state. A society devastated by militarism and monetarism had managed to recompose many of its social networks and fight back. This new trend, as Lechner notes, was also influenced by the neo-liberal conceptions of the state and the individual, and inevitably took an ingenuous liberal flavour.[41] It led, however, to a recognition of the plurality of social interests: 'the working class' was no longer. Or, as Laclau and Mouffe put it, 'there is no single underlying principle fixing — and hence constituting — the whole field of differences'.[42] Society was no longer seen as a self-defined totality. The democratization process would not simply imply the political activation of pre-constituted social subjects. Rather, the transition to democracy would at one and same time forge new subjects and collective identities while it constructed a new institutional order. In the new, more fluid, conception of politics, political identities could be decomposed and recomposed. It was not only the existing corporative institutions that would participate in the democratic game. As the democratic game was opening up, so the rules of the game had to be established. Much of the process occurred at the level of discourse, and it was sometimes the new social forces which most successfully articulated the democratic interpellations.

Disenchantment of the left

To the general 'crisis of Marxism' we must add the more specific crisis of perspectives in the Latin America left in the wake of the demilitarization process. The idea of a socialist Utopia has long since evaporated, but there is now a real crisis of identity of the left. As Lechner asks: 'What transformations do they propose? What is the possible and desired order? What does socialism mean today in these societies?'[43] Socialism may still exist as a far-off dream, but more often it is simply out of fashion. Daily life under the military regimes has left a bitter legacy of fear, mistrust and individualism which may have overriden whatever experiences of solidarity existed. For the party left, the dissipation of its traditional reference points has led to a bitter process of splits and recriminations. Against the compromises of the new democracies, some traditional left sectors still raise the dusty banners of 'Liberation or Dependency'. The slogan of dependency would reduce all the complex antagonisms and differences within society to the over-arching conflict with 'imperialism' or, more simply, the International Monetary Fund. The new democracies are denounced for their merely 'formal' commitment to democracy, and the old recipes of state socialism offered up as an alternative. So, there is an old left which appears to have learned nothing from the experience of the last twenty years, and a new left which has not yet found its way in the new democracies.

The Latin American intellectual left's disenchantment with socialism has certain parallels with the disillusionment suffered by Western intellectuals with regards to the Soviet Union in the 1930s, which led to the 'God That Failed' syndrome.[44] Andre Gide felt at the time: 'Who can ever say what the Soviet Union had been for me? Far more than the country of my choice, an example and an inspiration — it represented what I had always dreamed of but no longer dared hope; it was a land where I imagined Utopia was in process of becoming reality'.[45] Then came the Moscow Trials, the bitter struggles within the Republican camp during the Spanish Civil War, and the failure to confront the rise of Hitler. Gide now felt that: 'The Soviet Union has deceived our fondest hopes and showed us tragically in what treacherous quicksand an honest revolution can founder'.[46] In Latin America, the disillusionment with the Cuban revolution was not so profound, but the general feeling that socialism was 'The God That Failed' is widespread. The swing towards revolution in the 1960s and early 1970s has left bitter memories among those who survived the military holocaust that followed. Arthur Koestler wrote, after his disenchantment in the 1930s, that 'as a rule, our memory romanticizes the past. But when one has renounced a creed or been betrayed by a friend, the opposite mechanism sets to work . . . the passions of that time seem transformed into perversions, the shadow of barbed wire lies across the condemned playground of memory'.[47] Those caught up in 'the great illusion in our time' often embraced 'a new addiction of the opposite type'.[48]

Democracy and socialism

In Latin America, the new addiction of the left is democracy. If that is not to be another God that failed, its limitations must be closely probed. Simply to counterpose democracy and authoritarianism is ultimately as debilitating as the previous socialism/fascism disjuncture. Just as there were political alternatives between the latter two, so the term democracy begs deconstruction. Arthur Rosenberg, in his classic study of democracy and socialism, argued that:

> In 1848 the concept of democracy generally embraced the labouring masses, in so far as they fought against the wealthy upper class. In the meantime, however, the concept of democracy had been taken over into the camp of the wealthy bourgeoisie. . . . While the older democratic movement had had a definite social content, now the social fighting slogans no longer belonged to the essence of bourgeois democracy.[49]

The desire for class conciliation in this now purely political form of democracy contrasted sharply with its social revolutionary origins. Whereas in 1848, 'the democratic idea had actually moved the masses and had carried them to the barricades', this was no longer the case, and as a general conclusion, Rosenberg notes that 'The democratic movement had been wrecked every time on its social contradictions'.[50] In relation to the new democracies of Latin America, there can be no evasion of the social contradictions they bear within themselves. Only the fully egalitarian socialist extension of democracy can move towards a resolution of the grievous social and economic problems of the continent.

That socialism is still necessary in Latin America (and elsewhere in the Third World) seems clear, but the question then arises as to what type of socialism. The bureaucratic socialism of the actually existing 'workers' states' is hardly an attractive alternative. For Andrew Levine, in his *Arguments for Socialism*, 'communism requires precisely what radical democratization fosters: autonomous individuals capable of coordinating behaviour without coercive restraint'.[51] Socialism, if it is to fulfil its objectives as a transitional stage to full communism, must perforce be democratic. Certainly, democratic socialism in this sense has never been historically realized. The point is, as Levine stresses, that 'had he [Marx] reason to think socialism realizable only in the state bureaucratic form, there would hardly be a case for socialism even in theory'.[52] To make socialism a viable and attractive option, its democratic form must be thought through and made realizable. No one can act on behalf of the working class; mass participation in the ruling bodies of society is a prerequisite. As classical Marxism stressed, only the working class can free the working class. Furthermore, as Rousseau insisted, only real popular control educates. Genuine control by people over all the social, political, economic, cultural and other aspects of their life depends on a full exercise of democracy. In a sense, if socialism must be democratic to achieve the objectives it sets out to achieve, one could argue, conversely, that the full flowering of democratic principles across society demands a post-capitalist breakthrough. A theory of socialist democracy barely exists today, confused as the term often is with social democracy or with 'actually existing socialism'.

Democracy and liberalism
One area where the new socialist democracy can learn from 'bourgeois democracy' is in the field of individual rights. Liberalism continues to thrive, as Norberto Bobbio argues, because 'it is rooted in a philosophical outlook which, like it or not, gave birth to the modern world: the individualistic conception of society and history'.[53] The left has scarcely come to terms with this fact and has continued to advocate an organicist view of society, where the individual is subsumed by the collectivity. Not surprisingly, the new liberalism of the new right finds a popular audience that has become disenchanted with statist social democracy. To deal with this situation it is not necessary for socialism to take on board wholesale (or even piecemeal) the doctrines of the new right. For Bobbio, the task of democratic socialism is to seek a new theory of social contract, different from that put forward by the neo-liberals, which would start from the 'incontestable individualist conception of society' while striving to implement 'a principle of distributive justice' to make it compatible with the principles of socialism.[54] In Latin America, this type of debate has sprung from two quite different impulses: firstly, the undoubted resonance of Friedmanite policies across wide layers of society, and, secondly, the more restricted but probably deeper impact of the human rights campaigns during the military dictatorship. Individual rights are not a bourgeois illusion or a luxury; a recognition of individual interests need not lead to a Hobbesian society. Marxism has traditionally closed itself off from these issues, to its own disadvantage.

Certainly, democratic socialism will not result from a naive (or Machiavellian) marriage between Marxism and liberalism. A concept worth pursuing to break out of this impasse would be that of 'autonomy'. As with 'freedom' or 'liberty', the term is subject to diverse interpretations, but can be defined as the power or right of self-government. The Italian new left set the category of *autonomia operaia* (workers' autonomy) on the political map; the women's movement imposed their political and organizational autonomy; and now we have the 'autonomy of politics'. In their different ways, all three moves represented a refusal of bureaucratic socialism. Autonomy, for Levine, implies 'freedom from the deliberate imposition of ends' and allows people to 'seize control of their lives and their destinies'.[55] It is the means whereby the 'free development of each' is compatible with the 'free development of all', to recall the terminology of classical Marxism. In terms of the project of democratic socialism, autonomy entails a recognition of the diversity of social interests, the refusal of class reductionism and, above all, the refusal of economism. In the new democracies, this orientation would imply a turn towards the new social movements which have done so much to revitalize democracy. Above all, it leads to a 'new way of doing politics', which fully accepts the autonomy and validity of this dimension of society. As John Keane has shown, the pursuit of a socialist and pluralist civil society requires the weakening of all bureaucracies and the establishment and strengthening of spheres of autonomous public life.[56] Socialism does not imply an 'end of politics', as some Marxist formulations would imply, nor under capitalism should socialists vacate this terrain.

Democratic socialism can also be associated with the Gramscian strategy of hegemony. As Anne Sassoon notes, 'the building of hegemony, the gaining of widespread consent, and a democratization as the practice of politics is an integral part of the socialist revolution in Gramsci's conception.'[57] The democratic socialist parties (single-party Leninism being incompatible) need not only to practise internal democracy, but to maintain democratic (not vanguardist or elitist) relations with the working class and other oppressed layers in society. Whereas both Leninism and social democracy look towards institutional engineering as a means to change, Gramsci directs our attention instead to the need for a prefigurative strategy of change. It is not on the magic day of the revolution that social, cultural and ideological transformation will take place. A strategy of hegemony entails the building of prefigurative (of socialism) practices and institutions in the here and now. This is very far from the statist and instrumentalist conception of politics, held by Leninist 'professional revolutionaries' and social reformers alike. In today's post-modern culture, a new political realism is both possible and necessary, as politics become secularized. As Lechner argues, this new political realism may also lead to 'a new sensibility of what is possible, an ability which might help to reduce the distance between political programmes and the daily experiences of the people'.[58] A hegemonic and prefigurative practice by democratic socialism is in keeping with the post-modern de-dramatization of politics.

Democratic practice

Finally, we can consider the practical politics of democratic socialism. The political modernization school of the 1950s set great store by the concept of 'civic culture'. Almond and Verba wrote that, 'The civic culture appears to be particularly appropriate for a democratic political system. It is not the only form of democratic political culture, but it seems to be the one most congruent with a stable, democratic system'.[59] That is to say, democracy depends not only on institutions, but also on the political culture of the people involved in them. Marxists, if they heard this 'interpellation' at all, would respond that revolutions were not tea parties, or, in another culinary analogy, that omelettes cannot be made without breaking eggs (heads). In the heady days when revolution was around the corner, civic culture was the last thing on people's minds. Now, in the new democracies of the southern cone, there is a fruitful and passionate debate on the culture of democracy. In more general terms, Gavin Kitching has argued that:

> A socialist world must necessarily be a world very different from the one we know, a world permeated at every level with what the ancient Athenians called the principle of 'civic virtue', where citizens' duties are stressed as much as their rights — and indeed, in which the performance of such duties is an important safeguard of rights.[60]

If this is the case for post-capitalist societies, it is a principle that must apply to democratic socialist political practice here and now, in keeping with the spirit of hegemony and prefigurative politics.

At this stage, it could be objected that the conception of socialist democracy being advanced has no bearing on the Third World, given the pressing and immediate economic and social problems that dominate politics. In this conception, the failure to achieve economic democracy is seen as a kind of constraint or limit on the prospects of political democracy. Another variant sees in the foreign debt a sword of Damocles hanging above the path of the advancing democracies. Yet democracy has flourished not only under prosperous and secure economic conditions. As with all forms of economism, these variants on the 'economic constraints' argument deny the autonomy of the political realm. Democratic institutions are no less 'real' because social and economic inequality prevails: it would be absurd, anyway, to expect the reversal of historical patterns in a few years. We can say not only that democracy is an objective in its own right, but that it sets the most favourable terrain to pursue the interests of the oppressed in society. There can be few thinking people in Latin America today who believe that dictatorship exposes the true face of capitalism and imperialism, and will thus galvanize the masses into action. We also need to reject any fanciful notion that the new democracies have been placed in power (and allowed to remain there) by their imperial and military masters only to act as 'fall guys' for the economic crisis. The popular acclaim for the various austerity programmes under the new democracies ('democratic austerity' being a concept the left cannot comprehend) in itself shows the limits of this notion as a guide to political practice.

Paul Baran wrote in the mid-1950s that, 'socialism in backward and underdeveloped countries has a powerful tendency to become a backward and underdeveloped socialism'.[61] Thirty years later, experience shows this warning to be perfectly valid. We need to evaluate the precise role of external counter-revolutionary pressures in Third World socialist states, but we cannot escape the conclusion that democracy has been conspicious mainly by its absence. Arguably, it is only the fullest democracy which can prevent the emergence and consolidation of a new ruling class, no matter how 'revolutionary' the elite may be. Even if we accept that the advance of capitalism in the once peripheral areas of its global expansion is 'progressive' in a general historical sense, this is not a recipe for political quietism. It does imply, however, an honest re-evaluation of 'actually existing socialism' in the Third World — its economic, political and social strategies. The militarized Leninism that guides political struggle also needs reassessing, as it seems to foster bureaucratic practices. Above all, Third World Marxism needs to reconsider its attitude to democracy, which is not only a luxury of the far-off imperialist centres, nor merely a sham introduced by opportunist political leaders. As Andrew Levine puts it so eloquently: 'Marxian politics represents an extreme valorization of democratic values. It is radical democratic politics, inscribed in the framework of the Marxian theory of history'.[62] If the implications of this statement were accepted, 'underdeveloped socialism' would not be so prevalent today.

Notes

1. T. Karl, 'Petroleum and Political Pacts: The Transition to Democracy in Venezuela', in O'Donnell et al, *Transitions from Authoritarian Rule*, p. 198.

2. J. Cotler, 'Military Interventions and "Transfer of Power to Civilians" in Peru', in Ibid, p. 151.

3. L. Whitehead, 'Bolivia's Failed Democratization, 1977–1980', in Ibid, p. 70.

4. Ibid, p. 71.

5. L. Trotsky, *Writings, 1938–39*, (Pathfinder, New York, 1974), p. 326.

6. K. Remmer, 'Redemocratization and the Impact of Authoritarian Rule in Latin America', *Comparative Politics*, Vol. 17. No. 3, 1985, p. 269.

7. O. Landi, 'Conjeturas Políticas sobre la Argentina post-Malvinas', in *Revista Mexicana de Sociología*, 4/82, 1982, p. 1246.

8. Inter-American Development Bank, *Economic and Social Progress in Latin America*, (Washington, 1987), p. 33.

9. Ibid. p. 38.

10. Ibid. p. 19.

11. Ibid. p. 67.

12. Ibid. p. 67.

13. L. Martins, 'The "Liberalization" of Authoritarian Rule in Brazil', in O'Donnell et al, *Transitions from Authoritarian Rule*, p. 94.

14. F. H. Cardoso, 'La Democracia en América Latina', *Punto de Vista* No. 23, 1985, p. 8.

15. F. Fanzylber, 'Democratization, Endogenous Modernization, and Integration: Strategic Choices for Latin America and Economic Relations with the United States', The Wilson Center, *Working Papers*, No. 145, 1984, p. 32.

16. F. H. Cardoso, 'La Democracia en América Latina', p. 5.

17. N. Lechner, *La Conflictiva y Nunca Acabada Construcción del Orden Deseado*, (FLACSO, Santiago, 1984), p. 179.

18. A. Przeworski, 'Some Problems in the Study of the Transition to Democracy', in G. O'Donnell et al, *Transitions from Authoritarian Rule*, p. 58.

19. N. Lechner, 'Epílogo', in N. Lechner, (ed.) *Estado y Política en America Latina*, (Siglo XXI, Mexico, 1981) p. 324.

20. A. Flisfisch, 'El surgimiento de una nueva ideología democrática en América Latina', in *Critica y Utopía*, No. 2 (1984), p. 12.

21. W. Ansaldi (ed.) *La ética de la democracia*, (CLACSO, Buenos Aires, 1984), p. 14.

22. A. Flisfisch, 'Derechos humanos, politica y poder' in W. Ansaldi (ed.), *Le ética de la democracia*, p. 107.

23. *Disappeared! Technique of Terror* (Zed Books, London, 1986).

24. J. C. Portantiero, *La democratización del estado*, (CLADE, Montevideo, 1986), p. 29.

25. L. de Riz, 'Notas sobre parlamento y partidos en la Argentina de hoy', in H. Sabato and M. Cavarozzi (eds), *Democracia, orden político y parlamento fuerte* (Centro Editor de América Latina, Buenos Aires, 1984), p. 12.

26. See E. P. Thompson, *Writing by Candlelight*, (Merlin, London, 1980).

27. B. Fine, *Democracy and the Rule of Law*, (Pluto Press, London, 1984), p. 175.

28. Ibid, p. 175.

29. M. dos Santos, 'Acuerdos sociales y procesos de transicion,' in M. dos Santos et al, *Concertación Social y Democracia*, (CED, Santiago, 1985), p. 13.

30. A. Flisfisch, 'El surgimiento de una nueva ideología democrática', p. 25.

31. L. Colletti, *From Rousseau to Lenin*, (New Left Books, London, 1972), p. 193.

32. G. O'Donnell, *Pactos Políticos y Pactos Económico-Sociales*, mimeo, São Paulo, 1985, p. 2.

33. Ibid. p. 4.

34. A. Przeworski, *Capitalism and Social Democracy*, (Cambridge University Press, Cambridge, 1985), p. 180.

35. Ibid, p. 197.

36. Ibid, p. 265.

37. Cited by C. Pierson, *Marxist Theory and Democratic Politics*, (Polity Press, Cambridge, 1986) p. 35.

38. E. Tironi, *La Torre de Babel*, p. 36.

39. Ibid, p. 37.

40. N. Lechner, 'De la revolución a la democracía', in *La Ciudad Futura*, No. 2, Oct. 1986, p. 33.

41. Ibid. p. 34.

42. E. Laclau and C. Mouffe, *Hegemony and Socialist Strategy*, (Verso, London, 1985), p. 14.

43. N. Lechner, 'De la revolución a la democracía', p. 35.

44. A. Koestler, et al, *The God That Failed*, (The Right Book Club, London n.d.)

45. Ibid. p. 183.

46. Ibid. p. 198.

47. Ibid. p. 63–64.

48. Ibid. p. 64.

49. A. Rosenberg, *Democracy and Socialism*, (Beacon Press, Boston, 1965), p. 302.

50. Ibid, p. 153.

51. A. Levine, *Arguing for Socialism*, (RKP, London, 1984), p. 114.

52. Ibid, p. 196.

53. N. Bobbio, *The Future of Democracy*, (Polity Press, Cambridge, 1987), p. 116.

54. Ibid, p. 117.

55. A. Levine, *Arguing for Socialism*, p. 35.

56. J. Keane, *Public Life and Late Capitalism*, (CUP, Cambridge, 1984).

57. A. Sassoon, *Gramsci's Politics*, (Croom Helm, London, 1980), p. 223.

58. N. Lechner, *La Democratización en el contexto de una cultura pos-moderna*, (FLACSO, Santiago, 1986), Documentos de Trabajo No. 292, p. 10–11.

59. G. Almond and S. Verba, *The Civic Culture*, (Little Brown and Co., Boston, 1963) p. 366.

60. G. Kitching, *Rethinking Socialism*, (Methuen, London, 1983), p. 45.

61. P. Baran, *The Political Economy of Growth*, (Monthly Review Press, New York, 1957), p. 9.

62. A. Levine, *Arguing for Socialism*, p. 225.

Bibliography

This is divided into a general and a country-by-country section. Given the recent nature of the new democracies I have included articles as well as books, contrary to normal practice. Furthermore, and for the same reason, I have not restricted entries to English language material, as in *Politics and Dependency in the Third World*. Chile is included as a case of failed democratization.

General

Ansaldi, W., (ed.) *La ética de la democracia*, Buenos Aires, CLACSO, 1986.

Brunner, J., *Los Debates Sobre la Modernidad y el Futuro de América Latina*, FLACSO, Santiago, 1986– Documentos de Trabajo No. 293.

Cammack, T., (ed.) *Symposium: The Rebirth of Democracy, Bulletin of Latin American Research*, Oxford, Pergamon, Vol. 4, No. 2, 1985.

———— (ed.) *The New Democracies in Latin America*, London, Croom Helm, 1987.

Cardoso, F. H., 'La democracia en América Latina', *Punto de Vista*, Buenos Aires, Vol. VI, No. 2/3, 1985.

Cheresky, I. and Chonchol, J. (eds), *Crisis y Transformación de los Regimenes Autoritarios*, Buenos Aires, EUDEBA, 1985.

Drake, P. and Silva, E., *Elections and Democratization in Latin America 1980–85*. San Diego, Centre for Iberian and Latin American studies, 1986.

Flisfisch, A., Lechner, N. and Moulián, T., *Problemas de la Democracia y la Política Democrática en América Latina*, Santiago, FLACSO, Documentos de Trabajo No. 240, 1985.

Foxley, A., *Para Una Democracia Estable*, Santiago, CIEPLAN, 1985.

Garretón, M. A., *Dictaduras y Democratización*, Santiago, FLACSO, 1984.

Germani, G. et al, *Los Limites de la Democracia*, 2 vols, Buenos Aires, CLACSO, 1985.

Handleman, H. and Sanders, T., *Military Government and the Movement Towards Democracy in South America*, Indiana University Press, 1981.

Herman, E. and Petras, J. '"Resurgent Democracy": Rhetoric and Reality', *New Left Review* No. 155, 1985.

Hertz, J., *From Dictatorship to Democracy: Coping with the Legacies of Totalitarianism*, Westport, Greenwood Press, 1982.

Lechner, N., (ed.) *Estado y Política en América Latina*, Mexico, Siglo XXI, 1981.

López, G. and Stöhl, M. (eds), *Liberalization and Redemocratization in Latin America*, London, Greenwood Press, 1987.

Martin del Campo, J. L. (ed.), *Los nuevos procesos sociales y la teoría política contemporanea*, Mexico, Siglo XXI, 1986.

O'Donnell, G., Schmitter, P. and Whitehead, L. (eds), *Transitions from Authoritarian Rule. Prospects for Democracy*. Baltimore and London, The Johns Hopkins University Press, 1986.

Peeler, J., *Latin American Democracies: Colombia, Costa Rica, Venezuela*, University of North Carolina Press, 1985.

Portantiero, J. C., *La democratización del estado*, Montevideo, CLADE, 1986.

—— Portes, A. and Kincaid, D., 'The Crisis of Authoritarianism: State and Civil Society in Argentina, Chile and Uruguay', in R. Braungart (ed.), *Research in Political Sociology*, Vol. 1, JAI Press, 1985.

Remmer, K., 'Redemocratization and the Impact of Authoritarian Rule in Latin America', *Comparative Politics*, Vol. 17, No. 3, 1985.

Rouquie, A. and Schvarzer, J. (eds), *¿Como Renacen las Democracias?*, Buenos Aires, Emece Editores, 1985.

Rustow, D., 'Transitions to Democracy: Towards a Dynamic Model', *Comparative Politics* II, April 1970.

Slater, D. (ed.), *New social movements and the state in Latin America*, Amsterdam, CEDLA, 1985.

Stepan, A., 'State Power and the Strength of Civil Society in the Southern Cone of Latin America', in Evans, P., Rueschemeyer, D. and Skopcpol, T. (eds), *Bringing the State Back In*, Cambridge, Cambridge University Press, 1985.

Thorp, R. and Whitehead, L. (eds), *Latin American Debt and the Adjustment Crisis*, London, Macmillan, 1987.

Wiarda, H. (ed.), *The Continuing Struggle for Democracy in Latin America*, Boulder, Westview Press.

Argentina

Alfonsín, R., *Ahora: Mi propuesta política*, Buenos Aires, Sudamericana, 1983.

Amérique Latine (Paris) No. 11, 1982, Special Issue: *Argentine, le pays de la crise permanente*.

Colombo, A. and Palermo, V., *Participación y pluralismo en la Argentina contemporánea*, Buenos Aires, Centro Editor de América Latina, 1985.

Crítica y Utopia, No. 10/11, 1983 Special Issue: *La Argentina en Transición*.

Cuadernos del Bimestre, No. 3, 1984, *Del colapso militar al triunfo de Alfonsín*.

Delich, F., *Metaforas de la Sociedad Argentina*, Buenos Aires, Editorial fundamencana, 1986.

Feijoo, M. C., *Las luchas de un barrio y la memoria colectiva*, Buenos Aires, CEDES, 1984.

Ferrer, A., *Puede Argentina pagar su deuda externa*, Buenos Aires, El Cid Editor.

—— *Vivir con lo nuestro*, Buenos Aires, El Cid Editor, 1984.

Fontana, A., *Fuerzas Armadas, Partidos Políticos y Transición a la Democracia en Argentina*, Buenos Aires, Estudios CEDES, 1984.

Gilly, A., 'Argentina despues de la dictadura', *Coyoacán*, Mexico, Vol. VIII, No. 16, 1984.

Jelin, E. (ed.), *Los nuevos movimientos sociales*, 2 vols, Buenos Aires, Centro Editor de America Latina, 1985.

Landi, O., 'Conjectura sobre la Argentina post-Malvinas', *Revista Mexicana de Sociología*, 4/28, 1982.

Landi, O., *El discurso sobre los posible*, Buenos Aires, Estudios CEDES, 1985.

Lavergne, N., *El debate sobre el programa económico del gobierno Constitucional*, Buenos Aires, CISEA, Cuadernos del Bimestre, No. 2, 1983.

Leis, H., *Sobre Cultura Democracia en Argentina: Testimonio de un Todavia Exiliado*, Notre Dame, Kellogg Institute Working Papers.

Mainwaring, S. and Viola, E., 'New Social Movements, Political Culture and Democracy: Brazil and Argentina in the 1980's', *Telos*, No. 61, 1984.

Makin, G., 'The Argentine Process of Demilitarization 1980–83', *Government and Opposition*, Vol. 19, No. 2, 1984.

Maronese, L. et al, *El Voto Peronista '83*, Buenos Aires, El Cid, 1985.

Oazlak, O. (ed.), *'Proceso', crisis y transición democratica*, 2 vols, Buenos Aires, Centro Editor América Latina, 1984.

Pion-Berlin, D., 'The Fall of Military Rule in Argentina: 1976–1983', *Journal of Inter-American Studies and World Affairs*.

Riz, L. de, et al, 'El movimiento sindical y la concertación en la Argentina actual', in Comisión de Movimientos Sociales (CLACSO), *El Sindicalismo Latinoamericano en us ochenta*, Santiago, CLACSO, 1986.

Rouquie, A., 'Argentina: the departure of the military — end of a political cycle or just another episode', *International Affairs*, 59, 1983.

Rozitchner, L., *Las Malvinas: de la guerra 'suica' a la guerra 'limpia'*, Buenos Aires, Centro Editor de América Latina, 1985.

Sábato, H. and Cavarozzi, M. (eds), *Democracia, orden político y parlamento fuerte*, Buenos Aires, Centro Editor de América Latina, 1984.

Strasser, C., *La Democratización en la Argentina Hacia 1985*, Buenos Aires, FLACSO, Documento No. 20, 1985.

Unamuno, Barbaro, Cafiero et al, *El Peronismo de la Derrota*, Buenos Aires, Centro Editor de América Latina, 1984.

Unidos Vol. IV, No. 9, 1986, special issue: *El Alfonsinismo: Navegaciones y Enigmas*.

Brazil

Abramo, L. W., *Empresarios e Trabalhadores: Novas Ideias e Velhos Fantasmas*, São Paulo, Cadernos EEDEC, No. 7, 1985.

Alves, M. H. M., *State and Opposition in Brazil*, Austin, University of Texas Press, 1985.

—— Amérique Latine, Paris, No. 10, 1982, special issue: *Brésil: une transition problématique*.

Bresser Pereira, L., *Os Limites da 'Abertura' e a Sociedade Civil*, São Paulo, Cadernos CEDEC, No. 4, 1984.

Bunker, S., 'Debt and Democratization: Changing Perspectives on the Brazilian State', *Latin American Research Review*, Vol. XXI, No. 3, 1986.

Carneiro, R. (ed.), *Politica Economica da Nova Republica*, São Paulo, Paz e Terra, 1986.

Cunningham, S., 'Brazil in Transition: Perspectives on Economy and Society', *Bulletin of Latin American Research*, Vol. 6, No. 2, 1987.

Diniz, E., 'A Transição Política No Brasil: Uma reavaliação da Dinamica da Abertura', *Dados*, Rio de Janeiro, Vol. 28, No. 3, 1985.

Koutzii, F. (ed.), *Nova República: Um balanço*, São Paulo, L. & P. M. Editores, 1986.

Lamounier, B. and Moura, *Política Econômica e Abertura Politica 1973–1983*, São Paulo, Textos IDESP, No. 4, 1984.

—— and Moszynski, J., *A eleção de Janio Quadros*, São Paulo, Textos IDESP, No. 16, 1986.

Mainwaring, S. and Viola, E., 'Brazil and Argentina in the 1980's', *Journal of International Affairs*, Vol. 38, No. 2, 1985.

Martins, L., 'The "Liberalization" of Authoritarian Rule in Brazil', in O'Donnell, G. et al, *Transitions from Authoritarian Rule*.

Morais, R., *Pacto Social. Da Negociacao ao Pacote*, São Paulo, L. & P. M., 1986.

Moreira, M. M., 'Political Liberalization and Economic Crisis', *Government and Opposition*, Vol. 19, No. 2, 1984.

Novos Estudos CEBRAP, No. 10, 1984, Special Issue: *A Oposicão no Poder*.

Philip, G., 'Democratization in Brazil and Argentina', *Government and Opposition*, Vol. 19, No. 2, 1984.

Política e Administração, Vol. 1, No. 2, 1985, Special Issue: *Movimentos Sociais no Brasil*.

Sader, E., 'The Workers' Party in Brazil', *New Left Review*, No. 165, 1987.

—— (ed.), *E Agora P.T.?*, São Paulo, Brasiliense, 1986.

Selcher, W. (ed.), *Political Liberalization in Brazil*, Boulder, Westview Press, 1986.

Stepan, A. (ed.), *Democratizing Brazil*, Yale University Press, 1987.

Tavares de Almeida, M. H., 'Sindicalismo Brasileiro e Pacto Social', in Comisión de Movimientos Laborales (CLACSO), *El Sindicalismo Latinoamericano en los Ochenta*, Santiago, CLACSO, 1986.

Velazco e Cruz, S. and Martins, C. E., 'De Castello a Figueiredo uma incursão no pre-historia da "abertura"', in Sorj, B. and Tavares de Almeida, M. C. (eds), *Sociedade e Política no Brasil pós-64*, São Paulo, Brasiliense, 1983.

Chile

Amérique Latine (Paris), No. 6, 1981, Special Issue, *Chile: un projet de révolution capitaliste*.

Angell, A., 'Why is the Transition to Democracy Proving so Difficult in Chile?', *Bulletin of Latin American Research*, Vol. 5, No. 1, Oxford, Pergamon Press, 1986.

Autogestions, No. 17, 1984, Special Issue: *La Democratie Souterraine. Chile 1973–1984*.

Barrerer, M. et al, *Trade Unions and the State in Present Day Chile* Geneva, UNRISD, 1985.

Boeninger, E., 'La Concertación Política y Social: Problema y Exigencia de la Consolidación Democrática', CED, *Documentos de Trabajo*, No. 21, 1985.

Brunner, J., *Politicas Culturales de Oposición en Chile*, FLACSO, *Documentos de Trabajo*, No. 78, Santiago, 1985.

Campero, G. and Valenzuela, J., *El Movimiento Sindical en el Regimen Militar Chileno 1973–1981*, Santiago, ILET, 1984.

Garretón, M. A., 'The Political Evolution of the Chilean Military Regime and Problems in the Transition to Democracy', in O'Donnell, G. et al, *Transitions from Authoritarian Rule. Escenarios e Intineranos Para la Transicion*, Santiago, FLACSO, *Documentos* No. 35, 1986.

Gomariz, E., *Movilización politica, Fuerzas Armadas, y transición democrática*, Santiago, FLACSO, *Documentos* No. 35, 1986.

Jilberto, A. E. Fernandez, *Dictadura Militar y Oposición Política en Chile 1973–1981*, Amsterdam, CEDLA, 1986.

Labouring Under the Junta. The union movement in Chile, London, Chile Solidarity Campaign, 1987.

Lechner, N., *La Conflictiva y Nunca Acabada Construcción del Orden Deseado*, Santiago, FLACSO, 1984.

—— 'El projecto neoconservador y la democracia', in Martin de al Campo, J. L. (eds), *Los nuevos procesos sociales y la teoría política contemporanea*, Mexico, Siglo XXI, 1986.

Leiva, F. I. and Petras, J., 'Chile's Poor Struggle for Democracy', *Latin American Perspectives*, Vol. 13, No. 4, 1986.

Lozza, A., *Chile Sublevado. Reportaje al FPMR*, Buenos Aires, Editorial Antarca, 1986.

Maza, G. and Garces, M., *La Explosión de las Mayorias. Protesta Nacional 1983–84*. Santiago, Educcación y Comunicación, 1985.

Moulián, T., *Democracia y Socialismo en Chile*, Santiago, FLACSO, 1983.

Moulián, T. and Vergara, T., 'Estado, ideología y politicas economicas en Chile', Santiago, Estudios CIEPLAN, No. 3, 1980.

Raczynski, D. and Serrano, C., *Vivir la Pobreza: Testimonio de las Mujeres*, Santiago, CIEPLAN, 1985.

Rosales, O., *Planificación y Mercado en un Projecto Democrático para Chile*, Santiago, CED Documentos No. 132, 1986.

Smith, B., *The Church and Politics in Chile: Challenges to Modern Catholicism*, Princeton, Princeton University Press, 1982.

Tironi, E., *La Torre de Babel. Ensayos de Critica y Renovacion Politica*, Santiago, Ediciones Sur, 1984.

Valenzuela, J. S. and Valenzuela, A. (eds), *Military Rule in Chile. Dictatorship and Opposition*, Baltimore, Johns Hopkins University Press, 1986.

Vargara, P., *Auge y Caida del Neoliberalismo en Chile*, Santiago, FLACSO, 1985.

Uruguay

Aguiar, C. et al, *Apertura y Concertación*, Montevideo, Ediciones de la Banda Oriental, 1985.

Bonino, L. C., *Crisis de los partidos tradicionales y movimiento revolucionario en Uruguay*, Montevideo, Ediciones de la Banda Oriental, 1984.

Bruschera, O., *Las Decadas Infames — Análisis Politico 1967–1985*, Montevideo, Linardi y Risso, 1986.

CIESU, *7 Enfoques Sobre la Concertación*, Montevideo, Ediciones de la Banda Oriental, 1984.

CINVE, *La Crisis Uruguaya y el Problema Nacional*, Montevideo, Ediciones de la Banda Oriental, 1984.

Errandonea, A., 'Sindicatos y democracia tutelada', *Cuadernos de Marcha*, Montevideo, Vol. 11, No. 9, 1986.

Garguilo, M., 'El Movimiento sindical Uruguay en los 80', in Comisión de Movimientos Sociales (CLACSO), *El Sindicalismo Latinoamericano en los Ochenta*, Santiago, CLACSO, 1986.

Gillespie, C., Goodman, L., Rial, J. and Winn, P., (eds), *Uruguay y la Democracia*, 3 vols, Montevideo, Ediciones de la Banda Oriental, 1985.

Gillespie, C. G., 'Uruguay's Transition from Collegial Military–Technocratic Rule' in O'Donnell, G. et al, *Transitions from Authoritarian Rule*.

Gonzalez, L., 'Uruguay 1980–81: An Unexpected Opening', *Latin American Research Review*, Vol. 18, No. 3, 1983.

El sistema de partidos y las perspectivas de la democracia Uruguaya, Montevideo, CIESU, Documentos No. 90, 1985.

La Táctica del Partido Comunista del Uruguay en la Lucha Contra la Dictadura 1973/1984, Buenos Aires, (no publisher named), 1984.

Martorelli, H., *Transición a la democracia*, Montevideo, Ediciones de la Banda Oriental, 1984.

Perelli, C., *Matrices ideológicas y discurso político*, Montevideo, CIESU, Documentos No. 185, 1985.

—— *Someter o Convencer: El Discurso Militar*, Montevideo, Ediciones de la Banda Oriental, 1986.

—— and Rial, J., *De Mitos y Memorias Politicas*, Montevideo, Ediciones de la Banda Oriental, 1986.

Revista Mexicana de Sociologia, Vol. XLVII, No. 2, 1983, special issue: *Uruguay en la Transición*.

Rial, J., *Partidos Políticos, democracía y autoritarismo*, 2 Vols, Montevideo, Ediciones de la Banda Oriental, 1974.

—— *Uruguay: Elecciones de 1984*, Montevideo, Ediciones de la Banda Oriental, 1985.

—— *La izquierda partidaria frente a la redemocratización*, Montevideo, CIESU, Documentos de Trabajo, No. 109, 1985.

—— *Las Fuerzas Armadas: ¿soldados–políticos garantes de la democracia?*, Montevideo, Ediciones de la Banda Oriental, 1986.

Sierra, G. de, *Sociedad y Politica en el Uruguay de la Crisis*, Montevideo, Librosur, 1985.

—— *Sistema y Partidos Políticos en el Uruguay de la Crisis*, CIEDUR, Documentos de Trabajo, No. 25, 1985.

Sosnowski, S. (ed.) *Represión, Exilio y Democracia: La Cultura Uruguaya*, Montevideo, Ediciones de la Banda Oriental, 1987.

Index